Marty Meitus and Patti Thorn

FUN PLACES
to Go with
Children in

Colorado
2ND EDITION

CHRONICLE BOOKS

SAN FRANCISCO

Printed in the United States of America.

Library of Congress Cataloging-in-Publication Data available.

ISBN 0-8118-1915-9

Cover design: Anne Galperin
Book design and illustration: Karen Smidth
Composition: Words & Deeds
Maps: Ellen McElhinny
Cover photograph: © Vail Photo by Jack Affleck

Distributed in Canada by Raincoast Books,
8680 Cambie Street, Vancouver, B.C. V6P 6M9

10 9 8 7 6 5 4 3 2 1

Chronicle Books
85 Second Street
San Francisco, CA 94105

Web Site: www.chroniclebooks.com

M.M. To Doug, Melissa, and Jacob—and to my traveling pals on many a car trip, Judy, Richard, Sandi, Claudia, Marvin, Amanda, Rob, and Jackie. And to my Mom and Dad.

P.T. To my very special traveling companions, Harold, Erin, and Sam, who made research an adventure and who held down the home fort when I was gone. And to Nancy, Sonny, and Devera, who set the standard in car trips.

A special thank you to Margaret Carlin and Kristi Hanks. And to the many other young friends who lent us their time and opinions.

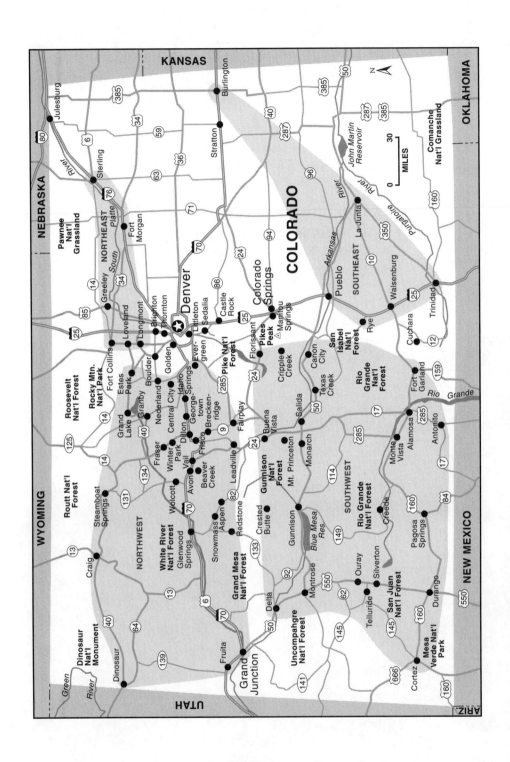

Contents

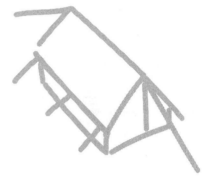

Introduction

IF YOU'RE A PARENT, you know that traveling with children is more than packing your bags and slipping the sing-along tape into the cassette player. You need crayons, coloring books, snacks, an assortment of shoes and coats for any weather—but most of all, you need a battle plan. With their notoriously short attention spans, children require plenty of diversions on any trip.

You could open your average guidebook, but where to begin? That historical museum may sound good on paper, but how will it be when you let your 2-year-old loose inside?

In researching this book, we visited hundreds of attractions in Colorado with our own children in tow. We looked for places that would engage them, and whether we were traveling to the Great Sand Dunes in the south or to the Colorado National Monument in the west, we found gems all along the way.

In this book, you'll find quiet attractions as well as those that tempt tourists with giant roadside billboards. You'll find museums and stops with educational value as well as hot springs and amusement parks where kids can simply let down their hair.

We have included only those attractions that we felt were worth a visit, even a cursory one. We were looking for good value for the dollar, keeping in mind that traveling with families can be an expensive proposition. We have tried to include information that will help you make your own decision as to the worth of the experience in time and money. For instance, a museum that will keep you busy for only 30 minutes may not be worth a stop on a busy summer day—but should the weather change abruptly, you'll be glad for an indoor option. We have also indicated the ages we feel are ideal for each attraction.

In addition, you'll find a black diamond (♦) marking our very favorite attractions: places that we and our children loved, that were reasonably priced, and that we wouldn't hesitate to visit time and again if we were in the area. Some of them are major sites with national recognition; others are small local finds.

Colorado boasts an abundance of outdoor activities, including white-water rafting, skiing, hiking, and camping. We offer tips on how to navigate the many choices offered here.

We have tried to be as accurate as possible with prices and hours; however, be sure to call ahead, since hours in Colorado often vary from season to season. For example, in Creede, the excellent Underground Mining Museum is open for only a few hours in the afternoon in the winter, subject to change; call ahead, however, and they're happy to accommodate you. In Aspen, a well-known bakery shortens its hours during the off-season. When is the off-season? Said one bakery clerk, "Whenever the slopes close—and that depends on the snow."

Along those lines, a word of warning about the climate. As the bakery clerk noted, weather in Colorado is highly variable. You may find the sun out in one location only to find blizzard conditions a short distance away. Pay attention to weather reports and always allow a little extra time.

In addition, remember that the distances between major cities and resort towns can be vast. Denver to Aspen is four to five hours driving time—in good weather. You need to be prepared for long stretches of driving with only isolated countryside for viewing. Because of the rugged terrain, drive time may be longer than anticipated. On the way to visit Bishop's Castle between Rye and Westcliffe, we planned a 30-minute trip off the main highway; we didn't know that the attraction is located along a winding mountain road, and in fact, it took closer to an hour to reach it. Despite the inconvenience, we were thrilled to encounter a family of deer at the side of the road and later a bobcat that streaked out of sight.

So expect the unexpected and get ready for adventure. Colorado, a land known for its majestic peaks and fertile valleys, will provide you and your children with memories that will last long after your bags are unpacked—and the crayons, coloring books, and tapes are stashed away.

And, by the way, if you know of a place we missed or disagree with one of our choices, please let us know. We'll be on the lookout for more places to go for the next edition. Write to us care of: Chronicle Books, 85 Second Street, Sixth Floor, San Francisco, CA 94105.

Hiking

WE'LL NEVER FORGET THAT MOMENT on our first hike when someone put his finger to his lips and pointed. We stopped, motioning to our
children, and followed his line of vision. Deer—a family of four—were
staring at us just as we were staring at them. Then, with a flick of their
white tails, they were gone, miragelike, leaving us all in awe.

Such are the wonders of hiking in Colorado terrain. Whether it's a
crystal-clear lake with a mountain backdrop, a field of wildflowers, or a
family of deer, you'll find nature in all its bounty, sure to leave an indel-
ible impression on your children.

While we recommend several hikes and hiking areas in this book,
if you're a serious hiker, you may want to read one of the numerous books
written exclusively on hiking with children in Colorado, such as *Best Hikes
with Children in Colorado* by Maureen Keilty (Seattle: The Mountaineers,
1991). Choose a book that rates the difficulty of the suggested trail, gives
the mileage, and locates points of interest. Parks will also have information
and trail guides to help you make decisions. You might want to consider
brushing up on some of the native plants and wildlife in Colorado. We
find it adds interest to the hike if we act as tour guide—pointing out birds,
flowers, animal tracks, and the like so that the kids are engaged throughout. Several of the nature centers will lend you binoculars for short hikes;
if you're hiking elsewhere, consider bringing a pair of your own.

Despite the beauty of the surroundings, we've found that our most
successful hikes with children were those that aimed for a specific destination, such as a waterfall, a swinging bridge, or a mountaintop lake. If you
just set out aimlessly, the kids will pepper you with everyone's favorite
question: when are we going to get there? By heading for a specific place,
you will have an answer—and something for everyone to look forward to.

Here are some other tips for successful hiking:

- If you're hiking in the mountains, **start out early in the day.** Thunderstorms roll in almost every afternoon—even on days that start out clear and cloudless. If you see a storm coming, it's best to head for a lower elevation.

- **Dress in layers**—short-sleeve shirt, sweatshirt, jacket. In some spots, you may find intense sun (don't forget the sunscreen); in others, intense shade. The exertion may leave you hot, but cloud cover may roll in suddenly and leave you shivering. Bring inexpensive waterproof ponchos for each member of the family. Wear comfortable sneakers with good support. Hiking boots are great, but don't make the investment unless you're planning to take frequent hikes.

- **Pack plenty of snacks and drinks.** If the kids are flagging, we pass out little bags of snacks—trail mix, sandwich cookies, cheese circles—so they can eat as they go. We also pack a lunch—the kids always rally when it's time to look for that perfect picnic spot.

- **Bring your own water and drink often** to replenish your body, even when you're not thirsty. Don't drink lake, stream, creek, or any sort of mountain water. No matter how inviting, you risk getting giardiasis, which will cause cramps and diarrhea, from an organism that has infected much of the mountain waters.

- **Don't underestimate altitude sickness,** a common ailment for people who aren't used to mountain heights. If you feel lightheaded, faint, or ill as you climb, it's best to head back down to a lower elevation.

- **Be aware of the possibility of getting ticks.** Ticks are most prevalent from March through July and particularly from April through June. The National Park Service advises wearing long pants instead of shorts, spraying all your clothes with a good insect repellant suitable for ticks, and tucking in any loose-fitting clothing. Check for ticks frequently on your clothes and skin, especially in vulnerable areas such as the back of your neck. Stay calm; most ticks can be removed with a tweezer. If you're unable to dislodge a tick, contact a doctor immediately.

Camping

SEVERAL YEARS AGO, a friend took his then 3-year-old on his first camping trip. As luck would have it, it rained incessantly. Outside their tent, the lightning flashed, the thunder boomed, and the little boy, his eyes as big as saucers, held tightly to his father. They told ghost stories, ate peanut butter and jelly sandwiches, and fell asleep close together to the drumming of the rain. They still recall it as the best camping trip they ever took.

That's the joy of camping in Colorado—where the unexpected makes for treasured memories. And those memories can come from a variety of experiences.

Camping can be as simple as pulling your recreational vehicle up to a campground and as complicated as hiking into the backcountry and staking a site.

If you've never been camping, start by buying a book specifically about camping to help you plan the kind of experience you'd like and to direct you to the most appropriate facility. The *Complete Colorado Campground Guide,* for instance, lists all campgrounds by location, with directions, available facilities, and other pertinent information, including specific phone numbers so you can call each directly. Find the guide at book and sporting goods stores, or write to Outdoor Books, P.O. Box 417, Denver CO 80201, or call (800) 952-5342 ($12.95 plus $3.50 postage and handling). In this book, you'll find entries on some of the major state and national parks that offer campgrounds.

Before you set out, here are some general tips on camping with kids:

- **Choose a campground and book early.** Parks and reservoirs are popular sites and fill up quickly. Rocky Mountain National Park, for instance, has five roadside campgrounds: three are open on a first-come, first-served basis, two by reservation only.

- **Pick a campground that has interesting day hikes** close by.
- **Choose a secluded spot** at the campground, near a creek, river, or lake, to give the kids the added entertainment a body of water provides—wading, skipping stones, looking for signs of insect and animal life.
- Because a camp fire can be so much a part of the camping experience, **ask about the rules for building fires at the site.** Many campgrounds have fire pits and will provide wood. Don't forget to bring the ingredients for s'mores, the gooey marshmallow, chocolate bar, and graham cracker confection that's a natural in the outdoors.
- **Rent your equipment for your first outing.** Stores that specialize in outdoor gear will rent everything from sleeping bags to tents to stoves. If you decide camping isn't for you, you won't be stuck with a lot of expensive equipment.
- Given that it can snow in the high country at any time, **be prepared with warm clothing**—even in the summer. Just as important, don't forget the rain gear. Rainproof ponchos are an inexpensive but good way to cover up.
- **Keep the food simple.** Pack a cooler with hot dogs and other perishables. Bring hot chocolate and oatmeal packets for breakfast. Be prepared not to cook in case of bad weather—bring the peanut butter and jelly and bread. Fill water bottles and bring an assortment of powdered drink mixes, always a hit with kids.
- **Bring flashlights and a book of ghost stories** for bedtime. Cards, games, and a battery-powered radio will help pass the time if you're caught in the tent by bad weather.
- **Bring garbage bags and a first-aid kit.**
- **Advise your kids on what to do if they wander away and can't find the campsite.** One suggestion is to give all the kids whistles to wear around their necks and teach them to blow three times if they're in distress.

Types of Campgrounds

In Colorado, campgrounds generally fall into four categories:
- **Private campgrounds:** These are owner-operated campgrounds that usually offer full services, such as water, electrical hookups, gasoline, and grocery stores. Choose from 230 private campgrounds in Colorado, many with pools and playgrounds and aimed at attracting families. For a free list of private campgrounds, cabins, and

lodges, write to *The Colorado Directory,* published by the Colorado Association of Campgrounds, Cabins, and Lodges, 5101 Pennsylvania Ave., Boulder CO 80303, or call (303) 499-9343 or check the Web site, http://www.entertain.com/wedgwood/caccl/.

- **State parks:** Colorado has 40 state parks with first-rate camping facilities. Although you might not find grocery stores or gasoline on the premises, you'll usually find restrooms, washing facilities, and electrical hookups. State parks are an excellent choice for first-time campers and usually have lots of things to do, from swimming beaches to boat docks to playgrounds. The state parks fill up fast, especially on three-day weekends, so you may want to consider making a reservation. For a free list of state parks with information on locations and facilities, write to Colorado State Parks, 1313 Sherman Street, #618, Denver 80203, or call (303) 866-3437 or check the Web site, http://www.dnr.state.co.us/parks/.

- **National parks:** Many of Colorado's 10 national parks offer opportunities for tent and backcountry camping. A few have full-service facilities like the state parks. The best known is Rocky Mountain National Park, and reservations are strongly advised; call the national reservation system, at (800) 365-CAMP or check the Web site, http://www.nps.gov/romo. For a free list of national parks in Colorado, write to National Park Service Information Desk, P.O. Box 25287, Denver CO 80225-0287, or call (303) 969-2000.

- **U.S. Forest Service:** The state's 11 national forests offer the largest number of campgrounds in the state, with 348 campgrounds, 29 group campgrounds, and 7,477 campsites. Many are rustic; some have picnic tables, grills, and running water. Many sites will accommodate tents and motor homes. About half the sites can be reserved, the rest are first-come, first-served. Campers can generally hike throughout the national forests and set up a tent anywhere, as long as they follow the rules and regulations. For a free list of national forest campgrounds in the Rocky Mountain Region, write USDA Forest Service Regional Office, Attention: Visitors Service, P.O. Box 25127, Lakewood CO 80225, or call (303) 275-5350.

Trout Ranches

FISHING IS ONE OF THE MOST POPULAR recreational sports in Colorado, and you'll find fishermen along every lake, creek, river, and stream. Invariably, when children see people casting their lines for the hundredth time, they are going to ask the obvious: why can't we grab a pole and join in the fun?

Enter the trout ranch. These commercial enterprises, some of them no more than a well-stocked fish pond by the side of the road, cater to kids and offer all of the fun of fishing with none of the hassle. No fishing license is required. The ranch supplies the pole, the net, the bait, and a 30-second crash course in fishing.

Attracted by the big sign that read "Public Invited," we stopped at one such place, **Pinecrest Trout Ranch,** 4121 Highway 103, in Idaho Springs, just at the turn-off for Mount Evans and Echo Lake. (Phone: 303-567-4017. Open daily, 9 A.M. to 5:30 P.M., and closed end of September to first or second week in May, depending on weather.) The pond was lined with people, including children as young as 3 and 4 holding fishing poles—and their excited parents, cameras at the ready. Pinecrest awards certificates for catching your first fish—a nice touch for the thrilled kids.

Other trout ranches throughout the state offer similar experiences. Before choosing one, make sure that they will clean your trout for you. Many of these trout ranches also list nearby restaurants that will cook your catch if you're on the road. You'll need to have ice and a cooler along if you're planning to take the fish along for the ride. Most of these ponds do not allow you to catch the fish and release it, so it's a good idea to know ahead of time what you plan to do with your catch.

Also, beware that the cost can really add up. The admission and pole at this particular ranch cost $4 per person; the fish was 42 cents an inch.

Since our trout turned out to be 13½ inches, the total for one trout: around $10. A restaurant will charge you even more to cook your fine fish du jour. Nevertheless, we spent a fun couple of hours—and we have the pictures to prove it.

Whitewater Rafting

YOU'VE DONE YOUR SHARE of fishing. You've hiked and camped
with abandon. Now you're ready for a new adventure. Something unusual.
Something thrilling. Something you'll remember long after the experience
is over. It's inevitable: you'll be whitewater rafting soon. "The rapids are
fun and exciting. There is an element of risk and that's part of it," says
Steve Reese, park manager for the Arkansas Headwaters Recreation Area,
one of the most popular spots for rafting in the state. "The scenery, the
weather, it all combines to create a great atmosphere." It's an atmosphere,
Reese adds, that families can enjoy together, to everyone's benefit. "Family
boating is a wonderful thing," he says. "It brings families together. They
laugh together, have fun together, are in the outdoors together. It's as
healthy as can be. There's something about a river that relaxes people;
barriers come down."

Colorado offers more than its share of opportunity for families, with
more than a hundred named rivers, including the Arkansas, which boasts
65 outfitters on its banks alone. The state can serve up gentle rivers that
will calmly propel your boat along or rollicking water that will give you
the ride of your life. While the choices can be comforting, they also
present a dilemma: How to select the right experience for you and your
family?

It's not difficult, once you know a few basics about the sport. First,
it's important to consider the type of water you'll be rafting, taking into
account your children's ages. River waters are classified according to their
roughness and the degree of skill it takes to navigate them. Class I waters
are the easiest to navigate, Class VI, the hardest (see Rapid Ratings Scale,
page 20). Most outfitters recommend waiting until your children are
at least age 7 before tackling Class III water and above. Many suggest a
minimum of age 4 before tackling any raft trip at all—but much depends
on your children's comfort level in and around the water. It's best to

explain to outfitters your child's skill level and ask their opinion, as they are the most familiar with the waters they raft. (Outfitters may also require your children to take a swim test, depending on the trip planned.)

If your children are older and age is not an issue, outfitters generally recommend Class III water as a starting point. These trips will be exciting enough in spots to ensure no one leaves feeling bored. "I don't know too many kids who want to sit and just watch the scenery for four hours," says Reed Dils, an outfitter for more than 20 years and former chairman of the Colorado River Outfitters Association.

As you peruse the various brochures advertising raft trips, take note that they'll generally say what class of water the trip passes through. You can then compare the trips in the types of water you feel most comfortable tackling.

Just as important as the river you choose is the outfitter with whom you plan to make the run. Outfitters provide the boats, lifejackets, wet suits (when necessary), and first aid. They plan the runs and load the boats. All outfitters are required to be licensed, which guarantees some training, experience, safety knowledge (for example, all guides are required to know CPR and first aid), and certain equipment standards. A license also guarantees the outfitter is properly insured. Those who are members of trade groups such as the Colorado River Outfitters Association or the Arkansas River Outfitters Association have also pledged to abide by a code of ethics and bylaws that go beyond the state's requirements.

Ask the outfitters you are considering if they are licensed and how long they have been in the business. Experience, in this field, counts heavily. You might also ask for the names and phone numbers of others who have taken trips with the outfitter.

Here are some other tips for planning your rafting trip:
- **Consider the time of year.** Generally, rivers are at their roughest at the peak of the snowmelt, which is May and June for most rivers in the state. In addition to causing more activity on the river, snowmelt also affects water temperature; the more snow melting into the river, the colder you can expect the water to be. First-timers may want to wait until midsummer, when the water is warmer and a bit calmer. With children, especially, this may make the difference between a fun and a miserable experience.
- **Plan a relatively short trip your first time out.** Outfitters generally offer half- or full-day trips; some also offer quarter-day runs. With children, it's best to opt for a small taste of the sport. If they hate it,

you'll be back on shore soon. If they love it, you can plan a follow-up trip.

- **Plan a morning trip when possible.** Afternoon showers are legendary in Colorado.
- **First-timers should consider requesting an oar boat** instead of a paddle boat. In oar boats, guides use oars to control the boat's movement; passengers can simply hang on while someone else does the work. In paddle boats, each passenger is given a paddle to help with the steering. Children who have never rafted before (and parents, too!) may feel safer using their hands to hold on rather than to paddle.
- **Ask if the outfitter has self-bailing boats.** These boats are less likely to fill up with water and your feet won't be immersed most of the trip. In addition, no one will have to abandon paddling (if you're in a paddle boat) to bail the boat out. A self-bailing boat tends to be less heavy and hard to maneuver, and you will subsequently have more control. "It's a much safer experience," says Dils.
- **Ask if the outfitter has equipment specifically for children.** If not, the lifejackets may not fit properly and the outfitter may not be able to supply wet suits for the kids.
- **Check the lifejacket** to make sure the size is correct; the jacket should say how many pounds a person must weigh to wear it safely.
- **Ask what kind of equipment you'll need to bring** in case of rain or rides that promise to be extremely wet. Many outfitters provide ponchos (but some may charge an extra fee for their use); some rent wet suits and booties, which can be worn on cold days. Dils suggests that if the combined water and air temperature is less than 100 degrees, you may be more comfortable in a wet suit. The money spent on this "extra," he adds, will be more than made up in comfort.
- On a normal summer day, **wear shorts, T-shirt, tennis shoes, hat, and lots of sunscreen.** Bring a change of clothes for the ride home, in case you return drenched.
- **Ask outfitters about special outings for children;** some combine rafting with other adventures, such as looking for fossils or exploring Indian ruins.
- **Don't shop for an outfitter by price alone.** Those who offer cut-rates may be skimping on the quality of their equipment.
- **Make reservations whenever possible.** Trips tend to fill up on weekends in June and July; they are less full during the week and late summer. During the busy season, outfitters advise planning two weeks ahead to ensure yourself a spot.

- **Call a few days ahead to see what the river conditions are.**
  When the water is extremely rough, outfitters may change the minimum age of their passengers. A call will avoid disappointment on arrival for all concerned.

Rapid Ratings' Scale*

River ratings are based on normal water levels and can vary with water fluctuations.

Class I—Easy. Small waves and no experience required.

Class II—Medium. Moderately difficult rapids, clear passages.

Class III—Difficult. Waves numerous, irregular, and high, with rocks and eddies, requiring expert skill in maneuvering.

Class IV—Very Difficult. Long rapids; powerful waves; irregular, boiling eddies; powerful and precise maneuvering required.

Class V—Extremely difficult. Large and violent rapids; highly congested routes almost always requiring scrutiny from shore; critical and complex maneuvering required.

Class VI—Unrunnable.

* Provided by the Colorado River Outfitters Association.

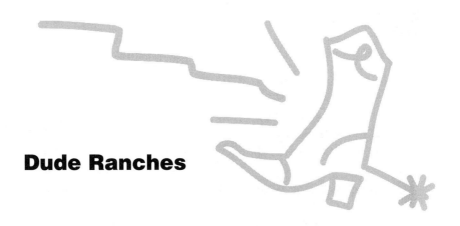

Dude Ranches

IN THE MOVIE *CITY SLICKERS*, Billy Crystal found his smile on a
cattle drive in Colorado. He wasn't the only happy camper. Dude ranch
owners have been grinning from ear to ear ever since the movie made
ridin' and ropin' at a dude ranch more desirable than a week in
Disneyland.

Dude ranches were started in the 1800s when wealthy people came
out West and took up the cattle business. When freeloading relatives
began to arrive, these people realized they could open their homes to
guests who wanted to see their lifestyle—and charge for the privilege.

Colorado has 38 dude ranches that are members of the Colorado Dude
& Guest Ranch Association, a kind of AAA of dude ranches. A dude ranch
differs from a hotel or resort in that the owner lives on the premises year-
round. Many of the ranches, in turn, are open to guests year-round. The
ranches provide an all-in-one package: accommodations, food, and activities, with horseback riding as the theme. Some of the ranches are rustic;
others have luxurious facilities with pools and racquetball courts.

At one time folks chose a dude ranch for the Western experience.
Now they're just as likely to choose one for the children's programs. Every
dude ranch offers a family program of one sort or another, whether it's
hayrides, barbecues, line dancing, or singalongs. Most offer a separate
supervised program for children so that kids go one way, parents another.
Kids' activities might include guided nature walks, swimming, camp-
outs, and, of course, riding. Adults can choose from a similar menu of
activities.

Here are some tips from Wright Catlow, director of the Colorado
Dude & Guest Ranch Association, and others for choosing a dude ranch
that's right for your family:

- **Ask the owner to describe the children's program** and what
  the kids will do during a typical stay. What does the ranch offer for

toddlers? Preschoolers? Teens? Some of the ranches feature supervised programs only for ages 3 to 12; others offer special tot and/or teen programs.

- Because it is the cornerstone of dude ranches, you'll want to **inquire about the riding program.** Children under age 6 are usually not allowed to ride alone, so find out what provisions they make for the preschool and toddler set. At some ranches, young children are led around the ring on a horse to get them used to the animal. Dude ranches will not allow parents to ride with their child on a horse.

  In many cases, a child is assigned his or her own horse and there's a "rodeo" at week's end where children can show off their new horseback riding skills. Find out what the ranch does if a child doesn't like horses in general or his or her assigned horse in particular. Nothing ruins a horseback riding excursion faster than having a horse that a child can't warm up to, for whatever reason.

  If you know before you book a ranch that your child really doesn't like horses, Catlow advises rethinking your vacation plans. "If you have one kid who doesn't like horses and other kids in the family who do, you'll have to weigh the consequences. Do you mind, for instance, taking the child with you on your jeep trip or swimming?"

- **If it's a cattle drive you're after,** there are a few ranches that allow guests to help move cattle from one pasture to another. There are also a couple of true working ranches where you can participate in the real business of keeping the place up and running. These types of dude ranches are unsuitable for younger kids, although they may be able to accommodate teens.

- **Choose a dude ranch that's a member of the association.** Member dude ranches are inspected regularly by the board of directors. To receive your copy of the Colorado Dude & Guest Ranch Association booklet, write to P.O. Box 300, Tabernash CO 80478, or call (970) 887-3128 or (970) 887-9248.

● C Lazy U Ranch
P.O. Box 379, Granby. (970) 887-3344.

The crème de la crème of Colorado's 38-member Dude & Guest Ranch Association is the C Lazy U Ranch in Granby, which has achieved both the Mobil Five-Star rating and the AAA Five-Diamond. Although the rooms have neither telephone nor television, the kids will have more than enough to do to while away the time. Among the activities are fishing, tennis, racquetball, a game room, paddleboats, and hayrides.

The 3-to-5-year-old set has its own program, geared to their age group, including pony rides and time to play on the well-designed playground. Each child over age 6 is assigned a horse for the week, and the week is devoted to learning about horses and riding, culminating in a "Showdeo." The children are whisked away after breakfast each day and spend the rest of the time into the evening with counselors. Even the teens aren't forgotten, with a program of their own that includes horseback riding, fishing, swimming, and hiking. The family meets up again after "adult" dinner for any evening events.

The C Lazy U is open late May to late September, and late December through March; it is closed April and November. The ranch costs $1,750 per person per week (plus tax and 15 percent service charge) for adults and children over the age of 6 during the peak summer season. Children 3 to 5 receive a discount. Prices drop during the rest of the year, particularly from January to March. Call for rates. Babies are not invited without a nanny except during specific "baby weeks" each summer.

Skiing

OBVIOUSLY, ONE OF THE MAIN REASONS people come to Colorado is to ski. With 25 areas boasting more than 24,000 acres of skiable terrain—along with plentiful sunny days and breathtaking mountaintop views—the state rarely disappoints. For every skier, there's the perfect run; for every vacation preference, there's the perfect resort. And now more than ever before, for every family, there are literally scores of ski options to choose from—everything from instruction to child care to ticket packages. After years of catering to twenty-, thirty-, and fortysomething skiers, who most often left their young children at home, ski areas have heard the call of the ever-vocal baby boomers, who are now vacationing more often with children. And they are responding in a big way—with package deals for beginning skiers offering lively instruction, complete with skiing cartoon figures and special mountain "adventures" for children as young as 3 and plentiful day-care facilities for children who aren't old enough or don't care to ski. Parents who head to the hills will find ski areas eager to serve them and that, in fact, are marketing to them aggresively.

So much for the good news. The bad news is that all this accommodation comes with a price. No matter how you slice it, skiing is an expensive proposition. The sport not only requires pricey lift tickets (anywhere from $8 to $59 per day for adults), but special equipment, clothing, and often, instruction. Multiply all of that for a family of four, and one outing can bury your budget faster than an avalanche.

Even when budget problems have been overcome, skiing with children, especially those who have never tried the sport before, presents unique obstacles: what happens when your 4-year-old, for example, decides he's had enough after an hour—and you've bought full-day lift tickets for the whole family? Or what do you do when you've driven 200 miles, only to discover the weather in the mountains is miserable and, suddenly, so are your kids? We recall one obstinate youngster who took a look at the snow swirling madly outside the car window and promptly declared: "I'm not getting out of this car." Needless to say, her parents hadn't foreseen the problem.

Patience, as always, is a virtue. But some careful planning can also help you navigate this vacation slalom. Below, we offer a few tips:

ON PRICE

- **Look for discounts.** Ski areas market to two distinct skiers: the vacationing family, who will likely spend a week or so at a resort, and the locals, who drive up to the mountains for a single day of skiing. Ski executives know that the former, who have planned and saved for vacation, are generally willing to spend more money than the latter, who are simply squeezing the outing into their many other day-to-day expenses. Ski areas, therefore, offer plentiful discounts to Denver metro skiers as enticements to get them up to the hills.

  If you are arriving in Denver and know where you will be skiing, check out major grocery stores and gas stations and other retail outlets that sell discounted ski tickets. You can save anywhere from a couple dollars to $5 or $6 per ticket, which can add up to a substantial savings for a family. Also, keep your eye open for coupons in local publications and coupon booklets; during nonpeak ski weeks, these are plentiful.

- **Ski out-of-the-mainstream areas.** As with anything, demand inflates price. It's no concidence that the most popular ski areas are also the most expensive. When you're skiing with beginners, do you really need the challenging bowls that make Vail a hot spot? Or the variety of slopes and the prestige that Aspen offers? More likely, you'll be looking for gentle runs, a nonthreatening atmosphere, and cordial staff with time to care about you and your children. Colorado offers plenty of smaller ski areas with all of these qualities—and much lower prices to boot.

- **Price shop for equipment.** For vacation skiers, it's generally less expensive to rent equipment, especially if you're only skiing a few days and can find a package deal that includes rental, lesson, and lift ticket. But good deals are also available for those who buy. Some Denver retail outlets allow you to buy children's equipment, use it for a season, then turn it in the next year for bigger sizes for a relatively small fee. Buying used equipment is also a good option, since children generaly outgrow their equipment long before they wear it out.

- **Buy unisex.** If you plan to be a skiing family, it behooves you to buy clothes and equipment in colors both boys and girls can use. You'll be grateful you can drag out gloves, boots, jackets, warm-up pants, and so on when the next child has finally grown into them!

ON PLANNING A SKI OUTING WITH KIDS

- **Try to hit a nice day with first-timers.** There's nothing that will destroy a child's enthusiasm for this sport faster than a frigid day. If possible, plan your trip in the spring, when good weather days (with temperatures often in the 40s and 50s) far outnumber the bad. Or plan a vacation that's long enough to allow for a few days of rest and relaxation if the weather proves troublesome. Then you can sit out the bad days and wait until the sun reappears.
- **Don't push your child to ski.** As one parent whose 4-year-old daughter ended up in the nursery after a half-completed, $60 ski lesson put it: "That was the most expensive day of child care we've ever had." While many children may need some coaxing, be sure they are basically receptive to the idea. It will save everyone from a tense, unsuccessful outing.
- **Look for resorts with child-friendly instruction.** Most resorts now offer programs specifically geared to children. Among the many recent developments, some resorts offer cartoon cutouts and amusement park style settings, such as tepees and re-created mining towns, on the training slopes; special ski attachments to help children keep their skis together on their first few tries; and skiers dressed in animal costumes. While some of these amenities are just window dressing, a bright atmosphere can also help hold a timid beginner's interest.
- Parents with children who aren't ready to ski should **shop resorts based on day-care facilities.** Look at cost, ratio of supervisors to children, the physical set-up of the facility, and how easy it is to get to the facility from the slopes, should you want to check in on your child during the day. Does the area accommodate infants? (Some don't.)

ON HOW TO DRESS FOR SKIING

As always, layering is essential for uncertain mountain weather. Standard ski clothes for children should include:
- long underwear (tops and bottoms)

- wool socks
- turtleneck
- wool sweater
- waterproof pants
- ski parka
- knit hat
- scarf
- waterproof gloves (Don't bring knit mittens and gloves; when they get wet, they stay wet. Waterproof gloves are essential.)
- sunglasses
- goggles

It's not necessary to buy fancy name brands, especially if you aren't certain your children will enjoy the sport. Buy or borrow clothes that seem warm (thickness in parkas, however, is not necessarily an indication, as new materials offer less bulk and warmth at the same time). If your children are prone to cold hands, visit a ski shop and ask for "hand warmers." These are small, inexpensive packets under various brand names that give off heat for six to eight hours when put inside a glove. We know parents who swear by these relatively new ski accessories.

It is also wise to give children backpacks to carry on their skiing adventures. This way, they can take off hats, scarves, and so on should the weather turn warm. And sunscreen is a must, even on cloudy days. Remember: you'll be at high altitude, where the sun is at top strength. In addition, the sun often bounces off of the white snow in the mountains, doubling the doses of exposure.

Ski Areas

Below, we offer child-related information on Colorado ski areas. Note that these are the prices available at time of publication, but be advised that prices change rapidly from year to year, as well as from peak ski season to less-busy times. Ski instruction and day-care programs are also constantly in flux, so be sure to call first to confirm.

A diamond (◆) next to a ski resort indicates that we consider the area exceptionally child-friendly. Our picks range from pricey destinations to those where a family can ski relatively inexpensively. But always, we have considered value: does the area offer enough amenities to justify the price? We have also considered whether the area offers child care, ski instruction programs that cater to children, and special events and discounts.

● Arapahoe Basin, Keystone

(970) 468-2316. Adults, $39; ages 6 to 14, $12; ages 5 and under, free. Child-care facilities for ages 18 months and older. Reservations recommended.

All ski programs include lift ticket, equipment rental, full- or half-day lesson, and lunch (for full day). Ski lessons for ages 4 and up. Snowboard lessons for ages 9 and up. New children's ski theme area.

● Aspen Highlands, Aspen

(800) 525-6200 or (970) 925-1220. Tickets can be used at any of the four Aspen areas: adults, $59; ages 7 to 12, $35; ages 13 to 27, $39; ages 6 and under, free.

Ski programs include lessons, lift, and lunch for ages 3½ to 6 (the program is called Snow Puppies). For ages 7 to 12, lunch and lessons (lifts are additional). Beginners can use a special chairlift.

● Aspen Mountain, Aspen

(800) 525-6200 or (970) 925-1220. Tickets can be used at any of the four Aspen areas; adults, $59; ages 7 to 12, $35; ages 13 to 27, $39; ages 6 and under, free.

No beginner runs; intermediate and expert skiers only. Ski programs for adults only (over 18).

● Snowmass, Aspen

(800) 525-6200 or (970) 925-1220. Tickets can be used at any of the four Aspen areas: adults, $59; ages 7 to 12, $35; ages 13 to 27, $39; ages 6 and under, free. Child care for children ages 6 weeks to 12 years; includes indoor and outdoor activities.

Ski programs: for 3-year-olds, includes equipment, special "contoured for kids" ski area, "magic carpet" to take children to the top of the hill; 4 years through kindergarten, includes snow games; first grade through 12 years, includes full-day (lunch included) and half-day programs; ages 13 to 19, a full-day program that does not include lunch.

Three-day learn-to-ski-or-snowboard packages for ages 7 to 19 includes lift ticket, lessons, rentals (lunch included for ages 8 to 12 only).

Snowmass claims its half-pipe for snowboarders is the longest in North America.

Free shuttle from Aspen. Also, a free shuttle called Burnie the Bear travels throughout Snowmass Village area, picking up children and bringing them to and from ski school.

● Buttermilk, Aspen ◆

(800) 525-6200 or (970) 925-1220. Tickets can be used at any of the four Aspen areas: adults, $59; ages 7 to 12, $35; ages 13 to 27, $39; ages 6 and under, free.

The most child-friendly of Aspen's ski areas, with primarily beginner and intermediate runs.

Ski programs: for children ages 3 to 6, includes private ski hill and chairlift, lunch, and snacks; first grade to 12 years, includes full-day lessons; ages 13 to 19, includes full-day lessons. Three-day learn-to-ski-or-snowboard program for ages 8 to 19 includes lift tickets, lessons, and rentals (lunch included for ages 8 to 12 only).

Children are invited to congregate at Fort Frog, a children's learning and video center, with lookout towers, old wagons, a jail, a saloon, and an Indian tepee village outside. Fort Frog hosts children's races, barbecues, Mexican theme parties, and more. Children and adults are invited to have their skiing videotaped and to watch the playback at the fort.

Fort inhabitants include characters like Max the Moose, Colonel Frog, and No Problem Joe. Children can trace their adventures by using the children's trail map, which takes them through Dead Bird Mine, Bear Jump, Devil's Gut, Grandma's Trail, and more.

The area also boasts weekly ski races against Max the Moose. If your children beat Max, they'll receive a button that says, "I Waxed Max." If not, they get a button that says, "I made tracks with Max."

Also, bus service picks up kids at the gondola building at Aspen Mountain and drives them to the area; parents can then ski at other Aspen resorts without driving kids to ski school.

The area also offers a snowboard park and snowboard half-pipe.

● Beaver Creek Resort, Avon ◆

(970) 949-5750. Adults, $54 ($56 during holidays); ages 5 to 12, $35; ages 4 and under, free. Child care for ages 2 months to 6 years. Reservations required.

Ski programs: children age 3, includes lessons, lunch, and free play (must be potty trained); ages 4 to 6, includes lesson, lunch, lift ticket, ski-through attractions (re-created mines, hibernating bear caves, tepee villages, and more), visits by the Western Gang, a weekly fun race with ribbons for everyone, and before- and after-lesson child care; ages 6 to 12, includes lift ticket, ski-through attractions, and weekly ski school race, with ribbons for everyone. Snowboard lessons, offered in program, similar to skiing.

Children can ski on Children's Adventure Mountain, which features the story of a miner and trapper as they search for gold. The area offers five ski-through attractions, such as a ghost town and an Indian village. Young skiers receive a Children's Adventure Mountain merit button, consisting of six circles, each representing one of the five ski-through adventures and one for understanding skier safety. After visiting an attraction and mastering the terrain, children receive a merit sticker.

● Breckenridge Ski Resort, Breckenridge

(970) 453-5000. Adults, $47; ages 5 to 12, $17; ages 4 and under, free. Child care for children 2 months through 5 years.

Ski programs: for children ages 3 to 5, full- and half-day program includes lesson, lunch (full-day only), snacks, and child care (reservations required); for ages 6 to 17, full- and half-day lessons, include lunch (full-day only) and user-friendly lifts. Snowboarding instruction also available.

● Copper Mountain Resort, Copper Mountain ◆

(970) 968-2882. Adults, $45; children, 6 to 14, $18; ages 5 and under, free. Multiday tickets, in increments of three days or more, are $12 per day for children ages 6 to 14. They are valid all season long. Free lift tickets for children under age 14 whose parents purchase special lodging packages from mid-November to mid-December, January to mid-February, and April to closing. Child care for children 2 months to 4 years; includes cookie baking (cookies are presented to parents after they return from skiing), outdoor play, and a "soft skiing" experience for children ages 3 and older. Reservations required. Discounts for three or more full-days.

Ski programs: for ages 4 to 12, includes full- and half-day (lunch included) lessons. Discount packages for lesson, rental, lift ticket, and lunch.

Children's ski school is located at "Kid's Headquarters," a child-friendly facility with play area, child-sized cafeteria, and so on. The resort also offers Family Ski Areas: 30 acres of mostly easy terrain, isolated from the rest of the mountain.

● Crested Butte Mountain Resort, Crested Butte ◆

(800) 444-9236, (800) 544-8448, or (970) 349-2333. Adults, $47; ages 12 and under pay their age for lift ticket with a paying adult. During preseason (mid-November to mid-December and last two weeks of April), everyone skis free; first-time skiers ages 13 and up may take lessons for $10. Child care for 6 months to 7 years; includes snow play, games, arts and crafts. Reservations recommended.

Ski programs: for age 3, includes full- or half-day lesson, lunch (full day only), rental, and child care (children must be potty trained); ages 4 to 7, includes equipment rental, child care and lunch; ages 8 to 12, includes full- and half-day lessons (no lift tickets, rentals, or lunch); ages 13 to 17, full- or half-day lessons. Rip session, for 8-to-17-year-old adventurous skiers (must be level 8 or 9 skier), lessons but no lift ticket or rentals. Snowboard lessons, ages 8 to 12, includes rental but no lift ticket.

Tag-a-Long lesson allows parents, proficient in skiing, to ski with their children and an instructor for one to three hours. Parents will learn information on how to help their child progress and ski safely after the lesson.

● Cuchara Valley Resort, Cuchara

(719) 742-3163 or (888) 282-4272. Adults, $29.95; ages 7 to 12, $19.95; ages 6 and under, free with paying adult. Night skiing begins around 6 P.M.; $12.95, all ages. Child care for infants to age 13; includes games, crafts, and lunch. Reservations advised.

Ski programs: for ages 3 to 13, includes full- and half-day lessons, rental, lunch, and snowplay for the younger children once they tire of skiing. Snowboarding lessons available.

The area features several special events, such as a costume day or a fun day with races.

● Eldora Mountain Resort, Nederland

(303) 440-8700. Adults, $30; children, ages 7 to 12, $16; ages 6 and under ski free with an adult lift ticket purchase.

Ski programs: ages 3 to 4, includes one-hour morning and one-hour afternoon lessons, rentals, and child care; ages 4 to 6 and 7 to 12, includes lift, lesson, rental, and lunch (or any combination of these). Eldora also offers numerous ongoing programs for local children. Call for details.

The mountain features outdoor forts, obstacle courses, "Eldorable Bear" mascot, wooden character cutouts, and more.

● Howelsen Ski Area, Steamboat Springs

(970) 879-2170. Adults, $10; ages 12 and under, $5.

Gentle slopes, free tow for beginners. Extremely reasonable season-pass rates.

● Keystone/North Peak/The Outback, Keystone

(970) 496-4181 (Children's Center) or (800) 468-5004. Adults, $47; ages 5 to 12, $17; ages 4 and under, free. Child care for children

ages 2 months to 12 years, includes lunch with both full- and half-days.

Evening hours available for those who plan to night ski. Parents who leave children in the nursery may ski with beepers to keep in touch with the Children's Center while skiing. The Children's Center also offers snowplay—including sledding, building snow forts, gondola rides, and more—for children ages 3 and up. Reservations required.

Ski programs: for children ages 3 to 16, includes full- and half-day lessons, lift tickets, ski rental, and lunch (for full days). Small discounts for multiple-day lessons.

Keystone offers Gold Rush Alley, a kids-only terrain where children ski through "mines" and around colorful cutouts.

● Loveland Ski Areas, Georgetown

(303) 569-3203. Adults, $35; ages 6 to 14, $17; ages 5 and under, free. Child care, ages 1 to 12 years. Reservations recommended.

Ski programs: for ages 3½ to 4, includes rentals, inside instruction, 30 to 45 minutes outside lunch, quiet time, then more outside instruction, small surface lift for children; ages 5 to 14, includes all-day lessons, rentals, lunch, and lift ticket. (Partial-day lessons are available, but discouraged.) Snowboarding programs: for ages 8 to 14, includes all-day lesson, rental, lunch, and lift ticket.

● Monarch Ski & Snowboard Area, Monarch

(719) 539-3573 or (888) 996-7669. Adults, $32; children, ages 7 to 12, $18; ages 6 and under, free. Child care for ages 2 months to 6 years. Reservations required.

Ski school program: for ages 2 to 6, one-hour private lesson with child care; ages 7 to 12, two-hour ski lesson includes ski rental and lift ticket (snowboard lessons also available).

Never-ever ski package: for children, all ages, who have never skied before; includes lift ticket, ski rental, and two-hour lesson.

● Powderhorn Resort, Grand Junction

(970) 268-5700. Adults, $31; students ages 7 to 18, $23; ages 6 and under, free. Child care for children ages 2 to 6. Half-day includes one-hour ski lesson, rental equipment, and snacks; full-day includes two one-hour ski lessons, rental equipment, snacks, and lunch.

Ski programs: ages 7 to 12, includes various packages, full- and half-day lessons.

The Magic Forest with cutout forest animals is on the beginner hill. The E-Z Rider beginner lift is free for all ages.

● Purgatory-Durango, Durango

(970) 247-9000. Adults, $40; ages 6 to 12, $18; ages 5 and under, free. Child care for ages 2 months to 5; reservations required.

Ski programs: age 3, includes play on cross-country skis (skis included), plus full- or half-day child care; ages 4 and 5, includes lift ticket and full-day (with lunch) and half-day lessons with major emphasis on skiing, but also includes storytime, playtime, and games; ages 6 through 12, includes full- and half-day lessons, lift ticket, lunch (with full-day). Experienced skiers, age 6 through age 12, can take advantage of supervised skiing to work on NASTAR racing bumps and parallel turns.

Children's adventure park offers a maze, miner's cabin, and more. The area also offers private ski lessons for those with disabilities. Snowboarding lessons available for ages 6 to 12, with the same program as skiing, above.

● SilverCreek Ski Area, Silver Creek ◆

(800) 448-9458. Adults, $32; ages 13 to 17, $28; ages 6 to 12, $15. Child care for children ages 1 to 8 years, with discounts for additional children in the same family. Child care is available for infants, 6 months to 1 year, but reservations are required.

Ski programs: full-day or half-day lessons, including rental, lift ticket, and lunch (for full day), for ages 3 to 5, 6 to 7, and 8 to 12. Special "learn to ski or your money back" packages for ages 13 and older.

Four Silver Bear Ski Weeks throughout the season allow children ages 12 and under to ski free if their parents are skiing two days, and it includes magic shows, ice cream parties, and teddy bear parades (weeks vary, call for information). Lollipop Races throughout the season are designed for children ages 3 to 12, with lollipop-shaped gates and free lollipops for those who complete the course.

SilverCreek also offers snowboarding and skiing under the lights from 5 to 9 P.M. for $5 lift ticket; tubing from 1 to 4 P.M. and 5 to 9 P.M.; snowmobiling and snowbiking (a bike on skis). Lessons available for snowboarding and snowbiking.

● Ski Cooper, Leadville

(719) 486-3684. Adults, $25; ages 6 to 12, $15; ages 5 and under, free. Child care, ages 2 to 8. Reservations required.

Ski programs: ages 4 to 10, includes full-day lesson, lift ticket, rentals, and lunch. Snowboard programs: two-hour lessons, ages 6 and older; rental not included.

● Steamboat Springs

(970) 879-6111. Adults, $48; ages 13 to 18, $36; ages 12 and under, $28. Child care for children 6 months through kindergarten.

Ski programs: for ages 2½ to 3½, includes one-hour private ski lesson and all-day child care with lunch; ages 3½ through kindergarten, includes own lift, designated ski areas, and lunch; ages 6 through 15, includes their own area on the mountain, with a "skiing skills" playground in a Western theme.

Children age 12 and under ski free when parents purchase a five night/five-or-more-days lift ticket package. Kids Adventure Club at night is for 2½-to-12-year-olds, and includes indoor crafts, activities, games, climbing gym weekly. The club happens 6 to 10:30 P.M. so parents can have a night out; hourly rates are charged. Snowboarding lessons for ages 8 and up.

● Sunlight Mountain Resort, Glenwood Springs

(970) 945-7491. Adults, $28; ages 6 to 12, $19; ages 5 and under, free. Child care for children ages 6 months to 6 years. Fifty percent discount off the full-day rate for each additional child.

Ski programs: for ages 3 to 6, full- and half-day programs include lift ticket, lesson, rentals, day care, and lunch (full-day only); ages 7 to 14, various options. Beginner package includes lesson, lift, and rentals.

Sunlight offers a hill for children with mazes, obstacles, cartoon figures, a bridge, and more.

● Telluride, Telluride

(970) 728-4424 or (800) 801-4832. Adults, $49; ages 6 to 12, $26; ages 5 and under, free. For skiers enrolled in ski school, lift ticket is $12. Child care for ages 2 months to 3 years. Reservations advised.

Ski programs: for ages 3 to 5, includes 1½-hour lesson (children must be potty trained) plus supervised play; ages 6 to 12, includes two-hour lesson in morning, lunch, and two-hour lesson in afternoon. Students learn about Telluride's heritage of mining, the Ute Indians, and the town's history while skiing. Day care before and after ski lessons is available for those who sign up for multiday lessons. Snowboarding programs for ages 6 to 12; same as skiing program, above. Children 5 and under ski free.

● Vail, Vail

(970) 476-5601.

See Beaver Creek entry.

● Winter Park/Mary Jane, Winter Park

(970) 726-1551 or (303) 780-6551 (for Denver metro callers). Adults, $45; ages 6 to 13, $15; ages 5 and under, free. Early November to early December and early April to mid-April, adults $27; ages 6 to 13, $15; ages 5 and under, free. Child care for children 2 months to 5 years. Reservations required.

Ski programs: for ages 3 to 4 (must be potty trained), includes nonintensive ski experience and indoor and outdoor games; ages 5 and 6, includes first ride on the chairlift; ages 7 and 8, includes somewhat faster-paced instruction; ages 9 through 13, includes skiing according to their ability out and about on the mountain. During peak ski periods such as Christmas vacation and spring break, teenagers ages 13 to 16 may take less structured lessons that allow them to ski with their peers.

Winter Park offers a Learn to Ski Park for beginners: 20 acres of trails isolated from more advanced trails. The area features a variety of chairlifts to teach beginners confidence on each.

Winter Park is recognized for its outstanding ski program for disabled people, the largest such program in the world. Adaptive equipment allows the area to meet the needs of more than 40 different disabilities.

● Wolf Creek Ski Area, Pagosa Springs

(970) 264-5629. Adults, $34; ages 12 and under, $22.

Ski programs: for ages 5 to 8, includes full- or half-day instruction, lift ticket, "magic carpet" ride to the top of the learning hill (half-day includes snack; full-day includes lunch and snack); ages 9 to 12, includes full- or half-day lesson, and lift ticket. Snowboarding programs: for ages 9 and up; beginner package includes one-day lift ticket, four-hour lesson.

Younger children enrolled in ski school receive special Wolf Creek pins; older children receive medals.

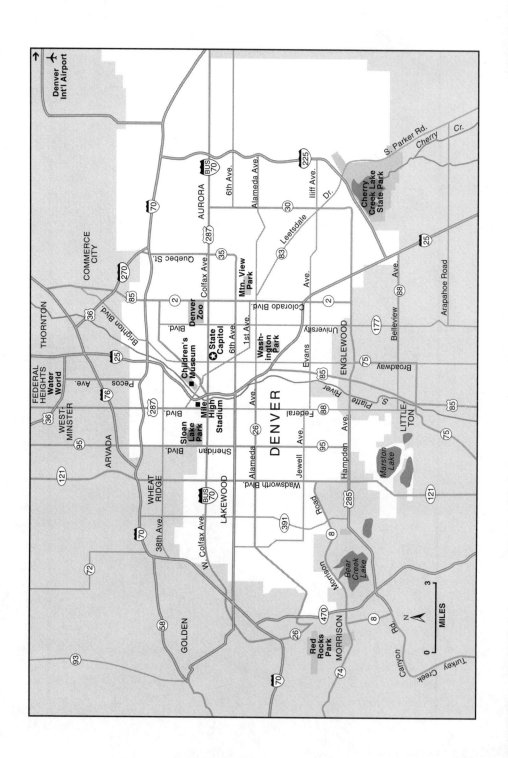

Denver

VISIT DENVER ON A CLOUDLESS DAY and you'll see why 1.9 million people have settled in the city and its surrounding suburbs: blue skies, sweeping, uncluttered horizons, a proud downtown skyline, all within a few hours of some of the most spectacular scenery you will find anywhere in the country. Denver may be flat as a table—they don't call her the "Queen City of the Plains" for nothing—but on a clear day, you can practically touch the rugged peaks in the distance that give the city her focal point and her allure.

Denver is 340 miles from the exact center of the continental United States. As such, it has become a cultural oasis, of sorts, for the midsection of the country. It boasts a beautiful center for the performing arts, which brings in performers of national and international repute; a first-rate natural history museum; and an art museum known nationwide for its impressive collection of Native American art. At the same time, those who live here also enjoy an abundance of offerings that many cultural meccas, such as New York and Los Angeles, lack: plentiful bike paths, hiking trails, nature preserves, and lakes for boating and other recreational activities. It's easy to find a good balance here between the high brow and the down to earth.

When it comes to children's activities, you'll find similar diversity. One could, theoretically, take the kids to a museum in the morning, a ballet in the afternoon, and a ballgame in the evening. The city offers a nationally ranked zoo, one of the nation's larger children's museums, an abundance of parks and recreational centers, and as many street fairs as there are weekends to hold them. If you're looking for ethnic flair, Denver has modest Italian, Hispanic, and Asian neighborhoods—and the attendant annual festivals that showcase many of these communities' special traditions.

In researching this book, we were struck, above all, by the number of serene, out-of-the-way spots the city affords, where children can take a small hike, watch for urban wildlife, or throw sticks into a creek while their parents take in the beauty of the day.

It all adds up to a city adventure of your own design. So assess your children's interests, browse through the many entries offered here (they are arranged alphabetically), and take some time to explore. The "Queen" and her court of many moods await.

● Barnes & Noble

960 South Colorado Boulevard. (303) 691-2998. Daily, 9 A.M. to 11 P.M. **Ages 3 and up.**

Barnes & Noble opened in Denver at this store and has since expanded to numerous locations throughout Colorado. The mega-bookstore offers endless aisles of well-organized sections and two added bonuses: an attached Supr Software store and a Starbucks coffee outlet.

But forget adult pursuits. Children will gravitate to their own room, labeled Barnes & Noble Jr., where they can choose everything from Clifford to Baby-Sitter Club books from similar, well-organized shelves separated by wide aisles. There's plenty of room for children to sit on the floor and browse through books. The room also offers a small table and chairs, as well as wooden benches near a stage used for storytimes.

The chain store offers similar outlets in Colorado Springs, Fort Collins, Grand Junction, Littleton, Pueblo, and Westminster. Each offer special storytimes geared to children ages 3 to 7, though all ages are welcome. Such events can last from 20 minutes to a half hour. A host of other children's events and parenting seminars also take place every month, including a Young Reader's Club. For more details, call the specific store for a monthly schedule.

● Big Bear Ice Arena

8580 Lowry Boulevard. (303) 343-1111. Public hours: daily hours change seasonally; call first. Admission prices: Still to be finalized, but probably adults, $5; ages 17 and under, $4. Skate rental: hockey skates, $3, and figure skating skates, $3. **Ages 5 and up.**

As of this writing, Big Bear Ice Arena, a brand-new $6 million facility, was just about to open its doors in a hangar at the former Lowry Air Force Base. The arena has two indoor ice skating rinks for hockey and public skating, and come spring of 1998, developers begin construction on two in-line skating rinks. Just in case your children are more comfortable with both feet on the ground, there's still entertainment aplenty. The

90,000-square-foot building has laser tag, an arcade, party rooms, and a concessions stand, with more plans in the works as time goes on.

● Black American West Museum and Heritage Center

3091 California Street (at 30th and California). (303) 292-2566. June to September: Monday to Friday, 10 A.M. to 5 P.M.; Saturday and Sunday, noon to 5 P.M. Rest of year: Museum is closed Monday and Tuesday and hours are shortened (call for schedule). Adults, $3; ages 13 to 17, $1; under age 13, 50 cents; under age 3, free; seniors, ages 65 and up, $2. Informal guided tours. **Ages 8 and up.**

This charming little museum, located in the heart of Denver's African-American community, celebrates African-American history through artifacts and pictures, with particular emphasis on the African-American cowboy. The museum is actually the former home of Justina Ford, the first African-American woman doctor in Colorado. The building was rescued before the wrecking ball destroyed it and moved to its present site.

Some of the museum centers on Ford's practice as an obstetrician. Our guide, in fact, was delivered by Ford in 1919. The heart of the museum is the collection of Paul Stewart, who has gathered material from all over the West. The museum is best suited for elementary school kids and older who have some sense of history.

● Bladium Sports Club of Denver

8787 Montview Boulevard, Building 65. (303) 320-3033. Hangar Skate Park: daily, weather permitting; hours vary by season (call first); $12 a day. Indoor in-line hockey rinks: public hours vary according to hockey league schedule (call first), $10 during open rink. Visitors are welcome to watch league hockey games for no admission charge. **Ages 6 and up.**

If your child is fascinated by skateboarding, in-line skating or BMX bicycles, he or she can live the fantasy at this skate park in the vicinity of the former Stapleton Airport in Denver. The outdoor Hangar Skate Park has ramps, rails, hips, gaps, and more, where kids can jump and twirl to their hearts' content. We watched for about 20 minutes as young kids bladed, biked, and rode their skateboards from ramp to ramp as easily as if they had wings. To participate, you must bring your own equipment and an approved helmet with a chin strap, knee and elbow pads, and wrist guards (for skating only). The sports shop on site also has some helmets and pads available for daily rental.

Inside, the Bladium has a fitness center and two hockey rinks where hockey leagues battle it out on a regular basis. There's an upstairs and downstairs viewing area where you can stand against the railing and watch the action. When the teams aren't in play, the rinks are open to the public for in-line skating (generally weekdays only until about 2 P.M., but call first). At that time, the rinks switch to hockey pick-up games (anyone can play but you need to make a reservation). Weekends are generally reserved for hockey league play. For indoor in-line skating, you can rent equipment and helmet and pads at the sports shop.

● The Bookies

4315 E. Mississippi Avenue. (303) 759-1117. Monday to Saturday, 10 A.M. to 6 P.M.; Sunday, noon to 5 P.M. **Ages 3 and up.**

There's a bowl of pretzels on a table within reach of the kids, toys overflowing from a corner nearby, and baskets of puppets and stuffed animals that virtually invite small friends to come and play. And yes: there are books. Thousands of books. The storefront to this delightful spot in a midtown strip mall is deceptive: this is no generic children's bookstore. It's loaded with a personality all its own—thanks to owner Sue Lubeck, who started the business out of her home years ago and now heads a 4,000-square-foot book adventure.

The store boasts 40,000 titles—everything from how to save the rainforest to how to save yourself from the classroom bully to Beatrix Potter, Mercer Mayer, and other kids' favorites. The Bookies offers an extensive section of educational books for home schoolers, a large multicultural section, not to mention puzzles, games, craft items, and great kid knickknacks.

Nearly everything in the store is priced at 10 percent (for credit card purchases) and 15 percent (for cash or check purchases) off suggested retail price. Bring the kids—who will have no trouble keeping busy while you shop. And don't forget preschooler storytime: every Saturday at 10 A.M.

● Brown Palace Hotel Tea ◆

17th Street at Tremont and Broadway. (303) 297-3111. Afternoon tea: Monday to Friday, noon to 4 P.M.; Saturday and Sunday, 1 P.M. to 4 P.M. Luncheon salads are also available, Monday to Friday, noon to 2 P.M. All teas, $14 to $19. **Ages 6 and up.**

Oriental rugs. Burnished, red leather chairs. Marble tables. What could be more memorable than tea in this lovely historical hotel?

The world-renowned Brown Palace, built in 1892, has preserved the charm and dignity of a kinder, gentler era. Attentive tuxedoed waiters serve tea in the elegantly appointed lobby under its stained-glass ceiling. A harpist or a pianist provide melodic background music.

The prix fixe afternoon tea is a combination of light sandwiches, scones, and Devonshire cream and tea pastries for $14. Other options include Chocolate Sensations, a chocolates-and-scones tea, $15, or The Royale Palace tea, which includes The Brown's Kir Royale, $19. Each person is served an individual pot of the tea of his or her choice. (Other beverages are also offered on the menu.) If you come at lunch time, you can order salads from a limited menu for an additional cost.

Children are welcome, but the atmosphere lends itself only to those who enjoy dressing up and are of an age to sit quietly and enjoy the special nature of this outing. This was a particular favorite of the preteen and teen set, who never fail to ask if we can go back again—soon.

The lobby has limited seating, and the tea, particularly on Saturday, is extremely popular; to avoid disappointment, make reservations in advance.

● Buckhorn Exchange

1000 Osage Street. (303) 534-9505. Lunch: Monday to Friday, 11:30 A.M. to 2 P.M. Dinner: Monday to Thursday, 5:30 to 9:30 P.M.; Friday and Saturday, 5 to 10 P.M.; Sunday, 4 to 9 P.M. Reservations advised. Lunch, $6 to $15; dinner, $17 to $39; kids' menu, $5.50 to $9.75. **Ages 4 and up.**

More than one hundred years old, the Buckhorn Exchange is Colorado's oldest steakhouse and saloon. The building retains its original oak floors and decorative metal ceiling, and it proudly displays Colorado liquor license No. 1 over its 137-year-old, hand-carved oak bar in the upstairs saloon and Victorian parlor.

The interior is cozy, and kids can count and identify the stuffed birds and animals that line the walls—500 in all—or check out the Native American artifacts and antique firearm collections.

Befitting a restaurant of the Old West, the menu is suitably Western —buffalo, elk, pheasant, baby-back ribs, and steaks. Kids can choose buffalo and elk or more traditional fare such as ribs and hamburgers from their own menu.

● Byers-Evans House and Denver History Museum

1310 Bannock Street. (303) 620-4933. Tuesday to Sunday, 11 A.M. to 3 P.M. Adults, $3; ages 6 to 16, $1.50; under age 6 and Colorado Historical Society members, free; seniors, ages 65 and up, $2.50. **Ages 7 and up.**

In the shadow, literally, of the Denver Art Museum, the Byers-Evans House and its accompanying small history museum offer a solid slice of Denver history. Built in 1883 by William Byers, founder of the *Rocky*

Mountain News, the house was later sold in 1889 to William Gray Evans, a key developer of the Moffat Tunnel, which linked Denver to the West. The Evans family lived in the house until 1981. Visitors will learn about both families—as well as Denver when it was a mere town of 4,000—in an informational video. They then tour the house with a docent.

Older children will enjoy wending their way through the many rooms, from the lavish family and guest parlors to the more spartan bathrooms, one complete with an early bottle of Phillips Milk of Magnesia! The house is filled with interesting nooks and crannies bound to inspire those who have ever dreamed of discovering their own secret hiding place.

This is not, however, a tour young children can appreciate, as visitors are warned not to sit on or touch the furnishings—and plenty of easily accessible knickknacks are bound to tempt tiny hands. The tour lasts about an hour, so a fairly long attention span is required. Those with a cursory knowledge of Denver history, however, will appreciate the many beautiful things the house contains, and the lively stories of their use.

In addition, visitors are invited to stop into the Denver History Museum, in the service wing of the Byers-Evans House. A small facility, the museum offers changing exhibits, pull-out drawers with postcards, campaign buttons and other memorabilia, and interactive videos that allow patrons to choose and view topics related to Denver's history.

● Children's Museum ◆

2121 Children's Museum Drive (exit 211 off Interstate 25; the teal- and fuchsia-colored building is visible from the highway). (303) 433-7444. Memorial Day to Labor Day: daily, 10 A.M. to 5 P.M. Labor Day to Memorial Day: Tuesday to Sunday, 10 A.M. to 5 P.M. All year round: Toddler hour, 9 to 10 A.M., Tuesday and Thursday; first Friday of the month, open until 8 P.M. Ages 3 to 59, $5; 1- and 2-year-olds, $2; seniors, ages 60 and up, $3. Open all Monday school holidays, except Christmas. Also closed on Thanksgiving Day. **Ages 2 to 10.**

A must-visit attraction, the Children's Museum offers hours of hands-on fun. Permanent exhibits include the Wild Oats Community Market and Inventions, a hands-on exhibit where kids can assemble a car on an assembly line or build their own wooden toys in an expanded wood shop.

Toddlers can play in Goldilocks's house; older children can play games on color computers. At the TV station exhibit, kids get to "report" the local weather, right down to tracking the weather system on a map—all on camera. In the science lab, children can experiment with bubbles, explore a beehive, and draw with the pendulum-swinging pen. Far and away one of the most interesting exhibits is called SpokesPeople. Here children can wheel themselves around in wheelchairs, reaching for cereal, "cooking" in a specially designed kitchen, or playing ball from their wheelchairs on a small basketball-type court, gaining insight into the special needs of the disabled.

Exhibits change from time to time to keep the museum fresh and interesting. The museum also has a theater where visiting troupes perform plays and comedy skits for a minimal additional charge. Outside, there's playground equipment for the younger kids to continue the experience. Although the Denver Children's Museum is not as elaborate as some we've seen in other major cities, it's certainly a warm and friendly place that will engage your children for an afternoon of fun—and learning. While you're there, you may want to hit the slopes at KidSlope at the museum (see page 61).

● Colorado History Museum

13th and Broadway. (303) 866-3682. Monday to Saturday,10 A.M. to 4:30 P.M.; Sunday, noon to 4:30 P.M. Adults, $3; students over age 16, with an ID card, and seniors, ages 65 and up, $2.50; children, ages 6 to 16, $1.50; under age 6, free. **Ages 6 and up.**

Walk through Colorado history with the use of a pictorial time line, dioramas, and artifacts—everything from period clothing to a full-size covered wagon to heavy mining equipment. Even younger kids will enjoy the model depictions of life on the frontier. Older kids will take special interest in the model of Denver at the time of the great flood of 1864. La Gente is a permanent exhibit that uses furnishings and fashions to show the Hispanic influence in Colorado. There's a children's corner as part of the La Gente exhibit, where elementary school children can experience a little hands-on learning.

Of most interest for older children is a pictorial display of turn-of-the-century children and clothing, centered around the story of Irma, a young Denver girl born in 1888. Irma died at age 12, but her trunk of toys, school supplies, and other treasures of her brief life have survived through the century.

Although much of the museum is "don't touch," there's enough to keep kids interested for 45 minutes to an hour, or even longer—especially the older set, who can pause and read the fascinating entries by each exhibit.

● Colorado Midland Model Railroad

1701 Wynkoop Street, in the basement of Union Station. (303) 572-1015. The last Friday of each month (but closed in June, July, and August), 7:30 to 9:30 P.M. Free. **Ages 2 and up.**

If you have a model train lover in the family, you probably already know there's no sense fighting this fascination. Its pull is as strong as a mighty diesel engine. Might as well jump onboard and bring your child to Denver's only passenger train station, where a grand miniature train layout—75 feet by 90 feet—is kept in mint condition in the basement.

The oldest O-scale (train lovers will understand) club layout in the United States, this miniature setup was originally built in 1933 and has been continually expanded ever since by the Denver Society of Model Railroaders. Once a month, the society invites visitors to watch from large, cut-out windows as members run five narrow-gauge and five standard-gauge miniature trains on more than 20 scale miles of track. You'll see boxcars, miniature Amtrak passenger cars, and more wend their way through tunnels and over hills built to resemble Colorado's rocky terrain (in fact, some of the layout is made from actual sifted Colorado rock). Needless to say, your children's eyes will be riveted to the track if they are seriously into trains. And even if you can't understand their delight, you'll appreciate the attention to detail society members have given this elaborate layout.

When you've had your fill of the miniature trains, don't forget to stop upstairs and let your children peek through the passageway where the real trains pull into the station. They are bound to be impressed by the size of the real thing. Take a minute, as well, to appreciate the architecture of this grand old building, which, with its marble floors and dramatic archways overhead, was clearly a jewel for the city in an earlier era.

● Colorado Rockies Baseball ◆

Coors Field, 20th and Blake streets. (800) 388-ROCK or (303)-ROCKIES. Prices range from $4 to $28 in the club level. Seats in the "rock pile": adults, $4; children, under age 12 and seniors, ages 55 and up, $1. **Ages 4 and up.**

Coors Field in lower downtown Denver seats 50,200 and frequently sells out, except for the "rock pile," the seats farthest from the playing field. However, you should be able to get tickets for most games with a phone call ahead of time. Kids will enjoy the antics of the mascot, Dinger, a purple dinosaur that hatched at one of the games in 1994. The younger tots (under four feet tall) can play on a small playground on the concourse in the left-field corner of the stadium, next to a kids' concession stand called Buckaroos.

Although the seats are reasonably priced, figure on knocking one out of the ballpark when it comes to food. At around $8 to $10 per person for hot dogs, pretzels, peanuts, soft drinks, and the like, a family of four can easily spend $40. If your kids have smaller appetites, it's worth a stroll over to Buckaroos where the prices have been downsized, along with the portions.

The brick-and-steel girder stadium is one of Denver's showpieces, blending a wonderful '90s structure with an old-time baseball feel. Nothing quite beats a baseball game and nothing quite beats the excitement of a Rockies' fan.

● Colorado State Capitol

1475 Sherman Street. (303) 866-2604. Memorial Day to Labor Day: Monday to Friday, 9 A.M. to 3:30 P.M.; Saturday, 9:30 A.M. to 2 P.M. Rest of year: Monday to Friday, 9:30 A.M. to 3:30 P.M. Guided tours every 30 minutes in summer; every 45 minutes in winter. Self-guided tours are also permitted. Tours begin at the north entrance. Free. **Ages 8 and up.**

You can't miss the gold dome of the state capitol building if you drive through downtown Denver. Rising 272 feet above the ground, the dome is outfitted in the metal that was so important to the state's early economy and growth. The original gold was a gift from Colorado miners.

Kids will find lots of points of interest here, including the step outside the west entrance that marks the spot where Denver is one mile above sea level (found to be in error in 1969; a true mile high is three steps above the marker), the legislative chambers, and the hand-stitched wallhanging on prominent women created by 3,500 people. You can also climb the 93 steps into the dome. There, from indoor and outdoor observations decks, you'll find a panoramic view of Denver and the vicinity, including Pikes Peak, on a clear day.

Every school child in the city takes the tour of the capitol at one time or another, and a trip to Denver wouldn't be complete without a visit to this impressive hub of Colorado state government.

● Colorado's Ocean Journey

In Central Platte Valley (exit 211 off Interstate 25) immediately north of the Children's Museum. Opening May, 1999. **All ages.**

Riding a tidal wave of excitement, Ocean Journey will spring to life in May 1999. The aquarium plans to house 15,000 fresh and saltwater creatures, displayed in five major exhibits: Colorado River Journey, Sea of Cortez, Depths of the Pacific, Ocean Discovery Plaza, and Indonesia River Journey, the latter a flooded Asian rainforest. The first floor of the two-story building will feature a sea otter exhibit where visitors can watch the otters frolic in their simulated habitat; the second floor will bring visitors face to face with sharks. Already rising from the Central Platte Valley, Ocean Journey is expected to attract a million visitors a year.

● Coors Field Tours

Coors Field, 20th and Blake streets. (303)-ROCKIES. Tours are conducted Monday to Saturday, all year round. April to the end of September, generally 10 A.M. to 3 P.M., on the hour. Rest of year, generally 11 A.M. to 2 P.M., on the hour. Adults, $5; children, under age 12, and seniors, ages 55 and up, $3. **Ages 8 and up.**

This popular 75-minute guided tour takes you through the ballpark for a look at the suites, the press box, and the visitor's clubhouse. If you're a baseball fan, and you can't make it to a game, you'll love the inside look at the stadium. Tours are frequently sold out, so book in advance.

● Denver Art Museum

100 West 14th Avenue Parkway. (303) 640-4433. Tuesday to Saturday, 10 A.M. to 5 P.M.; Sunday, noon to 5 P.M. Adults, $4.50; students with ID and seniors, ages 65 and up, $2.50; under age 6, free. Saturdays are free to all. **Ages 5 and up.**

What could be more child accessible than this building that looks as though it were made of a giant pile of gray Legos? OK, so inside it's a relatively quiet, pristine environment, filled with adults talking in low, reverent tones. There's still plenty of fun to be had here for kids. You just need to know when to come—and where to look.

The best days for families at the museum are Saturdays, when admission is free and the facility offers a host of events geared to children. Every first Saturday, kids ages 5 to 9 are invited to attend art workshops, which are generally geared to an exhibit on display at the museum. For instance, children might make straw images in the style of a New Mexican folk artist, or create miniature Indian sculptures out of wire, wood, and stone. Times are 11 A.M., 12:30 P.M., and 2 P.M. Meet near the Kids Corner on the main floor.

On the second, third, fourth, and fifth Saturday of each month families can check out "Family Backpacks," also near the Kids Corner. Inside each pack are games and activities to use as you walk through the galleries. With the "Western Adventures" backpack, for example, your kids can don an explorer's hat, keep a journal, and use binoculars on their scouting mission. With "Granny's Adventures in Africa," you'll be treated to a trip to West Africa through Granny's letters and drawings.

And that's not all. Every day, children can:

Pick up "Eye Spy" games on each floor. The games offer pictures of items found on that floor; children are asked to seek them out as they walk around the gallery. Older children especially will enjoy this challenging treasure hunt. (The game can be frustrating, however, for the younger ones.)

Try an unsupervised art project in the Kids Corner. Children might make a jaguar mask one visit, an Asian puppet the next. This is a great way to get your children used to the museum environment—and they will love cutting and pasting on the multicolored carpet, where no one will admonish them for letting the scraps fly. The project changes each month.

Settle into video and reading areas on each floor. Here tapes explain everything from Indian myths to how common objects became pop art. Numerous books and reading materials are available.

While you could easily spend an entire day here, children will have their fill after a few hours. It's best to come for a specific activity or to target one or two floors per visit—and return later for more.

We especially recommend the third floor, with its excellent Native American displays. Children will enjoy seeing tepees, beaded clothing, and life-size models of horses. Kids will also be fascinated with the huge totem poles on the second floor.

● Denver Botanic Gardens

1005 York Street. (303) 331-4000. Daily, 9 A.M. to 5 P.M.; until 8 P.M. on selected summer evenings. May to September: adults, $4; students ages 6 to 15 and seniors ages 65 and up, $2; under age 6, free. October to April: adults, $3; students ages 15 and up and seniors ages 65 and up, $1.50; ages 6 to 15, $1; under 6, free. **All ages.**

Upon entering the Tropical Conservatory of the Denver Botanic Gardens, a delighted 5-year-old noted, "It looks like a jungle." The children can explore the conservatory indoors, which is, indeed, as thick as a jungle, with winding paved pathways and occasional bridges. As of spring 1998, an elevator disguised in a banyan tree takes visitors to a viewing platform where they can look down on the rainforest.

More likely, children will prefer to romp along the numerous paths outdoors that wind among the rose garden, the Xeriscape demonstration garden, the endangered plants garden, and the herb and vegetable gardens. Don't miss the Japanese garden with its authentic teahouse in the far northwest corner, designed by renowned architect Koichi Kawana. In the summer, look for the storybook garden with plants from the classic tales, such as the poppies from *The Wizard of Oz,* Mr. MacGregor's Garden from *Peter Rabbit,* and life-size topiary rabbits and bears from *Winnie the Pooh.* In spring and summer, the gardens are ablaze with color, but even in winter, children will enjoy the outing, looking for those pretty little flowers that still poke their heads through the snow.

The Botanic Gardens also host wonderful outdoor concerts in the summer—some adult-oriented, others geared to children. Either way, children are welcome. Bring a picnic dinner and enjoy a summer night.

● Denver Broncos Football

Mile High Stadium, 1900 Eliot Street (exit 210B off Interstate 25). (303) 433-7466. Box office (located at the stadium): Monday to Friday, 8 A.M. to 5 P.M. and Saturday before a home game, 9 A.M. to noon. Tickets, $20, $25, $34, $36, $42. **Ages 5 and up.**

Mile High Stadium seats around 76,000 people and is always sold out by game time. But some fans can get tickets for individual games with planning and a little luck. Call the box office and request a mail-order form. The box office begins mailing forms around the end of June and will process them on a first-come, first-served basis as soon as tickets go on sale in mid-July. Be aware that they don't have every price range for every game.

As for getting tickets around the actual day of the game, some single tickets might be available or you might get lucky and score a pair or two. Check with the box office for availability.

Note: There has been much talk of a new home for the Broncos, which is pending at this time. If plans go through, it's expected to be located in the same vicinity as Mile High Stadium.

● The Denver Buffalo Company

1109 Lincoln Street. (303) 832-0880. Main dining room: Monday to Saturday, lunch, 11 A.M. to 2:30 P.M.; dinner, 5 to 10 P.M.; Sunday, dinner only, 4 to 9 P.M. Deli: Monday to Saturday, 10 A.M. to 9 P.M.; closed Sunday. Trading Post: Monday to Thursday, 10 A.M. to 9 P.M.; Friday and Saturday, 10 A.M. to 10 P.M.; Sunday, 4 to 9 P.M. **Ages 5 and up.**

Where else can you sample a hot dog made of buffalo (the Buffdog), Buffalo Stroganoff, Buffalo Chile Verde Con Carne, and Buffalo Ravioli? The Buffalo Company was formed in 1989 and raises its own buffalo at a ranch east of Kiowa for the Denver restaurant. It serves up buffalo in every imaginable form in a fine dining area or in more limited forms in the adjoining deli. Perhaps as interesting as the food is the Trading Post, filled with artifacts of Western Americana and fine contemporary Western art.

Kids will be enchanted by the bronze buffalo that guards the outside of the restaurant, the Alaskan timber wolf and Lakota Indian chief in the entry way, and the stuffed buffalo in the Trading Post.

The kids' menu is a coloring booklet with games, including the Great Buffalo Hunt; children are asked to locate a totem pole, buffalo hide, Indian rug, and other items at the Buffalo Company to win a prize— usually an arrowhead from the Trading Post. Along with the requisite chicken fingers, the kids' menu also offers a Buffdog or Buffalo Burger for the adventurous visitor to try. (Kids like the Buffdog, in particular, which tastes like a lean beef hotdog.) The kids' menu is reasonably priced, but note that dinner in the fine dining room can be pricey. For a quick stop, grab a Buffdog at the deli.

● Denver Firefighters Museum

1326 Tremont Place. (303) 892-1436. Monday to Saturday, 10 A.M. to 2 P.M. Adults, $3; ages 11 and under and 55 and older, $2. **Ages 2 and up.**

This is a spit-polished place, with glistening red fire wagons standing proudly at attention. Located in Old Fire House No. 1, built in 1909, the small museum boasts authentic equipment from Denver's old days. You'll see an 1875 hose reel, an 1867 hand pumper, trampoline-like gizmos that were used to catch people jumping out of windows, old-time badges and uniforms, even a couple of helmets that were melted by the extreme heat of a fire. But for kids the biggest attraction by far is the shiny, white, modern fire truck that stands near the older pieces. While the other equipment is mostly hands-off for visitors, children are invited to climb up here and sit in the driver's seat. And they don't need to be asked twice. They play with the steering wheel, ring the bell, and flip the switches with enthusiasm.

Children are also welcome to try on firefighter's boots, coats, hats, and other clothing, to watch a video about fire featuring Donald Duck and Jiminy Cricket, and to listen to the tour guide tell stories of dramatic fires of yesteryear. A formal tour takes about one hour, but it's worth a much quicker stop just to let your children climb aboard a real fire truck.

● Denver Museum of Miniatures, Dolls, and Toys

1880 Gaylord Street. (303) 322-3704. Tuesday to Saturday, 10 A.M. to 4 P.M.; Sunday, 1 to 4 P.M. Adults, $3; children ages 2 to 16 and seniors ages 65 and up, $2. **Ages 4 and up.**

The world inside this museum is only inches high and populated with dolls who live in miniature luxury. Consider the 1839 Rhode Island home, complete with Oriental rugs, golden chandeliers, delicate wall-paper, and a croquet set laid out on the front lawn. (You'll wish you could move in!) You'll also see a miniature adobe house with tile floors and Indian pottery, a German milliner's shop from the early 1800s, tiny silver service sets, and an assortment of dolls and teddy bears. The museum consists of approximately nine galleries and a gift shop. If your children are observant and enjoy detail, this is a great place to stop. If not, how-ever, they may simply race through the rooms and be ready to leave long before you are.

The miniatures are housed in the Pearce-McAllister Cottage, built in 1899. After you are through looking at luxury in small slices, wander through the home's historic library on the bottom level. It contains origi-nal furnishings and memorabilia of the prominent McAllister family.

In addition, the museum offers birthday parties and periodic children's workshops on miniature art and other crafts. Call for upcom-ing classes.

● Denver Museum of Natural History ◆

2001 Colorado Boulevard (at Montview), City Park, adjacent to Denver Zoo. (303) 322-7009. Daily, 9 A.M. to 5 P.M.; closed Christmas Day. Adults, $6; ages 3 to 12 and seniors ages 60 and up, $4; under age 3, free. (Price includes Gates Planetarium.) **Ages 2 and up.**

(Gates Planetarium/Laser Fantasy and Imax Theater are located at the museum; see separate entries.)

The cavernous Denver Museum of Natural History was expanded and redesigned a few years ago when it had the chance to feature a special exhibit from Egypt. Since that time, the museum has had nothing but success, featuring wonderful changing exhibits, such as Imperial Tombs of China, along with perennial favorites. Recent special exhibits included such hands-on kid pleasers as Experiment Gallery and Whodunit, the science of solving crime.

The museum has regular exhibits of reconstructed dinosaur skel-etons—including dioramas, gems and minerals, and insects and butter-flies. One of our favorite exhibits is the pendulum near the planetarium, which knocks down strategically placed pins as it swings, showing how the earth is moving ever so slightly. The largest permanent exhibit is Prehistoric Journey, an award-winning display following the history of life on earth with replicas of dinosaurs and interactive computer games.

From a kid's perspective, the Hall of Life, a kind of museum within the museum, is the hands-down favorite. Here kids—and grown-ups—are issued a "credit" card that computerizes their personal data as they move from exhibit to exhibit within the hall, logging their knowledge of nutrition and the body for example, or their fitness and flexibility. At the exit, a computer reads the data and gives them a print-out on how they scored. The kids never tire of this hands-on chance to explore their personal best.

Note: If you want to see all the museum at one time, save the Hall of Life for last. Once you're there, the kids probably won't want to leave—and running through all Hall's exhibits could take 60 to 90 minutes, depending on the crowds.

● Denver Nuggets Basketball and Colorado Avalanche Hockey

McNichols Arena, 1635 Clay Street. (303) 893-3865 or (303) 830-8497 (to charge by phone), or you can buy tickets at the box office at the lower east entrance of the arena during business hours: Monday to Friday, 8:30 A.M. to 5 P.M.; Saturday, 10 A.M. to 3 P.M., during the seasons. Nuggets: Ticket prices: $10.50 to $27.50, upper level; $27.50 to $180, lower level. Tickets generally go on sale around the second Saturday in October. The season begins around the end of October and runs until the end of April. Games are generally in the evenings. Avalanche: Ticket prices range from $12.50 to $100. Tickets go on sale in September; games are generally sold out. Preseason begins in September; regular games in October. **Ages 5 and up.**

With the success of the Colorado Avalanche, hockey tickets are harder to score than a goal against Patrick Waugh. You're much more likely to get a seat at a Nuggets game—unless they become red hot once again. In 1999, the Avalanche and the Nuggets will be playing at a new stadium, the Pepsi Center, in the Platte Valley.

● Denver Public Library's Children's Library

1357 Broadway. (303) 640-8800. Monday to Wednesday, 10 A.M. to 9 P.M.; Thursday to Saturday, 10 A.M. to 5:30 P.M.; Sunday, 1 to 5 P.M. **Ages 2 and up.**

Every year, more than one million children's books are checked out of the Denver Public Library system. While branches are throughout the city, children will find the latest the system has to offer in this state-of-the-art main branch. Located on the first floor, the Children's Library boasts 12,500 square feet and includes a computerized Kid's Catalog designed by Denver librarians and others that uses pictures to help children navigate book choices, pictures to indicate the subject matter of books in various areas, computers with Internet access (parents note: access is uncensored), and cassette players. There are special areas for listening to audio tapes or reading, and when it's time for special events, such as story hours and author visits, children can congregate in an octagonal space with a striped ceiling that recalls the tents from *Arabian Nights.* Children will find their own, kid-size check-out desk located in the main hallway. (Look for the big stuffed teddy bear.)

Story times for preschool children (ages 2 to 5) are Wednesdays, 10 A.M., 10:30 A.M., and 1:30 P.M. and Saturdays, 11 A.M. The library also offers special entertainers, storytelling, and more each Saturday and Sunday, generally 2 to 3 P.M.

● Denver Puppet Theatre

3156 West 38th Avenue. (303) 458-6446. Thursday and Friday shows at 10 A.M. and 1 P.M.; Saturday shows at 11 A.M. and 1 P.M.; Sunday show at 1 P.M. Tickets, ages 1 and older, $3. **Ages 3 to 12.**

In today's glut of movies and TV, puppet shows seem to be relics of another era. But not here, where scores of brightly colored marionettes decorate the walls and a tiny stage sits like a king, front and center. The 3,000-square-foot theater consists of a performance room, with rows of chairs set in front of the stage, a room for birthday parties and other activities, and a gift shop. The shows, while not spectacular, feature fine puppets and a fair amount of audience participation. They are relatively short (approximately 40 minutes), but the audience is invited to roam the stage before and after, playing with puppets and behind various stages that are scatted throughout the theater. Children are also encouraged to create their own puppets before and after the show, using markers, paper, and glue. Preschoolers, especially, will enjoy the novelty of it all. Birthday parties and workshops are available.

● Denver Zoo

City Park, East 23rd Street and Steele Street (adjacent to the Denver Museum of Natural History). (303) 331-4110. Daily, winter, 10 A.M. to 5 P.M.; summer, 9 A.M. to 6 P.M. Adults, ages 13 to 61, $8; ages 4 to 12 and seniors ages 62 and up, $5; ages 3 and under, free. **All ages.**

Enter the Denver Zoo and spend an hour or spend the afternoon. Either way, with 3,500 animals housed on approximately 80 acres, there's more than enough to keep you busy. And with a park that is consistently rated among the top 10 in the country, you'll find clean, appealing exhibits with a fair amount of interactive learning experiences for the children. Visiting the underwater sea lion exhibit? Children are invited to press a button and compare how long they can hold their breath with a sea lion's average time. Just finished looking at the exotic animals in the Tropical

Discovery exhibit? Test your ability to recognize smells of the rainforest, such as cocoa and bananas. The zoo is constantly improving old exhibits and designing new ones to be even more child friendly.

To see the entire zoo, we suggest setting aside three to four hours. Keep in mind that this is a large park and restrooms can be hard to find, unless you know where to look. So you might want to stop at the facilities near the main entrance before heading into the park to avoid any problems later. Also, keep in mind that walking the entire park—especially with children in tow—can be exhausting. Strollers and wagons are available for rent.

After more visits here than we can count, we've come to approach the zoo in terms of layout: we head to the right or to the left on any given day, and plan to return another day to see what we missed on the other side. If you would like to do the same, here's the scoop: to the left, you'll find, among other animals, giraffes, lions, tigers, sea lions, polar bears, and the recently constructed Tropical Discovery building, which houses jungle animals, such as crocodiles, pythons, and exotic fish. On a tight schedule, this is a nice choice, offering fun exhibits—such as watching sea lions and polar bears swim underwater in the Northern Shores exhibit—with a relatively small amount of walking. Also, there is a snack bar and plenty of benches at the Northern Shores, where parents can take a breather while the children are entertained by the ever-entertaining seals.

If you head to the right, instead, you'll see elephants, hippos, gorillas, monkeys, all kinds of birds, including flocks of flamingos and more. There's decidedly more ground to cover on this side, a minus for those in a hurry. On the plus side, children love the new Primate Panorama building, which houses the gorillas, orangutans, and other monkeys. And a miniature train ride originates on this side, near the pachyderms. For 75 cents (ages 3 and under free with an adult), the train is always a hit with younger children. (One caveat: the train doesn't operate in bad weather.)

In addition, the zoo has recently instituted a free bird show, offered between Memorial Day and Labor Day at 11:30 A.M., 1, and 3 P.M., weather permitting. Located near the Hungry Elephant in a small theater setting, the show features birds of prey, including owls, macaws, and rare birds, in free flight. It lasts about 20 minutes and is worth a stop.

Whether you see the park in several trips or all in one visit, keep in mind that feeding times are a fun time to come. Generally, these are: penguins, 10:15 A.M. and 4 P.M.; sea lions, 11 A.M. and 2:30 P.M.; feline house, 3:30 P.M. (no feedings on Monday). Zoo officials also recommend coming in the fall and winter, when the animals aren't hampered by the hot sun and are more active. "It's a blast to go to the Northern Shores in the winter," says one spokeswoman. "The polar bears like to break the ice on their pond and play with the chunks."

For snacks, the Hungry Elephant Cafeteria near the main entrance offers indoor seating and serves full meals. The outdoor stands throughout the park feature mostly hot dogs, hamburgers, popcorn, and other snack food.

Note that the zoo is open every day of the year, including all holidays. It has wonderful special, seasonal events, including Wildlights during the Christmas season, in which the park is lit up at night and hot drinks are served; and Boo at the Zoo for Halloween visitors, who can enjoy face painting, fortune tellers, and more. Call the zoo for a schedule of upcoming events.

● Elitch Gardens Amusement Park ◆

2000 Elitch Circle (near Interstate 25 and Speer Boulevard). (303) 595-4386. Amusement park: Memorial Day to Labor Day, daily, generally 10 A.M. to 10 P.M. Open weekends early May to Memorial Day and Labor Day to November; hours vary. Water park: Memorial Day to Labor Day, daily, generally 11 A.M. to 7 P.M. Adults, $22.95; children 47 inches tall and under, $12.95; seniors ages 55 to 69, $15.95; ages 3 and under and seniors ages 70 and up, free. Parking, $4. Tickets allow admission to both parks. Season passes are available at a discounted rate. **Ages 2 and up.**

Want to please children of any age? This is no-miss, especially for those difficult-to-entertain teens and preteens. Elitch Gardens is situated on 70 acres in the Central Platte Valley near downtown. The park features two sections: an amusement area offering more than 40 rides and a 10-acre water park dubbed Island Kingdom.

In the amusement park, your children will enjoy such heart-stoppers as the Tower of Doom, which drops riders from the top of a 210-foot tower, 22 stories to the ground; the Mind Eraser, a daring loop that twists and turns and sends passengers upside down; and Shipwreck Falls, which catapults riders over a 50-foot waterfall. Your child must be 48 inches tall to go on most of the rides in this area. However, for smaller children, Kiddieland is a good option with rides geared for children up to age 7. In addition, you'll find carnival games and arcades—and free shows scattered throughout the park at various times of the day, including a spirited Wild West shoot-out, a flea circus, and magic shows.

At the adjacent water park, you'll find dozens of water slides and a five-story play structure with water spurting every which way. The area also offers a wave pool and places to simply relax in a lounge chair.

In order to juggle the clothing needs for both the amusement park and water area, we advise that children wear their swimsuits underneath their clothes. It works best to first enjoy the amusement rides (some, like Shipwreck Falls and Disaster Canyon, can soak a rider as thoroughly as any of the attractions on the water park side), then head to the water park. Towels aren't available for rent, so be sure and bring your own. You can stash them, along with a change of clothes, in lockers throughout the park (the larger lockers are in the water park). Most teens prefer to carry their things in backpacks, which they toss in a pile before boarding the rides (note, however, that that can be a risky proposition, as the attendant is not responsible for the bags).

While kids will have a blast here and can easily spend the entire day, be advised: this is unquestionably an expensive outing. In addition to the pricey admission fee, you will pay $4 to park; $5 for all-day use of the water park lockers ($2 will be refunded when the key is returned); and untold sums on food and drink (patrons are not allowed to bring food inside the park, although there are picnic tables available in grassy areas near the parking lot). Discount admission tickets are available at area retail outlets; call the main number for information.

Despite the cost, you'll get plenty of bang for the buck—and an outing that will leave your kids happy and satisfied.

● Forney Transportation Museum

1416 Platte Street. (303) 433-3643. Monday to Saturday, October 1 to April 30, 10 A.M. to 5 P.M. (other months, 9 A.M. to 5 P.M.); Sunday, 11 A.M. to 5 P.M. Adults, $4; ages 12 to 18, $2; ages 5 to 11, $1; children under age 5, free. **Ages 2 and up.**

Imagine a basement big enough to stash cars, hundreds of them. Then imagine the cars strewn about randomly—a 1915 Cadillac here, a Rolls Royce that once belonged to a royal family there. That's the Forney Transportation Museum, a funky warehouse filled endlessly with things on wheels—from toy buggies that were powered by the family dog to a gleaming train engine to a bicycle built for four. The museum boasts many rarities, including a car once owned by Amelia Earhart. But children aren't likely to be impressed by such name-dropping. They are bound to enjoy, however, cruising up and down the long aisles filled with shiny chrome and checking out the locomotives in the train yards outside—and don't forget to stop downstairs to see the miniature train setup. A quarter will set the tiny cars in motion.

● Four Mile Historic Park

715 South Forest Street. (303) 399-1859. April through September, Wednesday to Sunday, 10 A.M. to 4 P.M. Call for winter hours. Adults, $3.50; ages 6 to 15 and seniors ages 65 and up, $2; under age 6, free. Stagecoach/Wagon rides, weekends only, 11 A.M. to 2 P.M., $1. **Ages 5 and up.**

Chickens and turkeys strut their stuff at the Four Mile Historic Park, only a few miles from downtown Denver. Admission entitles you to stroll the 14 acres and take a tour of the oldest house in Denver (pay in the adjacent Bee House on the premises). The Four Mile House once served as a stage stop on the Cherokee Trail, survived the Cherry Creek flood in 1864, and became the center of a successful farming operation.

Guided tours of the house are given on the hour. Although the tour is lengthy, lasting about an hour, kids should find many points of interest, such as the long bunk bed where the original owner slept foot to foot with her daughter or the oversized toothbrush used by pioneer women. The original wing of the house stands in stark contrast to the lavish rooms added on by the second owner a short time later, a reflection of the quickly changing times.

In addition to the house, the premises have a well where the kids can pull up a bucket full of water, goats and draft horses to visit, and a full-size tepee they can sit in. From time to time, Four Mile Park has special activities featuring historical demonstrations such as quilting, blacksmithing, and spinning. Bring a picnic and buy a soft drink at the Bee House. There are restrooms and a water fountain as you first enter the park.

● Gates Planetarium and Laser Fantasy at the Denver Museum of Natural History

2001 Colorado Boulevard (at Montview), City Park, adjacent to Denver Zoo. General reservation and information, (303) 322-7009 or 800-925-2250. Planetarium, (303) 370-6351; Laser, (303) 370-6487. Planetarium: daily daytime performances; show times vary. Laser: evening performances; day and show times vary. Call for current information. Museum admission (includes planetarium but not laser shows): adults, $7; ages 4 to 12, $4.50; under age 4, free. Laser: any age, $6.50. Planetarium, **ages 8 and up;** *laser show,* **ages 12 and up.**

If your kids have never experienced a planetarium, this is a good place to meet the stars. The comfortable facility is relaxing, particularly after touring the museum.

In the evening, the planetarium turns from starry skies to lasers. The laser shows are geared to teens and adults, with lasers pulsing in syncopation to Pink Floyd, Jefferson Airplane, Steppenwolf, the Beatles, and Pearl Jam. Once in a while, laser shows suitable for the whole family are offered, and they are scheduled earlier in the evening. And by the way, the 3-D glasses that you can purchase from the nearby vending machine are not necessary to enjoy the show.

● Governor's Mansion
400 East 8th Avenue. (303) 866-3682. Limited hours on Tuesday afternoons and some evenings in June, July, and August and during the Christmas holidays; call for information. Free. **Ages 8 and up.**

The 30-minute tours of this beautiful, red brick, Colonial Revival mansion will give you a look at the place governors are allowed to call home while they serve the state of Colorado. The house was built around the turn of the century by Walter Cheesman, who died before it was finished. His wife sold the house in 1926 to wealthy businessman and philanthropist Claude Boettcher, who donated it to the state.

Of unforgettable appeal: the Palm Room, an all-white parlor with white marble floors, the site of many state receptions. Its windows look out onto the terraced gardens, designed by the original owner. Older children might enjoy this quick trip through another piece of Colorado history. Younger kids will probably be restless.

● Grizzly Rose
5450 North Valley Highway (exit 215 off Interstate 25, half mile south of 58th Avenue). (303) 295-1330. Sunday (family day), doors open 3 P.M. Admission is $3. Line dance lesson, 5 P.M.: adults, $2; ages 12 and under, $1 (line dance lesson not recommended for ages 8 and under). **Ages 2 and up.**

If your idea of Denver is country western music and cowboys and cowgirls, you won't be disappointed by the Grizzly Rose, a country western dance hall and saloon, reminiscent of Mickey Gilley's famous emporium.

On Sundays, the Grizzly Rose becomes a family affair, where young 'uns can have a taste of dancin' and country western music. If you want to learn a line dance, arrive in time for the 5 P.M. lesson, which lasts about an hour and is offered at a reasonable fee. The free 6 P.M. lesson is geared for younger children and their parents and teaches such dances as the Cotton Eyed Joe, the Chicken Dance, and the Hokey Pokey. It lasts about 30 minutes and falls into the you-get-what-you-pay-for category. Although it's lots of fun, it's short and sweet and will leave you hankering for more. After the lessons, a live band performs so you can kick up your heels on your own. There will be plenty of people sashaying their children—

toddlers on up—across the floor. About 8 P.M., teens tend to take over the dance floor.

The Grizzly Rose offers a full menu with plenty of kid-pleasing items for those who work up an appetite or just want to sit and watch others take a turn on the dance floor. (Note: the cafe doesn't begin serving until 5 P.M.) This is the place—finally—to wear that cowboy hat and those cowboy boots you bought just for your trip to Denver.

● IMAX Theater

At the Denver Museum of Natural History, 2001 Colorado Boulevard. (303) 322-7009, or (303) 370-8257 for the hearing impaired. Hours vary according to the show. Adults, $6; ages 3 to 12 and seniors ages 60 and up, $4; under age 3, free. Combination museum and IMAX: Adults, $9; ages 3 to 12 and seniors 60 and up, $6; under age 3, free. **Ages 6 and up.**

Sometimes bigger is better. And what better proof than the IMAX, where larger-than-life is the name of the game? At this theater, located in the front of the Museum of Natural History, the screen rises $4\frac{1}{2}$ stories tall. Here, movie subjects never cavort at a distance; they are up close and personal. If the subject is sharks, you'll see the plaque on their teeth. If it's Mount St. Helens, you'll duck from the lava.

It's best to leave preschoolers at home, since no one who leaves the theater is admitted back inside after the show has begun. (If a child has to go to the bathroom, or becomes frightened and wants to leave for a minute, you'll be stuck.) Also the shows start promptly. Unlike in a regular movie theater, you can't slide in a few minutes late.

● Josh & John's Naturally Homemade Ice Creams

1444 Market Street. (303) 628-0310. Daily, noon to midnight. Also in Colorado Springs and Boulder (see entries under those headings). **All ages.**

Josh Paris and John Krakauer grew up in Boston, where folks lined up for Steve's ice cream—homemade ice cream where you choose the mix-ins, which was a novelty at the time.

Josh and John's ice cream shops are reminiscent of Steve's. The ice cream is churned out front, and you choose the mix-ins and the flavors. As added incentive, they'll give you an ice creamometer card—a card that is punched every time you buy an ice cream; the colder the weather, the more punches you get. If it's below freezing and snowy, you get 15 punches and a free ice cream.

The young entrepreneurs, one of whom lives in Colorado, are hoping to do for this area what Steve's did for Boston and Ben and Jerry did for Vermont. There are several tables at the shops if you choose to make a rest stop here, or take a cone along for the ride. The Denver location is in lower downtown, near the Tabor Center and the historic Larimer Square district.

● KidSlope at the Children's Museum

2121 Children's Museum Drive (exit 211 off Interstate 25; the teal- and fuchsia-colored building is visible from the highway). (303) 433-7444. Memorial Day to Labor Day, daily. Labor Day to Memorial Day, Tuesday to Sunday. In-line skating, April to October only; snowboard and skiing, year-round. Two-hour lessons: 10 A.M., 12:30 P.M., and 3 P.M. Skiing, ages 4 and up; in-line skating, ages 6 and up; snowboarding, ages 8 and up. Skiing or in-line skating: $8. Snowboarding: $10. Equipment included. Ski or skate and museum admission: $11; Snowboard and admission, $13; Ski, skate, and admission, $18. Reservations advised. **Ages 4 and up.**

If you've always pictured yourself and your kids swooshing down a mountain but you haven't quite made it to the slopes, KidSlope will introduce you to the joys of skiing or snowboarding. Ski instructors provide a two-hour group lesson (ratio: five to one) on an artificial slope next to the Children's Museum. Participants are divided by age and ability. KidSlope will teach you the basics, without the hassle of lift lines: how to use equipment, the various ski positions, how to stop, and how to sidestep up the hill. Likewise with snowboarding and in-line skating, where you'll learn the basics, safety tips, and more, depending on ability. KidSlope also offers Sled Dogs, in which you wear a snowskate and "skate" down the hill.

The lesson here is pretty much the same as a beginner lesson you'll get at the resorts—for a lot less money. In one lesson, some kids have even been able to do a wedge turn; others have gone from a couple lessons here right to the slopes.

KidSlope is extremely popular. Lessons are frequently filled; you might want to book in advance to avoid disappointment. KidSlope also offers a special program for the disabled and their families (call for information).

● Liks

2039 East 13th Avenue. (303) 321-1492. Winter: daily, 11 A.M. to 10:30 P.M. Summer: daily, 11 A.M. to 11 P.M. **All ages.**

With ice cream like "chocolate decadence," "cherry cheesecake," and "creamy praline," this favorite neighborhood gathering spot (formerly known as Lickety Split) has won countless "Best Of" awards through the years. In central Denver, it's a great place to take a break if you're making

stops at downtown attractions. And if you have trouble choosing from
the plentiful selection, one friend of ours suggests ordering the "Piggy
split"—seven scoops of ice cream, five toppings, two bananas, whipped
cream, and sprinkles—and letting the whole family dig in.

● Molly Brown House Museum

*1340 Pennsylvania Street. (303) 832-4092. September to May: Tuesday to
Saturday, 10 A.M. to 4 P.M. (last tour, 3:30 P.M.), Sunday, noon to 4 P.M.
(last tour, 3:30 P.M.). June to August: Monday to Saturday, 10 A.M. to
4 P.M. (last tour, 3:30 P.M.), Sunday, noon to 4 P.M. (last tour, 3:30 P.M.).
Adults, $5; ages 6 to 12, $1.50; under age 6, free; seniors ages 65 and up,
$3.50. No strollers allowed in house.* **Ages 8 and up.**

You may have heard of the "unsinkable" Molly Brown from the famous Debbie Reynolds movie or, more recently, the film *Titanic*. Brown,
one of the more colorful Denver characters, earned her moniker for her
heroism during the sinking of the Titanic.

Her Victorian home, one of the best-known attractions in Denver, is
a picture-perfect look at upper-crust living at the turn of the century. The
dining room, bedrooms, and parlor are elegantly appointed; the kitchen
was state-of-the-art at the time. The house contains some of the original
furnishings, skillfully blended with period pieces.

The 30-minute guided tour, which begins in the carriage house/gift
shop/museum behind the mansion, is friendly and informative. Although
active younger kids will probably get fidgety, there's plenty to look at,
and the tour moves at a comfortable pace. Older kids should find the
Molly Brown story captivating: did she really burn her husband's money
in a furnace, or was that the stuff of movie legend? You'll know the answer by the end of the tour. The house is three blocks east of the state
capitol and in close proximity to all downtown Denver attractions.

● Platte Valley Trolley

*15th Street at Confluence Park to Sheridan Boulevard, with a stop at the
Children's Museum and at Ocean Journey (the latter opens in 1999; see entry).
(303) 458-6255. April, May, September, October: Tuesday to Sunday,
11 A.M. to 3 P.M. Summer: daily, 11 A.M. to 4 P.M. Rest of year: weekends
only, 11 A.M. to 4 P.M., weather permitting. Adults, $2; ages 3 to 12 and
seniors, ages 60 and up, $1; under age 2, free; for the hour round-trip, adults,
$4; ages 3 to 12, $2; under age 2, free; seniors ages 60 and up, $3. Tickets
are purchased on the trolley.* **All ages.**

The trolley runs a mile round-trip, with stops at the Children's Museum and 15th Street. On football days, you can park on 15th Street and

ride the trolley to Mile High Stadium. During the summer, the trolley runs other routes, including an hour round-trip ride through Lakewood Gulch; passengers are welcome to bring picnics on board. (Call for information.)

When the trolley pulls up alongside the Children's Museum, the kids will be clamoring to climb onboard. If they've never ridden a trolley, they'll find the short ride back and forth a novel experience.

● The Ski Train (Denver to Winter Park)

(303) 296-4754. Mid-December to early April, Saturday and Sunday. Leaves Union Station, 1701 Wynkoop Street, in downtown Denver at 7:15 A.M.; arrives in Winter Park at 9:15 A.M. Departs from Winter Park at 4:15 P.M. and arrives in Denver at 6:15 P.M. Coach class, $35. Club car, $55, includes Continental breakfast, private bar with attendant, and complimentary après-ski snacks. Train also runs on special excursions throughout the year; call for dates and times. **Ages 5 and up.**

For skiers, this is a hassle-free way to arrive at Winter Park for a day of skiing. But for skiers and nonskiers alike, this is a scenic ride that winds through beautiful countryside and the historic 6.2-mile Moffat Tunnel. Food and beverages are available in the two café lounge cars and at four snack bars. There are also restrooms onboard.

The train stops right at the base of the mountain. There are free shuttle buses into the town of Winter Park for those who aren't planning to ski.

Although the train seats 750 passengers, it's frequently booked, and reservations are a must. Bring your skiing equipment along; discount lift tickets are available aboard the train.

● Tattered Cover Book Store

2955 East First Avenue. (303) 322-7727. Monday to Saturday, 9 A.M. to 11 P.M.; Sunday, 10 A.M. to 6 P.M. **Ages 3 and up.**

What started as a neighborhood hole-in-the-wall has grown to one of the largest bookstores in the country, now occupying a building in the heart of Cherry Creek that once housed a department store. This is no staid environment: the store features plenty of stuffed chairs and couches for those who want to browse through the books. And at any time of the day, you'll find the place literally bursting with serious shoppers as well as with those who just came to sample the wares.

Children's books are featured on the lower level, and, as in the rest of the store, young patrons here are welcome to pick out some books, prop up their feet, and stay awhile. Children will love the look of this place, stuffed to the gills with all their favorites, as well as videos, cassettes, activity books, dolls, and storybook stuffed animals.

The store offers numerous story hours and book signings. Grab a "Rumpus Review" (the store's in-house newsletter) for current events. And don't forget to leave yourself—and your children—plenty of time to unwind. This is as good as a library—and without a librarian telling you to "hush."

The Tattered Cover also boasts a smaller, much quieter store in the downtown area, 1628 16th Street. Hours are: Monday to Thursday, 9 A.M. to 9 P.M.; Friday and Saturday, 9 A.M. to 11 P.M.; Sunday 10 A.M. to 6 P.M. Phone: (303) 436-1070.

● U.S. Mint at Denver

320 West Colfax Avenue. (303) 844-3582 for tour information; (303) 844-3331 or 844-3332 for ticket information. September to May: Monday to Friday, 8 A.M. to 2:45 P.M. (except Wednesday, when tours are from 9 A.M. to 2:45 P.M.); June, July, and August: Monday to Friday, 8 A.M. to 2:45 P.M. (except for the last Wednesday of each month, when tours are from 9 A.M. to 2:45 P.M.). Closed all legal holidays. Tours every 15 to 20 minutes. (Line begins at the Cherokee Street entrance.) Free. **Ages 5 and up.**

Half of all the country's coin production takes place in this grand old building. That's an average of 38 million coins a day, or $1.5 million dollars every 24 hours. Any way you count it, that's a lot of dough. And that's what this tour is all about: watching money pour out of giant contraptions as if they were Vegas slot machines. The rather quick tour—it lasts only about 15 minutes—will take you past giant windows where you can watch the money being made in rooms below. Unfortunately, much of the process is now automated, and there isn't much to see, other than money pouring out of presses, which stamp the pictures on both sides of the coin, and—in another room—machines that count the coins as they are being bagged.

Adults are likely to be interested in the tour guide's patter, and anyone is welcome to ask questions. But the main attraction for children will be seeing the money. Piles of it. On this count, they won't be disappointed.

At the end of the tour, children will also enjoy "making" their own souvenir. For $1, they'll receive a blank coin. A mint employee will then put the coin beneath a stamping press, ask your child to push a button, and—presto—the souvenir is ready. A wide variety of collector coins are also available for purchase at the end of the tour.

Admittance is on a first-come, first-served basis. In the summer, the wait to get inside can be up to 45 minutes. Plan accordingly.

● Washington Park

701 South Franklin Street. (303) 698-4962. Daily, 5 A.M. to 11 P.M.
All ages.

Where else but in this park can you see fathers on in-line skates pushing baby strollers? Women in Spandex racing around the park, baby joggers plowing the way? Men and women on bikes, babies sound asleep in their back carriers? It's yuppie heaven, to be sure, but Washington Park, located in the middle of the city, also offers great diversity, and you'll see all kinds of people gathered on a nice day. One of the favorite spots for families to congregate is the playground at the north end of the park. Near a large lake, the playground offers an extensive and unusually inventive play area, including a sandy area, tire swings, a fort-like structure with wheels, monkey bars, tunnels, and a myriad of other diversions. And when children tire of running and jumping, they can head over to the lake to watch ducks and geese. This is a no-miss spot for kids with energy to burn!

The park also offers beautiful flower gardens, a recreation center with a weight room, and swimming pool (call for hours and fees), and extensive paths shared by joggers, bicyclists, skaters, and those who get their exercise the old-fashioned way: walking!

● Watson's Pharmacy

900 Lincoln Street. (303) 837-1366. Monday to Thursday, 8 A.M. to 9 P.M.; Friday, 8 A.M. to 10 P.M.; Saturday, 10 A.M. to 10 P.M. **All ages.**

Lime Rickeys. Tin Roofs. Jersey Cows. This Denver institution—drugstore and old-fashioned soda fountain—with its black-and-white tile floors, jukebox, and marble-topped counter will have you toe-tapping down memory lane.

The kids can soak up the atmosphere of the good ol' days, twirling on red leather counter stools while Mom and Dad sip a taste of the past with flavored soft drinks, malts, sodas, phosphates, and egg creams.

● Wings Over the Rockies Air & Space Museum

7711 East Academy Parkway (formerly Lowry Air Force Base, Hangar No. 1). (303) 360-5360. Monday to Saturday, 10 A.M. to 4 P.M.; Sunday, noon to 4 P.M. Adults, $4; ages 6 to 17 and seniors ages 60 and up, $2; 5 and under, free. **Ages 6 and up.**

This cavernous facility houses a score of planes, from the huge B-IA bomber to the Eaglerock biplane. Although visitors are not allowed inside the planes or their cockpits, which are roped off, the sheer size of some of the aircraft alone is quite impressive and there's plenty of room to roam if you have toddlers in tow.

Although guides are only available for scheduled groups, hook onto the end of one and try to catch some of the fascinating history that comes with the planes. There is a mock space module, open for viewing, and the museum is planning special open-cockpit days where you can actually sit in the planes.

If you really want to make the kids happy, don't bypass the gift shop where we bought a cool "jet propelled" model plane for $2.

Denver Metropolitan Area

ARVADA

● Arvada Center for the Arts and Humanities

6901 Wadsworth Boulevard. (303) 431-3080. Children's theater performances, weekdays and selected Saturdays throughout fall, winter, and spring. General admission, $4 to $5. Summer shows for children in the outdoor amphitheatre, weekday mornings and evening performances, $3 general admission. Arvada Historical Museum: Monday to Friday, 9 A.M. to 5 P.M.; Saturday, 9 A.M. to 5 P.M.; Sunday, 1 to 5 P.M. Free. **Ages 5 to 11.**

The Arvada Center has fine performances for children with a cast of professional actors from the Denver area. Shows have included standards such as *Pinocchio* and original plays such as *The Dinosaur.* The summer-in-the-amphitheater performances showcase plays such as *The Frog Prince.*

Originally, the Arvada Center was built to house the Arvada Historical Museum, which is now a part of the gallery complex. Of most interest is an 1860s Denver log cabin, furnished in period pieces, that was moved to the site lock, stock, and timber. One corner of the museum also houses a dress-up corner where children can try on pioneer clothes and imagine living in days gone by.

AURORA

● Cherry Creek State Park

4201 South Parker Road (east entrance is 1 1/2 miles south of Interstate 225 on Parker Road; west entrance is near Dayton Street and Union Avenue). (303) 699-3860. Daily, 6 A.M. to 7 P.M.; during daylight savings time, 5 A.M. to 10 P.M. Per vehicle, $5; annual pass, $43. **All ages.**

Head down a nature trail early in the morning in this state park and you'd never know you were in the heart of a booming metropolitan area. Birds chirp, tall grass rustles, a duck glides quietly in a marsh—in short, this is the perfect place to make an escape from the hustle and bustle of modern life. Small wonder more than 1.5 million visitors flock here each year, making it one of the metro area's most popular recreational spots.

Cherry Creek State Park offers 3,915 acres filled with biking and hiking trails, picnic areas, campgrounds, and, best of all, an 880-acre reservoir open to boating and fishing. On a warm day, the reservoir is packed with colorful sailboats crisscrossing the water. Due to such crowds—and to protect its natural resources—the park limits the number of visitors at any one time. (Take note: on weekends and holidays, it's best to come early!)

Among the many offerings families will enjoy here:

Swim Beach. Located northwest of the east entrance, this is a great summertime diversion, complete with sandy beach, playground, first-aid station, and food concession. For those with toddlers and babies—or just lots of paraphernalia to carry—we suggest parking in the lower lot, which makes for an easier walk. Bring towels and plan to spend an afternoon. While the beach is technically open year-round, lifeguards are on duty and concessions are open only between Memorial Day and Labor Day. Beach hours are from 5 A.M. to 10 P.M. (Take note: lifeguards are not on duty the full day.)

Prairie Loop Nature Trail. At the south end of the park you'll find this well-marked, easy hike, where you are likely to see magpies, pheasant, and even an occasional great blue heron. The hike offers several small bridges to cross, and children will enjoy watching ducks swimming in the tiny creeks that run below the bridges. Park rangers offer interpretive walks in this area, as well as at Beaver Pond, Round-a-Bout, and Shop Creek nature trails. Call (303) 699-3860 for details.

Model Airplane Field. On a calm day, model airplane lovers head to this spot, also at the south end of the park, approximately two miles from the west entrance. Here, pilots send their remote-control planes racing down a mini runway and then diving and looping through the sky. On a good day, you'll see flocks of model planes buzzing overhead, as well as pilots working on their crafts in a gathering area. It all makes for a terrific free show, especially if you have young children who are interested in planes. No flying is allowed before 7 A.M., but any time after that and before the sun goes down, you're bound to find activity here if the weather is right.

The Marina. Located just northeast of the west entrance, the Marina offers power boats, sailboats, canoes, kayaks, and paddleboats for hourly rentals (with a sliding scale for longer rental times). It also offers sailing lessons. Even if you aren't interested in going out on the lake, this is a good place to simply stop for a snack at the nearby food concession and watch the sailboats darting about on the water. The Marina is open daily, April, May, September, and October, 10 A.M. to 6 P.M.; June, July, and August, weekdays, 10 A.M. to 8 P.M., weekends, 8 A.M. to 8 P.M. (closes early Wednesday evenings for sailboat races). (303) 779-6144.

Jet skis. These can be rented on the east side of the dam. This is a popular pastime, although extremely pricey ($45 for an hour, except Monday through Thursday, 10 A.M. to 1 P.M., when the price drops to $30). The concession stand is open daily, Memorial Day to Labor Day, 10 A.M. to 6 P.M. (303) 766-0766.

Horseback riding. South of the east entrance, you'll find stables where you can rent a horse for $14 an hour (two-horse minimum). Pony rides are also available ($7 per half hour); parents lead their children's ponies in a circle inside an arena. In addition, those interested in hay rides can set up the event anytime during the year by reservation (adults, $5; children under 12, $4; $75 minimum). Horses are available daily in the spring and summer, 9 A.M. to 6 P.M.; weekends only in the winter, weather permitting (hours vary). Rental is on a first-come, first-served basis (reservations recommended). Call (303) 690-8235.

● Plains Conservation Center

21901 East Hampden Avenue. (303) 693-3621. Open year-round for special events. Costs vary. **Ages 7 and up.**

In the far reaches of Aurora, where the housing developments stop and prairie lands take over, the Plains Conservation Center stretches for more than 1,900 acres. Home to pronghorn, jackrabbits, prairie dogs, owls, and eagles, the center offers a chance to leave the frenzy of everyday life behind for a few hours and walk through a prairie, study the smallest of plant life down to a blade of blue gramma grass, and listen to the buzz of nature. While the center isn't open to drop-in visitors (except some Saturdays in the summer), it offers regular programs that are well worth making the required reservation and paying a small fee.

One of the best is the monthly Moon Walk ($4 per person), which takes place once a month on the night of the full moon. Visitors follow a guide on an approximately 2½-mile hike; guides lecture on one aspect of nature during the walk, pointing out interesting plant and animal life along the way. (On our trip, we saw a coyote, an owl, and—to the delight of the kids—a small field mouse that scampered past our feet.)

As the walk progresses, the largest moon you'll ever see peaks over the horizon, then slowly rises, offering an awe-inspiring sight. A marshmallow roast over a bonfire, a big hit with kids, caps the evening. "It was perfect," said our 6-year-old as we headed home, quickly adding, "but tiring!"

Which brings us to our caveat: the walk is most likely too vigorous for very young children, and the guide's talk can prove too detailed for those with short attention spans. Our 6-year-old fidgeted somewhat during the longer parts of the talk. Children 8 and older are probably best suited for this mini-adventure.

The center also offers wagon rides each Friday night in July, August, and September; special activities, such as quilting and spinning demonstrations, on Saturdays in July and August (between 10 A.M. and 2 P.M.), and other events take place throughout the year. Call for prices and schedule.

BOULDER

● Boulder Creek Stream Observatory
Behind the Regal Harvest House, 1345 28th Street. (Parking available at the Harvest House.) Free. **Ages 2 and up.**

This quiet nook, hidden behind a foot path that winds along Boulder Creek, is a great place to stop and look at nature's offerings close-up. The observatory is simply four portholes that serve up an underwater view of the creek. On a good day, you can see rainbow, cutthroat, brown, and brook trout. A quarter will buy you a handful of fish food. Throw it over the wall and watch the fish enjoy the feast.

● Boulder Public Library
Main Branch, 11th Street and Arapahoe Avenue. (303) 441-3100. Monday to Thursday, 9 A.M. to 9 P.M.; Friday and Saturday, 9 A.M. to 6 P.M.; Sunday, noon to 6 P.M. Free. **Ages 2 to 11.**

The children's section in this library, designed for children up to sixth grade, is no stuffy, hush-hush affair. You'll find a puppet theater, complete with puppets children can play with, trees growing right in the middle of the room, plenty of pads and pillows for children to lounge on, and an aquarium with brightly colored tropical fish. Children will also enjoy looking at the library's Boulder Creek Habitat display, an aquarium filled with the varieties of trout that populate Boulder Creek. Storytimes are Monday to Saturday, 10:15 A.M.; Wednesday, 7 P.M.

● Boulder Skateboard Park

30th Street and Arapahoe Avenue, at Scott Carpenter Park (see entry). (303) 442-2778 or (303) 441-4421. School year: Monday to Friday, 2:30 P.M. to dark; Saturday and Sunday, 9 A.M. to 1 P.M., 1:30 to 5:30 P.M. Summer: daily, 10 A.M. to 2 P.M. and 4 to 8 P.M. $5 for each four-hour period or $30 for 10 sessions, $50 for 20 sessions. Rental: $1 each for helmet, knee pads, and elbow pads. **Ages 10 and up.**

If you're familiar with the terms "half pipe," "street course," and "hip-and-rail boxes," chances are you've got a serious skateboarder in your family. If so, you won't want to miss this unique Boulder spot. This "park"—a fenced-in area with specially designed curves and wicked inclines—caters to skateboarders, in-line skaters, and those who enjoy doing stunts on bikes. On a nice day, the area is filled with preteens and teens twisting, flipping, and jumping on their respective equipment. Which means, even if you don't skateboard, this is a great place to soak up some rays and watch the show.

The park is run by the YMCA of Boulder and offers supervision. But there's always the chance for injury. When this entry was written, the park was seven months old, and had already claimed a few broken bones to its name. "They were basically inexperienced riders, not sure of what they were doing," said one supervisor. Take heed.

● Celestial Seasonings ◆

4600 Sleepytime Drive. (Interstate 25 north to Highway 36, the Boulder exit. Take Highway 36 to the Foothills Parkway exit and continue on Foothills Parkway—it will become the Diagonal Highway—to Jay Road. Turn right on Jay Road, continue one mile east to Spine. Turn left on Spine—the area will look residential—but continue a half-mile north on Spine to Sleepytime Drive and turn left.) (303) 530-5300. Tours: Monday to Friday, 10 A.M. to 3 P.M., every hour on the hour. Tours are also given on Saturdays and Sundays, but the factory (the best part) may not be up and running on the weekends. Children under 5 are not allowed in the factory (the bulk of the tour) because of noise and safety issues. Free. **Ages 5 and up.**

When Mo Siegel started Celestial Seasonings in 1970, he hiked into the mountains to gather the ingredients for his herbal teas. Now the herbs are gathered worldwide, and Celestial Seasonings is one of the top names in tea.

Located on the outskirts of Boulder, the facility offers a tour that is fun and personal—no pressing your nose to glass to see the production. The tour takes at least an hour and begins with a short lesson in research and development: groups are asked to drink two versions of a tea and vote their preference. From there, you'll be guided through the mint room, where the strong minty smells elicit a collective gasp, and the production facility where you can watch the tea pour into tea bags. The excursion ends in a tasting room and gift shop where you can sample for free many of Celestial Seasonings' flavors in both hot and iced varieties—and buy a few boxes to take home, if desired. There's also a café on-site if you'd like to eat breakfast or lunch.

Our kids really enjoyed this very pleasant tour, right down to sipping their way through many of the different kinds of tea.

● Chautauqua Park ◆

900 Baseline Road. (303) 545-6924. Daily, 8 A.M. to 11 P.M. Quiet hours in the summer between 1 and 3 P.M. **All ages.**

Founded in 1898, Chautauqua Park was part of the once-popular national Chautauqua movement, which sought to provide cultural outlets to those in rural parts of the country. Chautauquas in various states offered lodging and summer camp-style programs for adults, who attended lectures, concerts, and other events. Boulder's Chautauqua was the only one west of the Mississippi. Today the park continues to pursue the goals of the movement, with myriad cultural activities.

Visitors to this lovely park bordered by the Boulder Flatirons will find 26 acres of rolling, grassy areas populated by people throwing Frisbees and walking their dogs. A playground has been recently renovated and children flock here on warm days; so do picnickers or those who just want to soak up the sun. (Note that the park enforces quiet hours between 1 and 3 P.M. in the summer, when loud music is banned and special programs are at a minimum.)

Another major draw are the extensive hiking trails that originate here. You'll see parents with babies in backpacks heading out to the Flatirons at any time of the day. Some of the trails provide easy hikes that children of any age can tackle; others are quite steep and difficult. For more direction, stop at the Ranger Cottage just inside the park entrance at the top of the parking lot. There, you can pick up a trail map that will offer guidance about skill levels required on each hike. The cottage is generally open from 8 A.M. to 4 P.M.

For those who prefer indoor activity, the park also boasts a cavernous concert hall, a landmark on the National Register of Historic Places, which brings in major artists throughout the year. While most of the shows are adult-oriented, in July the auditorium offers a silent film series, complete with pianist, which children thoroughly enjoy. The park also hosts a family film series in the auditorium throughout the summer, with movies that appeal to a wide range of ages, from toddlers on up.

A community house on-site also offers children's programs, everything from kite-making to entertaining physics demonstrations. And if all of this weren't enough, the park hosts various festivals throughout the summer. To keep current, it's best to call the number listed above and ask for a schedule of events.

From Memorial Day to Labor Day, the park opens a dining hall, which serves breakfast and lunch from 7 A.M. to 2 P.M. and dinner from 5:30 to 9 P.M. The food is good, and the hall offers a children's menu. There is also an ice-cream fountain, open from 8 A.M. to 9 P.M. A gift shop next door has recently been added; diners who are waiting for a table (the hall is often packed) can now browse in the three-room store, which offers an area specifically for children, featuring toys, coloring books, and other knickknacks to buy.

For a fun outing, plan to come to Chautauqua for a leisurely brunch, then spend the day enjoying its outdoor offerings. The splendid views alone are worth the trip.

● Collage Children's Museum

2065 30th Street in Aspen Plaza. (303) 440-9894. Monday, Thursday, Friday, and Saturday, 10 A.M. to 5 P.M.; Wednesday, 2 to 5 P.M.; Sunday, 1 to 5 P.M. $2 per person; $8 per family; under 2, free. Scholarships available to families and groups with special needs. **Ages 2 to 10.**

This small room packs a big punch, with activities designed to catch the eye every way you turn. Your children can try their hands at the museum's current art project, enclose themselves in giant-sized soap bubbles made with a bubble maker attached to a pulley, or design a quilt by computer.

The museum's Go Power display shows children how a battery works, and visitors can learn about animation by making their own film strip, placing it in a cylinder, and spinning it to see their "show" come to life. Collage also offers an area designed for toddlers. Many of the exhibits change every two to three months; Saturdays often feature special science programs at 11 A.M.

The drawbacks? The exhibits aren't always in good working order. Another problem is the size; if possible, avoid times that are likely to be crowded, such as weekends during the winter. We're told the best times during weekdays are between noon and 2 P.M., when school groups clear out for lunch breaks.

● Fiske Planetarium and Sommers-Bausch Observatory

University of Colorado at Boulder campus (Highway 36 to Colorado Avenue, turn left to Regent Drive, look for the silver dome). (303) 492-5001. Friday evenings, 7:30 P.M.; seasonally on Saturday afternoons. Laser shows: days and times vary; call for information. Friday evenings: adults, $3.50; ages 12 and under and seniors, ages 55 and up, $2. Saturday matinees: adults, $3; ages 12 and under and seniors, ages 55 and up, $1.50. Cash and checks only.
Ages 6 and up.

Fiske has found a way to distinguish itself from the area's many other planetariums. After the Friday evening show, visitors can walk next door to Sommers-Bausch Observatory and look through telescopes trained at different parts of the sky. Child-friendly helpers from the university adjust and fine-tune for the children so that everyone gets a chance to look at the moon and the stars.

Make sure you arrive a half hour before showtime to ensure seating. The kids will have no trouble passing the time with the hands-on exhibits, including prisms, magnets, and a telescope. Despite the generally child-friendly nature of the planetarium, the 45-minute show may prove too long for kids under age 6, who will probably be able to sit through it but who may get a little restless.

The planetarium does offer shows from time to time that may be suitable for younger kids, so ask about the age-appropriateness of the show when you call. The telescopes, however, are a great draw and should appeal to all ages.

● Josh & John's Naturally Homemade Ice Creams

1111 13th Street. (303) 440-9310. Sunday to Thursday, noon to midnight; Friday and Saturday, noon to 1 A.M. **All ages.**

See Denver entry for information.

● National Center for Atmospheric Research

1850 Table Mesa Drive. (303) 497-1174. Self-guided tours: Monday to Friday, 8 A.M. to 5 P.M.; Saturday, Sunday, and holidays, 9 A.M. to 3 P.M. Guided tours: mid-June to end of August, Monday to Saturday, noon; rest of year, Monday and Wednesday, noon. (No reservations required except for groups and clubs; tour lasts about one hour.) Free. **Ages 8 and up** *for displays;* **all ages** *for outdoor trails.*

Scientists from around the world come here to focus on the weather and climate-related studies, using the most sophisticated equipment, including radar, weather balloons, and supercomputers. Visitors are invited to tour the building, which offers many educational displays about the weather, the sun, and so on, as well as hand-outs to explain what is on view. Children who are interested in computers will especially enjoy viewing the large computer room on the lower level.

While the displays are highly scientific and will appeal only to children who are very technically oriented, plenty of families still enjoy this site—situated high upon a hill overlooking Boulder—for its peaceful nature trails behind the building. The trails offer informational signs about weather conditions unique to the area and are handicap accessible. This is a fine spot for a picnic, or for simply strolling around in search of mule deer and magpies.

● Pearl Street Mall ◆

On Pearl Street between 11th and 15th streets. Free. **All ages.**

When it comes to free entertainment, it doesn't get any better than this. Take a stroll on this outdoor mall lined with shops any summer evening and you'll find jugglers tossing fire torches, magicians, face painters, people turning balloons into inventive shapes, musicians of all kinds, and any number of other informal "acts." Children love this spot for its spontaneity and freedom (if the act is no good, kids have no problem leaving in the middle, running further on down the mall in search of the next show). And parents love the price. A few dollars in tips will buy you hours of fun.

For an impromptu playground, look for a spot in the middle of the mall that boasts large boulders and gravel. Children love to gather here to climb and slide. Also, there are several places to buy ice cream and cookies along the mall for an added treat.

● Scott Carpenter Park

30th Street and Arapahoe Avenue. (303) 441-3400 or (303) 441-3427 (pool). Pool open Memorial Day to Labor Day: Monday to Friday, adult lap swim, 11 A.M. to 1 P.M.; open swim, 1 to 5 P.M. Saturday and Sunday, adult lap swim, 11 A.M. to 1 P.M.; open swim, 1 to 6 P.M. Adults, $4.25; ages 4 to 18, $1.50; under age 3, free. Discounts available with resident pass. **All ages.**

This is one of Boulder's premier parks, and parents flock here with their children. The approximately 9-acre site offers a spacious playground (parents of toddlers will appreciate the fact that the toddler swings are set far apart from the older kids' swings); a 50-meter outdoor swimming pool, with attached diving pool, winding water slide, and separate toddler pool; a baseball diamond; a huge, grassy area for Frisbees and dogs; and paths for bikes and rollerskaters. The park also includes a skateboard park for boarders (see entry for Boulder Skateboard Park).

● University of Colorado Museum

On campus, at 15th Street and Broadway, just west of the University Memorial Center. (303) 492-6892. Monday to Friday, 9 A.M. to 5 P.M.; Saturday, 9 A.M. to 4 P.M.; Sunday, 10 A.M. to 4 P.M. Suggested donations: adults, $2.50; students through college and seniors, ages 65 and up, $1.50; ages 6 and older, $1. Closed holidays. **Ages 2 and up.**

This museum doesn't have the expanse of a big city museum. It also doesn't have the crowds, the high admission fees, and the distracting hoopla. The result is a quiet little museum where kids can spend time studying exhibits and even gain hands-on experience with magnifying glasses, bones, fossils, and more. Upstairs you'll find a room with dinosaur bones and fossils, including a triceratops skull, the limb bones of an imperial mammoth (giant elephant), which are as big around as tree trunks, and the skulls and bones of smaller prehistoric animals. There is also a Pueblo room with pottery and models of Indian mesas. Another room is devoted to changing exhibits.

Downstairs features the Discovery Corner, where young children can handle deer antlers, "try on" a giant tortoise shell, and test the joints of a human skeleton. The room also features a table with a microscope and a host of objects to look at under the lens: seashells, bone fragments, wood, pine cones, and other objects.

Your children will also enjoy studying the extensive stuffed animal collection downstairs and, in another exhibit, are invited to press buttons that trigger the sounds of various animals, such as the eerie buglelike call of an elk.

BRIGHTON

● Barr Lake State Park

13401 Picadilly Road. From downtown Denver, go north on Interstate 25 to Interstate 76. Stay on Interstate 76 to exit 22 (Bromley Lane) and turn right to Picadilly. (303) 659-6005. Park: daily, 5 A.M. to 10 P.M. Visitor center: Wednesday to Friday, 9 A.M. to 4 P.M.; Saturday and Sunday, 9 A.M. to 5 P.M. (Visitor center hours may vary by season.) $4 per car. **All ages.**

This 2,600-acre park surrounds a picturesque lake with the mountains as a backdrop. Bald eagles make their home here as well as 330 other species of birds. Stop at the visitor center and borrow (free) a kid's nature kit that includes a backpack with magnifying glasses, a bug box, and binoculars to spot the wildlife and birds that flock to the park.

Of major interest to kids: the boardwalk and gazebo that extends over the lake. From this vantage point—a short distance from the visitor's center—you have an excellent opportunity to sit on a bench and watch the birds at your leisure. Our kids were impressed by the feeling of having water surround them on all sides, as if they were in the midst of a flood. The park offers numerous interpretative programs throughout the year, including bird walks.

Barr Lake State Park is in Denver farming country. Although the 40-minute drive seems fairly tedious with miles of flat land, the park is worth a visit for its unique layout and setting. As you get near, the kids will find lambs, cattle, and horses grazing close to the road, which will perk up the ride. If you're planning to picnic—and there are some great picnic spots here—stock up near Denver. The visitor center has a soda pop machine and rest rooms but you'll have to drive extra miles on an already long outing to find the nearest food outlet.

COMMERCE CITY

● Rocky Mountain Arsenal Wildlife Tours

72nd Avenue and Quebec Street. (303) 289-0232. Visitor center open Saturday, 8 A.M. to 3:30 P.M. for drop-in visitors. Bus tours Saturday. Times vary seasonally. Call for schedule. Free. Reservations required. **Ages 5 and up.**

This could surely qualify as one of the most bizarre offerings in the state. This site was once used by the government for making chemical weapons and by Shell Chemical Company to manufacture pesticides—until both operations were shut down and a clean-up operation begun. In 1992, Congress declared that the Arsenal will become a National Wildlife Refuge once the process is complete.

Even as the massive clean-up continues, the Arsenal is home to more than 300 species of wildlife, including mule deer, bald eagles, coyote, great horned owls, and great blue heron. Each Saturday, the public is invited to board a bus and drive through the 27-square-mile facility as a tour guide points out the various species (as well as the eerie buildings that once housed the chemical operations). You'll see plenty of animals on this tour, and there's genuine excitement at every sighting, with visitors pulling out binoculars and cameras and positioning for the best view. Children enjoy being the first to spot an eagle or the ears of a deer popping up through the tall grass in the distance. When the crowd warrants it, the Arsenal rents a double-decker bus for the tour, another big hit with the kids. While officals insist the tour is safe and the contamination areas contained, note that there is still controversy on the issue.

Count on spending about two hours here, and keep in mind that different animals tend to be spotted at different times of the year. A return trip may be in order.

The Arsenal offers many special events throughout the year, including eagle viewing, nature hikes, moonlight hikes, and more. Call for a current schedule.

ENGLEWOOD

● Belleview Park

5001 S. Inca Drive at West Belleview. (303) 762-2680. Park: daily, 6 A.M. to 11 P.M. Lions Club train: Memorial Day to Labor Day, Tuesday to Saturday, 10 A.M. to 4 P.M.; Sunday, noon to 5 P.M., 50 cents per person; under age 2, free. Belleview Children's Farm: Memorial Day to Labor Day, Tuesday to Sunday, 9 A.M. to 4 P.M., 50 cents per person; under age 2, free. Park: free. **All ages.**

This park is affectionately known to locals as the "airplane park" because of the large plane propped high above the action at this busy place. The park boasts picnic tables and grills and two playgrounds, one with swings and equipment just right for the toddlers in your group, but the real showcase is the man-made stream that runs throughout the park. Children can wade, skip stones, and frolic in the ankle-to-calf-high water. It's best to bring shoes that the kids can wear into the sandy creek, such as waterproof sandals, and a towel, because most children wind up soaked despite the shallow depths. Parents in the know often bring their preschoolers in bathing suits ready for water play.

A train ride and petting zoo are designed for toddler to elementary school-age children. The train makes one circuit around the park, a trip that lasts less than five minutes—but the conductor invites children to scream loudly as they go through a small tunnel. Kids and noise? They'll beg you to go again. The petting zoo has ducks, rabbits, a pig, a cow, a few sheep, and some turtles, enough to keep the average child interested for around 20 minutes or more, depending on their age and affinity for animals. The whole park experience adds up to one great time; the creek alone draws a child-size crowd on lazy summer days.

● Country Dinner Playhouse

6875 South Clinton Street. (303) 799-1410. Performances every night except Monday; doors open at 6 P.M., show starts at 8 P.M. Also, Saturday and

Sunday matinees; doors open at noon, show starts at 2 P.M. Cost is $24.50 to $30.50 per person, depending on performance, and includes buffet-style meal, tax, and show. **Ages 7 and up.**

Theater and children often add up to an uncomfortable experience for all concerned—with children squirming in their seats long before the last curtain. But not here. The Country Dinner Playhouse has hit on a winning formula that accounts for its 20-plus years in business.

Tables at this theater surround a square stage that is situated on lifts. At dinnertime and between sets, the stage disappears into the rafters, only to be lowered to eye level—props and all—when the action is ready to begin! This alone creates a good deal of excitement for children, who won't soon forget the anticipation of a real, live show.

Whether you come for a matinee or an evening show, you'll line up for dinner, choosing from relatively typical buffet fare. Load up, because the line tends to be long and time often runs out before you've had a chance to get seconds.

After your meal, shows are always preceded by a singing and dancing troupe called the Barnstormers. The troupe usually consists of college-age musicians who sing a medley of popular songs (and who, by the way, double as your waiters and waitresses). At the end of their show, the Barnstormers sing happy birthday or happy anniversary to those celebrating in the audience and deliver cakes to the tables of those who have ordered them. If your child is having a birthday, the delight he or she will receive in being singled out is well worth the cost ($4 per cake, with enough to feed six to eight people).

Then, let the show begin! The Playhouse offers consistently well-reviewed plays, all family-oriented, most an average of two hours in length (including the Barnstormers). For young children, consider a matinee. And leave the youngest at home; we recommend taking only children ages 7 and older, as this is a long event.

● **Southshore Waterpark**
10750 East Briarwood Avenue (one mile east of Interstate 25 on Arapahoe Road). (303) 649-9875. Memorial Day to Labor Day, daily, 10 A.M. to 6 P.M. Adults, $12.50; ages 3 to 48 inches tall, $10.50; ages 2 and under and seniors, 62 and older, free. Special evening discounts after 3:30 P.M.
All ages.

Newer but much smaller than Hyland Hills Water World (see entry in Federal Heights), Southshore water complex boasts a five-story-high waterslide, a two-man inner tube slide, the Black Hole slide, and two high-speed slides. Or, you can catch the waves in the Breaker's Bay wave pool, an industrial-size pool where you can ride an inner tube or swim to shore.

The preschool and tot set have their own separate pool and waterslide, with the water starting at toe level and rising to a depth of one foot. A giant mushroom rises from the pool with constantly spewing water like a giant shower head.

Changing rooms, concessions by Paul's Place restaurants, rest rooms, and picnic areas are on-site. If you want to bring your own food and drink, you can use the picnic area provided outside the water park. No floating devices are allowed in the park; free life vests are available.

Spend a day, an afternoon, or a couple hours; it's a water park, so you can't miss.

● Trail Dust Steak House

Two locations, south and north of Denver, respectively. 7101 South Clinton Street, Englewood, (303) 790-2420, and 9101 Benton Street, Westminster, (303) 427-1446. Englewood location: Monday to Thursday, 11 A.M. to 2 P.M. and 5 to 11 P.M.; Friday, 11 A.M. to 2 P.M. and 5 P.M. to midnight; Saturday, 4 P.M. to midnight; Sunday, noon to 10 P.M. Westminster location: Monday to Thursday, 5 to 11 P.M.; Friday, 5 P.M. to midnight; Saturday, 4 P.M. to midnight; Sunday, noon to 10 P.M. Dinners, $8.99 to $21.99.
Ages 2 and up.

Little pardners and their big pardner parents will love the solid Western grub at this casual country joint. And we do mean casual. This restaurant's credo is "No neckties allowed!" ("This ain't no country club," explains the menu.) Men who show up in coat and tie are likely to find their ties cut clean off. If you don't believe it, just take a look at the walls, where person-less ties are pinned up and used for decoration like so many hunting trophies.

This is a kid restaurant to the max, with a tall slide in the middle of the room, a dance floor and country-western band for evening enter-tainment and plenty of cowbell noise every time a tie-offender is caught. (Monday to Saturday, the entertainment begins at 7 P.M.; Sunday, at 6 P.M.) In other words, don't expect much relaxation here. But the food— yes, it's meat and potatoes—is generally good, and the kids will have a blast.

A couple of tips: if you're bringing preschoolers or other children you want to keep an eye on, aim for a table near the slide; that's where your children will be spending most of their time. To get that table, come early. These are popular spots, and lines begin to form, even on weekdays, by 6 P.M. Come around 5. And eat fast: you are likely to be chasing down children or holding their hands on the dance floor most of the night. (Children under age 12 aren't allowed on the dance floor without an adult.)

FEDERAL HEIGHTS

● Hyland Hills Water World ◆

Pecos Street and 88th Avenue (Interstate 25 North to Exit 219 at 84th Avenue, west to Pecos, north to Water World). (303) 427-7873. Memorial Day to Labor Day, daily, 10 A.M. to 6 P.M. Adults, $17.95; ages 4 to12, $16.95; ages 3 and under and seniors ages 60 and over, free. Season passes available. **Ages 2 and up.**

Consider this park Disneyland with water, with 40 "rides" that range from monster water slides to Voyage to the Center of the Earth, a twisting water trip through a tunnel of surprises. This is the daddy of all water parks, a sort of city in itself, where you can easily spend a day exploring the offerings spread over 65 acres. Take a relatively calm trip down the Lazy River, where the current will carry you and your float along at a relaxing pace. Jump into one of two wave pools that simulate the motion of the ocean. Or take a hair-raising speed trip down the Screamin' Mimi, where it's best to close your eyes as you careen down the slide and skid across the top of the water at the bottom. Whatever your taste in thrills, there's something here to fill the bill.

If you're bringing young ones, the park offers a terrific spot for toddlers called Wally World. This well-landscaped area, on several levels, features pools of water that are about knee-high for toddlers. The area includes gentle water slides, tire swings that hang just above the water, and tiny fountains. Young children will also enjoy the water playground near the Screamin' Mimi, with its host of water-squirting and water-moving delights, such as squirt guns, water wheels, shower heads, and cascading waterfalls.

Our kids rank this one of the top attractions we have been to state-wide. The downside for parents is the expensive admission fee and a host of extras once you enter the park, including float rental for the wave pools ($4, with a 50 cent refund on return), lockers (50 cents; each time you open the locker, you must deposit another 50 cents to reuse it), and food, which is reasonably priced but can add up for a family. In addition, parents with children too young to explore the park without constant supervision will find the experience somewhat tiring. This is a large place, and to get to the start of each ride, you must climb uphill, usually carrying a rather cumbersome tube.

Still, the delight your children will experience should more than compensate. This is, quite simply, a remarkable water adventure. We starred it because we would return time and again—even knowing the drawbacks.

Note: It helps to have those popular nylon and rubber-soled shoes made to wear while swimming, as the cement can be hot, slippery, and rough on your feet. It is also a good idea to bring your own food, which will cut your costs considerably. Also, come early in the day to get your money's worth before afternoon showers threaten. Plan to spend at least three to four hours, to get acclimated and enjoy a fair number of rides.

FRANKTOWN

● Castlewood Canyon State Park

Interstate 25 to Castle Rock, turn east on Highway 86, go 6 miles to Franktown, turn south on Highway 83, and go five miles south to the park entrance. (303) 688-5242. Daily, summer, 8 A.M. to 9 P.M.; winter, 8 A.M. to 8 P.M. $4 per car. **All ages.**

Given its proximity to metro Denver, this is one of the truly amazing parks in the area. A spectacular canyon weaves through the 873-acre park, where you can picnic, hike, and experience the kind of canyonland beauty usually found in remoter areas of the state.

In addition to panoramic views of the Front Range and Pikes Peak, the park offers one trail that leads to the ruins of the 1890 Castlewood Canyon Dam, which collapsed in 1933. The visitor center or park ranger can give you a map of the area with trails rated for difficulty. Some of the cliffs have been designated for rock climbing and you can watch experienced climbers rappelling.

For the younger set, rangers have critter tales (storytelling) and other events on an ongoing basis; kids ages 7 to 12 can join the Junior Ranger Club and take part in their activities, which change monthly (call for specifics). In a state noted for beautiful park areas, this is a stand-out that kids of any age will enjoy. Rather than fitting in a visit to this park on your way elsewhere, plan to stop here when you have some leisure time.

GENESEE

● Buffalo Herd Overlook at Genesee Park

Interstate 70 West, Exit 254 (between Evergreen and Golden, in Genesee). Open daily, 5 A.M. to 11 P.M. Free. **All ages.**

Genesee Park is one of only two areas near Denver where you can see buffalo more or less in the wild. (See also Daniel's Park entry under Sedalia.) And even though you can see buffalo in the zoo, there's something thrilling about catching them in their natural state—and in such large numbers. You'll know if the animals are in sight by the number of cars pulled alongside the road. If you're lucky, you'll also spot the elk herd that calls the park home.

The overlook, part of a thousand-acre park, is on the way to a number of other attractions, including Buffalo Bill's Grave and Lookout Mountain Nature Center (see entries below). You'll also pass it as you head to the mountains.

The park is open for hiking and picnicking and has restroom facilities throughout.

Note: You're more likely to spot the buffalo close to the highway during the colder months because the Denver Parks Department supplements their feed then, drawing them closer for roadside viewing.

GOLDEN

● Adolph Coors Company Brewery

13th and Ford Street. (303) 277-2337. Monday to Saturday, 10 A.M. to 4 P.M.; tours offered continuously. Open to all ages; ages 18 years and under must be accompanied by an adult. Free. **Ages 10 and up.**

There's no denying that hometown pride is infectious in this tour of the Coors brewery. Tour guides cheerfully greet and shepherd you along every step of the way. You begin the tour by parking in the lot near Coors (follow the signs) where you board minibuses for the short ride to the brewery.

The tour includes a brief historical ride through Golden before entering the family-owned and operated brewery that has been a mainstay in Colorado for more than a hundred years. Because it is local, the history of the brewery is far more interesting than that of its competitor, the Anheuser-Busch brewery. As with Anheuser-Busch (see entry under Northeast), the tour winds up in the refreshment room where you can sample beer and soft drinks for free.

It's probably a toss-up which brewery tour kids will enjoy more—this one has the novelty of the minibuses and the tour itself goes down as easily as a smooth beer. But then, there are those Clydesdales. . . .

If choosing one over the other, we'd probably base the decision on which direction we're heading. Golden is closer to Denver; a visit to Coors and some of the other sights near Golden such as Buffalo Bill's Museum makes a nice day trip. A visit to Anheuser-Busch could be coupled with a pleasant day trip to Fort Collins.

● Buffalo Bill Memorial Museum and Grave

987½ Lookout Mountain Road (Interstate 70 West to exit 256). (303) 526-0747. May to end of October: daily, 9 A.M. to 5 P.M. Rest of year: Tuesday to Sunday, 9 A.M. to 4 P.M. Adults, $3; ages 6 to 15, $1; under age 6, free; seniors ages 66 and up, $2. **Ages 5 and up.**

When Buffalo Bill Cody, Wyoming-born government scout, pony express rider, and Wild West showman, died penniless in Colorado in 1917, Colorado and Wyoming nearly went to war over which state would claim burial rights. Colorado won, and Buffalo Bill's Memorial Museum and Grave attract more than 550,000 visitors a year and is one of the most popular tourist attractions in the Denver metro area.

Visitors park on the lower level next to the Buffalo Bill Museum, where they can pause and view the breathtaking vistas, take in the museum, stop at the gift shop, or continue up the short path to the grave site. The museum houses memorabilia, photos, paintings, and clothes from the Buffalo Bill era, including a Native American room with a buffalo head for the kids to pet.

View the time line and artifacts associated with his life, including many items from his Wild West show, such as a buckskin outfit; a Buffalo Bill mannequin astride a full-size horse; a stuffed buffalo; Native American artifacts; Western art; and antique firearms. Of special interest is a 15-minute video with actual footage from Buffalo Bill's show. (Buffalo Bill was one of the earliest filmmakers and recorded his show.) The museum will fire the imagination of children interested in the Old West. If you choose to bypass the museum and continue up the path, the grave site is free.

● Colorado Railroad Museum

17155 West 44th Avenue. (303) 279-4591 or (800) 365-6263. Daily, 9 A.M. to 5 P.M.; June, July, and August, 9 A.M. to 6 P.M. Adults, $3.50; ages 15 and under, $1.75; family (parents and children under age 16), $7.50.; seniors ages 60 and up, $3. **Ages 2 to 7.**

Talk about interactive. At this museum, your kids can climb all over the exhibits without a peep from the proprietor. This is a train lover's haven: 12 acres littered with old trains put out to pasture, more than 50 narrow- and standard-gauge locomotives, cars, and other railroad memorabilia. Kids are free to climb aboard, ring the bells, wave from the windows, and run through the cars at will—and they do so, with joy.

The grounds also boast an indoor museum: a replica of an 1880-style masonry depot, where you'll find a souvenir shop, railroad artifacts, and an elaborate miniature train layout downstairs. (Be sure to bring some quarters to make the train go.)

One caution: the trains are authentic—and so is the grease that can rub off onto your child's clothing. Don't dress them in anything that might be ruined by a brush with oil and grime.

● Golden D.A.R. Pioneer Museum

923 Tenth Street. (303) 278-7151. Winter: Monday to Saturday, noon to 4 P.M. Summer: Monday to Saturday, 11 A.M. to 4 P.M. Free. **Ages 7 and up.**

This museum, divided into four distinct areas, is chockful of memorabilia dating from the 1800s through the 1930s. (Beware of bringing toddlers—some of the items are within grabbing reach.) Visitors will see artifacts used by Native Americans, ranchers, miners, pioneers, and others. Among the items on display: beautiful period costumes, including children's dresses and bonnets, old-time kitchen implements, spinning wheels, an early record player, and more. Of special interest is the museum's extensive collection of Indian dolls, depicting individual tribes—and don't miss the fun quotes from the era posted around the room. We especially enjoyed this one by a farmer in 1936: "Brothers and sisters, I want to tell you this. The greatest thing on earth is to have the love of God in your heart. The next greatest thing is to have electricity in your house." You can easily tour this museum in one hour. It's worth a stop if you're in the area, especially if you're with older children.

● Heritage Square

Located between Interstate 70 and 6th Avenue on Highway 40 (take 6th Avenue west to Highway 40, turn left, watch for the sign on the right side of the road). (303) 279-2789. Monday to Saturday, 10 A.M. to 6 P.M.; Sunday, noon to 6 P.M. Extended summer hours. Free. **Ages 2 and up.**

There's no shortage of activity in this entertainment center about 20 minutes from Denver in the foothills. In fact, the problem may be that there is a glut of diversions. Shop 'til you drop? Ride the alpine slide? Enjoy the bumper cars? Pig out on ice cream and stick candy? It's hard to know where to start. OK. So the place lacks focus. So does Disneyland—and you won't hear the kids complaining there, either.

Heritage Square began as a Victorian-style shopping village, featuring mostly craft-type stores. Through the years, other features have been added. Now, it has the feel of a small city dedicated solely to fun and frolic. You can still browse through the 50-plus shops, which remain basically of the gift or craft variety, but it won't be long before your children lead you to the mini-amusement park, with rides for toddlers as well as older kids. In this area, you'll find standard fairground rides as well as bumper cars, paddleboats, and go-carts. As if this weren't enough, the park also features alpine and water slides (303-279-1664) (bring your own suits and towels) and a laser arcade (303-277-0990).

All this activity is bound to work up an appetite and you can dine in several sit-down restaurants, including a German beer garden. More likely, with kids in tow, you'll want to stop at a vending cart and get a less-expensive snack, such as a pretzel or ice cream cone.

Heritage Square also offers a matinee children's theater production each Saturday and dinner and melodrama productions during selected evenings in the Music Hall (303-279-7800), as well as Lazy H chuckwagon dinners with a Western show (303-278-1938).

While you could easily spend a day here, it may be best to stay just a few hours and couple this with a visit to one of the many other Golden-area attractions—for your own sanity. It can be quite overwhelming try-ing to navigate the many choices offered here. In addition, take note: while admission is free, many of the activities are not. The amusement rides, for instance, are $1 each, the alpine and water slides are priced at approximately $5, and you won't get past the ice cream stands without breaking open your wallet.

Also be aware that many of the activities most appealing to children are closed during the winter.

● Lookout Mountain Nature Center

910 Colorow Road. (303) 526-0594. Tuesday to Sunday, 10 A.M. to 4 P.M. Free. **All ages.**

The Lookout Mountain Nature Center is in a 110-acre wildlife sanc-tuary with a self-guided nature trail. On the weekends, the Nature Center features family programs, such as a Wild Tea Party, introducing kids to edible local plants, or Watchable Wildlife, finding animals in their natu-ral setting. The programs are around 2 hours and require 48-hour advance reservations. Some programs are geared for older children; some for younger.

The Nature Center also features year-round "Wild World" programs for children ages 5 to 10 after school. Special programs for toddlers under the age of 5 are offered some mornings. Advance reservations are also required.

If you're in the area and don't have reservations, you can make a quick stop at the Nature Center to get oriented and to look at exhibits on Colo-rado and its environs. Again with advance notice, you can check out an adventure pack with compass, hand lens, wind gauge, and bug boxes to explore nature on your own. The Nature Center is near Buffalo Bill's Grave and the Buffalo Herd Overlook (see entries above).

● Mother Cabrini Shrine

20189 Cabrini Boulevard. (Follow the well-marked signs from Interstate 70). (303) 526-0758. Daily: summer, 7 A.M. to 8 P.M. (gates close at 7:30 P.M.); winter, 7 A.M. to 5 P.M. **Ages 6 and up.**

Mother Cabrini, who was canonized in 1946, bought this property as a summer camp for orphans. It is now a shrine in her honor and in honor of the Sacred Heart of Jesus.

Take the short, winding drive up the mountainside to reach Mother Cabrini's shrine. Once you've arrived on the premises, you can park the car and walk the 373 steps to the 22-foot statue of the Sacred Heart. The climb is enhanced by the stations of the cross along the way and the Ten Commandments at the top. Also at the top is a glassed-in area where Mother Cabrini arranged white stones in the shape of a heart. During our visit, a number of children stopped and gathered stones to make their own cross and heart formations on the hillside adjacent to the statue.

Although the climb is arduous at this altitude, you'll be rewarded by a spectacular view of Denver and the environs. This is a remarkable place for the religious and nonreligious alike.

● The National Earthquake Information Center

18th and Illinois, School of Mines campus (building is marked: Department of the Interior, U.S. Geological Survey). (303) 273-8500. Tours available by appointment only, Tuesday to Thursday, 9 A.M. to 11 A.M. and 1 P.M. to 3 P.M. Free. **Ages 10 and up.**

When the big earthquake of 1994 struck in Northridge, California, this was the first place the world turned to for information. The National Earthquake Information Center monitors earthquake activity throughout the world and disseminates the information. Waverly Person, chief of the Information Center and a frequent tour guide, spent eight hours standing in front of TV cameras updating the information the day of that California quake. While we were there, his beeper went off, alerting him to a 3.4 tremor in Wyoming.

This isn't a tour so much as a session on earthquakes. The guide leads you into the earthquake monitoring room, explains the equipment and the who, what, where, and when of earthquakes, and then fields questions from adults and kids alike. Person handles the questions with humor and obvious love for his subject.

Although the information is not technical, the session, about 45 minutes, is best suited to the older child with a scientific bent. Tours are given as a public courtesy by busy geophysicists; preschoolers and younger kids really don't belong here.

While you're here, don't forget to stop at the display on the first floor where kids can play tic-tac-toe on earthquake trivia with a computer and jump on the ground and watch the seismometer record their own "earthquakes." Even grown-ups will want to take a turn.

● Ulysses Park

1205 Ulysses Street and 10th Avenue. (303) 384-8100 or 278-8365 (Batter's Up). Park: daily, 6 A.M. to 11 P.M. Free. **All ages.**

While younger kids are occupied on some very nice playground equipment here, older kids can hone their in-line skating and skateboarding skills.

This park is one of only a few in the state that has an area (no charge) set aside with first-rate skateboard and in-line skate ramps and platforms. Have your kids bring their own equipment. The park also has batting cages (Batter's Up), open Monday to Friday, noon to 9 P.M., and Saturdays and Sundays, 8 A.M. to 8 P.M., where you can hit balls for a nominal fee, using bats and helmets provided at the park.

This is a popular Golden park and a good place to relax after sightseeing in the area. If you plan to picnic, note there are pavilions but no grills.

HENDERSON

● Berry Patch Farms

83rd and Rosemary. (Five blocks southeast of Mile High Flea Market). (303) 286-0202 (recording). Spring, summer, fall: Monday, Wednesday, Friday, Saturday, 8 A.M. to 1 P.M. and Wednesday evenings, 4 P.M. to 7 P.M. (Hours subject to change; call first.) **Ages 2 and up.**

Looking for a really different excursion with the kids? Berry Patch Farms is a wonderfully child-friendly U-Pick-Em farm where the kids can run up and down the rows and pick vegetables, melons, raspberries, strawberries, and whatever else is in season. The owners update the recording weekly with a report on what's available for picking. Our kids had a blast—and were even willing to try some of the vegetables they had picked—a real bonus. Prices for the produce are reasonable; the experience invaluable. In the summer, go early in the day to avoid the hot sun. Season starts around beginning of June and usually closes around end of October, depending on weather.

● Mile High Flea Market

7007 East 88th Avenue. (Interstate 25 north from Denver to Interstate 76 East, exit at 88th Avenue and go right.) (303) 289-4656. Year-round, Wednesday, Saturday, and Sunday, 7 A.M. to 5 P.M. Admission, $2; ages 11 and under, free. **Ages 3 and up.**

If you love bargain hunting, you won't want to miss this giant flea market, with new and used items at cut-rate prices as far as the eye can see. Consider it the grandaddy of all garage sales! More than 2,000 vendors rent space here, in open-air spots as well as permanent structures. You'll find everything from garden tools to baby furniture, weight-loss cures to fresh fruit and vegetables in elaborate—and not-so-elaborate—set-ups. Need Band-Aids for the kids? Pick up a few boxes, $1 each. Looking for Hercules T-shirts? They're three for $10. You name it, it's here. All it takes is a good eye, strong legs—and an occasional snack or bauble for the kids to keep them interested!

There are endless miles of walking to be done here, so remember to dress children in comfortable shoes. You might also want to consider renting a grocery cart ($2, with an additional $3 deposit) or wagon ($4; must leave driver's license with vendor). In addition to giving the kids a break from walking, they are almost a necessity if you plan to buy numerous items.

Snack booths are located throughout the flea market, offering the usual food fare: hot dogs, nachos, pretzels, pizza, roasted corn on the cob, and more. In addition, keep in mind that there are three large, attended rest rooms at the east and west ends of the market and in the center.

Children will be overjoyed to find a smattering of carnival rides, usually near the center of the market (weekends only, March to October), and pony rides, generally at the east end of the market (summer only). But even without these diversions, kids seem perfectly happy to browse through the goods with Mom and Dad. Be forewarned, however: this browsing can cost you. Even at 50 cents or $1 for a knickknack, you may find you've spent more on throwaway items than you have saved on the purchases you actually wanted. Ah well. Chalk it up to the expense of the outing—and enjoy the thrill of the hunt!

LAKESIDE

● Lakeside Amusement Park

Interstate 70 and Sheridan Boulevard. (303) 477-1621. Weekends only in May. Memorial Day to Labor Day, Monday to Friday, 6 to 11 P.M. (main park), 1 to 10 P.M. (kiddie park); Saturday and Sunday, noon to 11 P.M. Admission, $1.50. Ride coupons, 25 cents each (most rides are two to six *coupons; all kiddie rides, two coupons). Unlimited rides, Monday to Friday, $10.75; Saturday and Sunday, $12.75.* **Ages 2 and up.**

On the western edge of Denver, just south of Arvada and east of Wheat Ridge, Lakeside is part of a tiny community of the same name. Built in 1908, it is a Denver landmark, its pink-capped citadel as recognizable to locals as any more stately historic site. One of two major amusement parks in the metro area (see also Elitch Gardens entry under Denver), Lakeside boasts 24 main rides, 15 kiddie rides, and a miniature steam train that takes riders one and a half miles around the lake that borders the park. The park also offers a traditional carousel dating to 1901, featuring all original animal figures. And, of course, visitors will find plenty of snack booths and arcade games as well.

While the design of Lakeside is decidedly fifties, with sign lettering that looks like it hasn't been updated in years, the park offers several strengths: the kiddie park is extensive and extremely reasonable; a child can play for several hours on less than $11 and will be thrilled with the choices (and adults don't pay excessive admission fees to accompany their toddlers). The miniature train ride is a delight (keep your eyes open for interesting birds landing in the marshy area around the lake; we even spotted a great blue heron on one trip). And the main rides are exciting for preteens without being heart-stopping for parents.

On the other hand, teenagers may feel the experience is a bit tame. They won't find the latest hot roller coaster or flume ride here, just the standards that have been around for years.

LAKEWOOD

 ● **Casa Bonita**

6715 West Colfax Avenue. (303) 232-5115. Daily, 11 A.M. to 9:30 P.M.; Friday and Saturday, 11 A.M. to 10 P.M. No reservations. **All ages.**

This Lakewood restaurant and entertainment center has been an institution in metropolitan Denver for more than 20 years. The gold-domed, pink adobe building is one of only two Casa Bonitas in the country—the other is in Tulsa, Oklahoma—and it features a 30-foot indoor waterfall, cliff divers, mariachi bands, puppet shows, and piñatas.

While you chow down on the all-you-can-eat Mexican food served cafeteria style, performers entertain in various skits—bad guys shoot it out with the sheriff, a gorilla escapes from its trainer, pirates kidnap the damsel in distress, and so on. In each skit, one performer always ends up diving into the pool below.

The building, 52,000 square feet, is designed to look like a Mexican village. The restaurant seats 1,100—and is often full to capacity. Diners are seated in a number of areas, including near the waterfall and pool or in pseudocaverns and mines. But no matter where you sit, the dining is secondary to the entertainment, and kids will quickly be up and about to watch all the action. Most kids, in fact, like to stand near the pool during the diving acts just to get splashed.

The all-you-can eat dinner is $8.39; the à la carte menu runs $5.49 to $8.49. The kids' meals are $2.99. Chips and salsa and sopapillas, those fried pillows of dough served with honey, are included in every meal.

This is a very popular place, especially in summer and during holidays. On Labor Day, there was a 90-minute wait to get in. Best bet during peak season is to try for the off-hours, such as midafternoon or just as it opens. Call ahead and ask what the wait looks like if you're pressed for time.

● Lakewood's Heritage Center

797 South Wadsworth Boulevard. (303) 987-7850. Tuesday to Friday, 10 A.M. to 4 P.M.; Saturday and Sunday, noon to 4 P.M. Guided tours every half hour, ending at 3:30 P.M. Tours: adults, $2; children ages 4 to 18, $1; ages 3 and under, free; no charge to stroll the grounds. Tours: ages 8 and up. Trails and duck pond: **All ages.**

Visit a country schoolhouse, complete with an apple on the teacher's desk; step into the 1920s home of a Russian Jewish immigrant family; take a look at a Model A car in the garage and a host of farm implements. It's all here at Lakewood's Heritage Center, a look at the history of the area from the turn of the century to the present.

Staffers have been busy revamping the exhibits and are still in a bit of flux, but if you're in the area, it's worth taking a moment to stop and tour the site. Volunteers will lead you through the historical buildings, and if you call first, they'll gladly open up one of their "discovery trunks"—filled with various artifacts, including Plains Indian clothes, bows and arrows, and more—to give your children a true, hands-on experience.

If your kids fidget during these kinds of "educational" jaunts, however, not to worry. Just take them for a walk along one of the extensive trails that wind through this 127-acre site, a slice of quiet in Lakewood's otherwise bustling landscape. We suggest heading to the lake north of the village. This is a beautiful spot, abundant with wild birds. From the covered bridge, your younger kids will love watching the many varieties of ducks and geese—which offer an educational value all its own.

The center sponsors special events throughout the year, including Cider Days in October, when the park is filled with antique tractor pulls, music, old-time refreshments, and more. Call for a schedule.

● White Fence Farm

6263 West Jewell Avenue. (303) 935-5945. Tuesday through Saturday, 5 to 9 P.M.; Sunday, 11:30 A.M. to 8 P.M. Closed Monday. Closed the month of January. **All ages.**

While you wait to dine at this ever-popular, ever-crowded restaurant and farm, children can pet the animals in the barnyard, play on the playground, climb in the elaborate treehouse, or tour the grounds in the horse-drawn carriage during warm weather. Families can also browse the country gift store while they wait.

The restaurant specializes in fried chicken with all the sides—bean salad, corn fritters, cole slaw—served family style. Kids get a token that entitles them to pick from the treasure chest at the end of the meal.

Although it's easy to pass the time, hungry diners will want to arrive immediately upon opening or later—after 7 P.M.—rather than early. No reservations are accepted for groups of less than 15 people.

LITTLETON

● Chatfield Arboretum

From Highway 470, take the Wadsworth exit south, turn west on Deer Creek Canyon Road, then watch for the entrance gate approximately one-third of a mile down the road. (303) 973-3705. Daily, 9 A.M. to 5 P.M. Adults, $1; Denver Botanic Gardens members and ages 15 and under, free. Children must be accompanied by an adult. **Ages 3 and up.**

Take a look at 19th-century farm equipment, a one-room schoolhouse dating from the 1870s with an old-time playground, a "survival garden"—filled with plants grown for medicine, food, or textiles—and more at this quiet attraction, just across from the Chatfield Dam and Visitor Center. The arboretum offers picnic tables and easy hiking trails along Deer Creek. It's low-key here, and kids are likely to get restless with the exhibits, but the calm surroundings, punctuated only by the sounds of nature, make it worth a short stop if you're in the area.

● Chatfield State Park

From Highway 470, head south on Wadsworth past three stoplights. Turn left into park entrance. General information, (303) 791-7275; visitor center, (303) 979-4120. Park: daily, 5 A.M. to 10 P.M. Visitor center: Monday to Friday, 8 A.M. to 4 P.M.; Saturday and Sunday, 9 A.M. to 5 P.M. (closed Saturday and Sunday in winter). Admission: $4 per car. **All ages.**

More than a century ago, settlers came to this area in search of gold, ignoring Indian warnings that it was "bad medicine" to settle in the area.

Their predecessors paid the price: rains flooded the area in 1933, 1935, and 1942. In 1965, another flood was responsible for 13 deaths and more than $300 million in damages. To avoid future problems, construction began on Chatfield Dam in 1967.

Today, the no longer flood-prone land has metamorphosed into a great family destination. The state park boasts 5,600 acres set aside for recreation, including hiking trails, picnic areas, boating, horseback riding, camping, fishing, and more. Out of the way for most Denverites, it is one of the metro area's best kept-secrets. After remarking that we couldn't believe we'd never been here before, one park ranger laughed. "We hear that all the time," she said. In addition to boating and camping, here's a range of suggested activities for families visiting the park:

Horseback riding. Horses can be leased at the Chatfield B&B Livery, southwest of Swim Beach. Ask for trail maps at the park's main entrance. Cost is $12.50 per hour. It's best to call ahead for reservations (303-933-3636). The livery also offers hayrack and sleigh rides in the winter.

Swim Beach. Open Memorial Day weekend through Labor Day weekend, this is one of the few sandy beaches you'll find in the metro area. Small wonder families flock here in the summer. The entrance fee is 50 cents per person (children under age 6 and seniors ages 63 and over are free) in addition to the park admission—well within reason. And the nearby concession stand is equally inexpensive (popcorn, 50 cents; sno-cone, 75 cents). Lifeguards are on duty. The water can be rather cold, but you'd never know it from the way the kids run in and out of the water with abandon!

Hiking trails. Ask for trail maps at the park's main entrance. Trails are both paved and dirt, so those with strollers will want to seek out the paved paths. Most provide easy, gentle hikes the entire family can enjoy.

Heron educational area. Head south from the park entrance and around the dam approximately two miles to this spot where you'll find informational signs about the great blue herons that populate the park. This area was originally designed as a heron overlook, where visitors could view these birds, which can grow to four feet with a six-foot wingspan. Unfortunately, the birds moved to other areas of the park, leaving visitors only with the educational signs. Stop for the information, then keep an eye out for the birds as you continue your visit.

Model airplane observation. Young children especially will enjoy watching these planes—each about three feet long—dip and dive in this special area of the park, just north of the heron educational stop. The area also boasts a small playground. On calm, warm days, plane enthusiasts begin showing up as early as 7 A.M., and you'll find action well into the evening hours.

Hot-air balloons. Close to the park entrance, balloon pilots take to the sky on mornings when conditions are right. And they aren't above performing some sky-high theatrics. "Some get a little crazy and try to skim the water," said one park ranger. It makes for a great show, best viewed from any high point in the park. Rangers suggest coming on those weekends when the weather is calm. Takeoff is generally "five minutes after sunrise," according to park officials.

Fishing. Fishing is allowed anywhere in the park except at Swim Beach.

Boat rentals. Just east of the marina, you'll find all kinds of boats available for rental between mid-May and mid-September. These include: paddleboats, ski boats, pontoons, fishing boats, power boats, and sailboats. You can also rent jet skis or take sailing lessons. Call (303) 791-6104 for times and prices.

Visitor center. North of the main entrance, it's a little out of the way but still worth a stop. Here you can pick up all the information you need on outdoor activities in the state and learn about the anatomy of a flood, among other things, in the center's educational area. The exhibits are lively—one display reenacts a dramatic moment in the lives of settlers facing the 1864 flood: "Jed! Jed! Help me!" shrieks a woman from the audio system—and even our 6-year-old wasn't bored during a quick walk-through.

● Littleton Historical Museum ◆

6028 South Gallup Street (next to Kettering Park), about 10 blocks off Littleton Boulevard. (303) 795-3950. Tuesday to Friday, 8 A.M. to 5 P.M.; Saturday, 10 A.M. to 5 P.M.; Sunday, 1 to 5 P.M. Free. **All ages.**

One of our favorite attractions, the Littleton Historical Museum is actually an elaborate park spread over 14 acres, featuring an 1860s homestead and an 1890s farm, complete with live farm animals. The grounds are expansive and beautiful, with sheep, horses, and cows in the paddocks, a large lake, and wonderful shady trees. It's a great place to walk around, even if you're not interested in the historical aspects of the museum.

At the home sites, guides in period costumes talk to children about life in their respective time periods, taking their cues from the kids' questions. One guide even showed our kids how to pet a chicken. The differences between the 1860s and the 1890s farms are startling, with plenty to explore, from the one-room cabin and schoolhouse to the more sophisticated five-room home of the 1890s. Visitors enter and exit the area through a small modern museum of period clothing, toys, and furniture.

You can easily spend a couple hours on the premises. If you're lucky enough to be in the vicinity in mid-October, call the museum and ask about the pumpkin festival. Kids can select their own pumpkins from the fields and enjoy hayrides, cider-pressing, and other demonstrations.

● Roxborough State Park

Interstate 25 to C-470 to Santa Fe exit, south on Santa Fe Drive to Titan Road, Titan Road becomes Rampart Range Road, go four miles and follow the well-marked signs to the park. (303) 973-3959. Daily: summer, generally 8 A.M. to 8 P.M.; winter, open daily but hours vary; call for times. Visitor center; hours vary monthly; call first. Admission: $4 per car. **All ages.**

There's an excellent chance you'll spot deer at this lovely park on the outskirts of Denver. The park has striking rock formations similar to Garden of the Gods (see entry under Colorado Springs) and well-manicured paths and trails. Bring binoculars for spotting golden eagles and other wildlife—bobcats, bears, coyotes—that frequent the park. We saw the flash of the white tail of a deer in the dense brush just outside the visitor center.

Spring is a popular time to visit the park; plan on an early start because parking is very limited and you may be forced to wait in line at the ranger's station if the park is crowded. As an extra bonus, call for the schedule of events that take place at the park—wildflower hikes, children's story hours, bird hikes, photo hikes, and puppet shows—and time your visit accordingly.

Most of the hikes are gentle loops. If you plan a hike of any length, bring a backpack of snacks for the kids. The visitor center has a soda machine, rest rooms, and a water fountain. You might also bring a picnic lunch to eat at one of the numerous benches along the trail.

MORRISON

● Dinosaur Ridge

Directly east of Red Rocks on Highway 26 (also known as Alameda Parkway). If coming from C-470, take the Morrison exit and drive west toward Morrison, then turn right onto the first frontage road, which is Rooney Road. Go north to Alameda Parkway and turn left. Continue until you reach the parking lot. (303) 697-3466. Open 24 hours a day. Visitor Center: summer, Monday to Saturday, 9 A.M. to 5 P.M., Sunday, noon to 5 P.M.; winter, Monday to Saturday, 9 A.M. to 4 P.M., Sunday, noon to 4 P.M. Free. **Ages 4 and up.**

This is truly one of the Denver area's most amazing secrets: dinosaur tracks and bones embedded on a ridge just a few miles from the city! Dating to more than 150 million years ago, these bones were first discovered in 1877. But, although the Dinosaur Ridge brochure calls the spot "a world-renowned geological and paleontological outdoor museum," you would be hard-pressed to find an average Denverite who has heard of it.

About 15 minutes from downtown Denver, Dinosaur Ridge is a hill circled by a public road. Visitors can park at either end of the mile-long road and walk up or down. You can also drive the road and pull over at various stops along the way, although traffic flow sometimes makes this difficult. Sixteen informational signs are posted to point out sites of geological and paleontological interest.

The most exciting of these stops is clearly No. 4, the giant dinosaur footprints marching up the hill. At the other end of the walk, you'll find camarosaurus bones buried in rock, but easily spotted. These are sure-fire hits with dinosaur-hungry kids (although the stops in between will be less interesting to younger children, who may be bored with the geological information presented).

The ridge is open any time, and takes about an hour to tour. Stop in for an informational video at the Visitor Center. We also recommend a stop at the Morrison Natural History Museum (see entry) as an educational complement to your visit. If you can time it right, the best days to come are Open Ridge Days—generally offered once a month from April through October—when the road is closed to traffic, tour guides are on hand to explain the sites, and buses are available to shuttle visitors back to where they started. Parents should keep a close eye on the little ones: the paths are narrow, and traffic can be busy on this road. Guided tours are also available for $25 for one to 12 people; reservations required.

● The Fort

19192 Highway 8 (Highway 285 to Highway 8—the Morrison/Evergreen exit. Turn right, the restaurant will be a couple hundred yards ahead). (303) 697-4771. Monday to Friday, 5:30 to 9:30 P.M.; Saturday, 5 to 9:30 P.M.; Sunday, 5 to 8:30 P.M. Children's menu featuring Western cuisine, $6 to $12; adults, $15 on up. Reservations accepted. **Ages 5 and up.**

The Fort isn't a restaurant; it's an experience. Built as a replica of Bent's Old Fort in La Junta, Colorado, The Fort restaurant combines history with authentic Western cuisine inside its thick adobe walls. In 1997, President and Mrs. Clinton hosted a dinner here for visiting foreign leaders, taking advantage of spectacular views and a one-of-a-kind place.

The restaurant has a center courtyard with a warming bonfire and a tepee for the kids to explore. The kids have no trouble passing the time until dinner. At the table they're given a cotton swab and one of those pictures that you touch with water to color, but they're usually equally entertained by the happenings around them. A mountain man strolls among the diners, and dinner is frequently punctuated by the beating of a drum to announce a birthday. The birthday person is given a coyote or buffalo hat to wear while having his or her picture taken. If that's not entertainment enough, ask your server to perform the mountain man's toast.

Owner Sam Arnold, Western historical culinary expert and author, oversees a menu that includes the infamous Rocky Mountain oysters, buffalo, trout, elk, and quail. Make no mistake: although you'll find warm and good-natured dining here, the food is first-rate Western cuisine and priced accordingly. If you're really lucky, Arnold himself will be on hand to deliver a toast or open a bottle of champagne with a tomahawk. As Arnold says in the very best tradition of the mountain man, "Waugh!"

● Morrison Natural History Museum

501 Colorado Highway 8 (half mile south of the town of Morrison). (303) 697-1873. Wednesday to Sunday, 1 to 4 P.M. Adults and children, $1; children ages 5 and under, free; families, $2.50. **Ages 4 and up.**

If you're planning a trip to Dinosaur Ridge (see entry), stop here first for a quick orientation. The museum, located a few miles from the ridge, offers a 20-minute video that discusses the history of the ridge and its offerings. When it's over, you can stroll through the small log cabin, where giant dinosaur teeth, a fossilized outline of the earliest known bird, a cast of the first dinosaur eggs ever found, and other dinosaur-related items are housed in glass display cases. This isn't an extensive collection, but what's here is fascinating to see.

The museum also features several hands-on exhibits for the kids. They can touch real dinosaur bones, handle live native reptiles, and take a tiny electric-powered drill in hand and chip away at a rock to find an embedded fossil of a stegasaurus. This is always a kid-pleaser—and a great lesson in how painstaking digging for fossils can be!

● Red Rocks Amphitheater

16351 County Road 93. (303) 697-8935. Open year-round. **Ages 4 and up.**

This attraction's name explains itself: these are giant red rock formations, thrust skyward years ago by earthquakes and other earth movements.

In 1929, humans took over, building an outdoor amphitheater between the rocks. Red Rocks is known predominantly for its first-rate concerts—geared almost completely to teens and adults—under the stars. Red Rocks offers a spectacular view of downtown Denver, and during nonconcert times, children will love climbing up and down the steps, checking out the stage area, and shouting to each other from yards away, since sound carries with ease. A major draw is the theater's Easter sunrise service, which attracts hundreds of worshipers every year.

The park also offers a trading post, where kids can buy a souvenir and you might enjoy a cup of coffee. In winter, the post is open daily, 9 A.M. to 5 P.M.; summer, 9 A.M. to 7 P.M.

After refreshment, you might consider taking the gentle, 1.4 mile hiking trail that begins just outside the trading post. Park naturalists are often on hand for guided walks here.

● World Famous Tiny Town and Railway

6249 South Turkey Creek Road. (303) 697-6829. Memorial Day to Labor Day: 10 A.M. to 5 P.M.; May, September, and October: Saturday and Sunday, 10 A.M. to 5 P.M. Adults, $2.50; ages 3 to 12, $1.50. Train, $1. Concession stand and gift shop. **All ages.**

This miniature town, which appears to be the work of elves, was originally built in 1915 by George Turner, who wanted to erect child-size buildings for his daughter. In 1920, the town opened to the public. After its initial success, however, Tiny Town fell into ruins, with only a few dollhouse remains to mark the spot.

In 1988, volunteers adopted Tiny Town, determined to restore it to its original luster, and they refurbished or re-created more than one hundred dollhouse and child-size buildings. Today, Tiny Town is back. Visitors can peer through the windows, and in some cases, pint-size visitors can climb inside. In addition to walking among the houses, you can ride an open-air train on its mile loop around the town. Tiny Town often has special activities on the weekends for its small guests, including face-painting, clowns, and other light entertainment. There's also a playground for the younger ones and picnic facilities. The toddler, preschool, and elementary school set will easily enjoy a half day at this special spot located about 30 minutes from downtown Denver.

SEDALIA

● Daniels Park

Interstate 25 to Castle Pines Parkway (exit 188), go west; parkway will dead-end into park. (Follow the dirt road.) Daily, 5 A.M. to 11 P.M. Free. **All ages.**

Daniels Park is one of only two places near Denver to see buffalo roaming in a natural setting. The other is the Buffalo Herd Overlook at Genesee Park (see entry under Genesee).

The thousand-acre park, with isolated mesas and spectacular cliffs and vistas, is a bit of an oasis in the midst of suburban housing developments at the southeastern end of metropolitan Denver. We saw kids scrambling sure-footed on the rocks at the overlook but we would advise holding tight, especially to younger children.

There are rest rooms, a shelter house, and picnic tables at the top. Daniels is a nice park to visit if you're on your way to Castle Rock or Colorado Springs or if you're visiting in this end of the metro area. The kids will have a quick chance to explore—and hopefully the buffalo will be roaming close at hand—while the grown-ups enjoy some of the beauty of the ever-varied Colorado scenery. Be aware, however, that you may not see the buffalo, depending on where they are in the park at the time of your visit.

THORNTON

● Thornton Recreation Center

11151 Colorado Boulevard. (303) 252-1600. Recreation center: daily, Monday to Friday, 5:30 A.M. to 10 P.M.; Saturday, 7:30 A.M. to 7 P.M.; Sunday, 8:30 A.M. to 8:30 P.M. Open swim: daily, but hours vary (call for schedule). Adults, ages 18 to 54, $5; ages 13 to 17, $3.50; ages 3 to 12 and seniors ages 55 and up, $2.50; 2 and under, free. **Ages 2 and up.**

What to do on a rainy day? If you're anywhere near Thornton, head for one of the only—if not the only—indoor wave pool in Denver. The recreation center is open to the public daily. In addition to the wave pool, you can shoot down a 150-foot slide on a tube into the small, lazy river or get splashed by a spewing mushroom-type cap; tubes are free. The little ones can play in the baby pool. If you tire of swimming, the center has a lounge with a big-screen television and video games to wile away the afternoon.

WESTMINSTER

● Adventure Golf

9650 North Sheridan. (303) 650-7588. March to October: weather permitting, Sunday to Thursday, 10 A.M. to 10 P.M.; Friday and Saturday, 10 A.M. to 11 P.M. Hours subject to change in spring and fall. Adults, $4.95; ages 4 to 12 and seniors ages 60 and up, $4.45; ages 3 and under, free. Second round, $3 with receipt from first round. **Ages 3 and up.**

Some miniature golf courses are just 18 green strips with 18 holes in them. Others are elaborate creations that make golfing a journey into someone's wild and wonderful imagination. This is the latter, one of the best mini-golf offerings in the city. Adventure Golf boasts three full courses, each with its own theme, situated among lush, colorful gardens. In the Lost Continent, a plane carrying a team of explorers has crashed. Golfers wend their way through the story, where they encounter the plane wreckage, a hand reaching out from quicksand, and more. During evening hours only, fire shoots up from the wreckage and a volcano explodes every nine minutes. Buccaneer Bay offers a pirate theme, while Adventure Cove is an Egyptian experience, filled with mummies and pyramids—each with special effects of their own. Staffers note that another course is planned for spring of 1998; it will no doubt be filled with terrific new surprises.

Adventure Golf has a concessions stand that sells soft drinks, hot dogs, nachos, ice cream cones, and other snacks at reasonable prices. We suggest you plan to come at night, when all special effects are operating, giving the experience an otherworldly glow.

● Butterfly & Insect Pavilion

6252 West 104th Avenue. (303) 469-5441. Tuesday to Sunday, 9 A.M. to 5 P.M. Adults, $6.50; ages 4 to 12, $3.50; ages 3 and under, free with paid adult (maximum of two free children per adult); seniors, ages 62 and up, $4.50. **Ages 2 and up.**

The Butterfly & Insect Pavilion is one of approximately six such facilties in the United States. The attraction includes two basic components. The first is a greenhouse-type room filled with—you guessed it— thousands of free-flying, colorful butterflies and lush tropical plants. Visitors are allowed to walk throughout the room, watching the butterflies, which often land on a shoulder or a head and flap their wings peacefully before taking off for the next destination. It is a spot of enchantment, and we guarantee your children will find the sight of so many butterflies in one place thrilling.

The other component is a room where exotic insects are housed in individual cages. For example, you can look at the Giant Sonoran Centipede, the largest in North America, or the Texas Brown Tarantula, among the largest spiders in the world. The accompanying informational signs are written to intrigue children with their "Did You Know?" teasers, and occasionally volunteers hold an insect or two that visitors are allowed to "pet."

It makes for a fun outing, although we offer one caveat: the price can be high for the amount of time you'll spend here. While the butterflies are captivating on first sight, kids tend to lose intererst rather quickly. The entire visit will probably last around an hour.

● Trail Dust Steak House

See Englewood entry.

WHEAT RIDGE

● Wheat Ridge Historic Park

4610 Robb Street. (303) 421-9111. Monday to Saturday, 10 A.M. *to 3* P.M. *Admission, $2.* **Ages 6 and up.**

This humble attraction features five historic buildings, including a sod house and log cabin, clustered on a small plot of land. Visitors first enter a brick bungalow, where historic items, such as typewriters and vacuum sweepers, are on display. From there, a volunteer will take interested parties through the sod house, furnished to reflect farm life in the 1880s and 1890s. The walls of this house were once nothing more than hardened dirt and prairie grass. "When I first saw it," said one volunteer, "it was covered with vines and bird's nests. It was charming, but it was melting away." The walls have since been plastered over. But visitors can still see the sod construction through a window set into the plaster.

A shed near the "soddy" holds early farm implements. And children will especially enjoy visiting the log cabin, built about 1863. The cabin consists of one room and a loft, yet two parents and six children once shared this tiny space!

The final stop is Wheat Ridge's first post office, a building recently moved to this site and restored. Visitors can look at the journals of early farmers, old children's books, and cookbooks.

The park is small and the tour fairly quick. But if you're in the area, this makes for an interesting and educational diversion. Of note are the park's special events. Mark your calendar for the May Festival, usually the second Saturday in May, and Apple Cider Day, the second Saturday in October. On these days, piping hot pumpkin cookies are offered straight out of the wood stove and cool cider comes fresh from the presses. One note: Other than the bungalow and post office, the buildings have no heat—except when the wood stoves are cranking on special event days. Bring sweaters.

Colorado Springs and Manitou Springs

WHEN GENERAL WILLIAM PALMER FIRST BEHELD the majesty of Pike's Peak in 1871, he decided at that moment to found a new, more sophisticated community to replace the miners' community nearby. Colorado Springs was formed from his hopes and dreams.

Today Colorado Springs thrives as both a first-class resort town and as a major defense center with several military installations and bases. Perhaps it's this diversity that accounts for the many—and unusual— number of attractions in Colorado Springs and neighboring Manitou Springs, once known for its spa waters. From the ProRodeo Hall of Fame to the May Museum of Natural History to the U.S. Olympic Training Center to the wondrous beauty of Palmer's inspiration, this area offers scenic splendors and more than its share of memorable places—all within 68 miles of Denver.

COLORADO SPRINGS

● American Numismatic Association Museum

818 North Cascade Avenue (at the campus of Colorado College). (719) 632-2646. Monday to Friday, 8:30 A.M. to 4 P.M. Free. **Ages 8 and up.**

You'll quickly find out what "numismatic" means at this museum. Rare coins and paper money are lovingly displayed at this friendly little spot, national headquarters for America's largest coin club.

The younger kids will be content to stop right at the door, where they're allowed to select one coin from the treasure box as a souvenir. Older kids will enjoy seeing paper money in denominations such as $10,000 and unusual coins, such as the 1913 Liberty Nickel, purchased at auction in 1967 for $46,500.

In order to make the most of what you're seeing, we suggest you call ahead and arrange for a tour. Tours are scaled to the audience; the guide even uses puppets for the younger children. A lot of information can be mined here, all on a fascinating subject.

● Bear Creek Regional Park Nature Center

245 Bear Creek Road. (Interstate 25 south to exit 141—Cimarron Street exit—go west. At 26th Street, turn left—follow signs for nature center. Go south on 26th Street two miles; 26th Street will become Bear Creek Road.) (719) 520-6387. Nature Center: Tuesday to Saturday, 9 A.M. to 4 P.M. Trails: Open daily, dawn to dusk. Free. **All ages.**

This picturesque spot features a Nature Center and some well-tended short trails—the longest is two miles—that loop uphill and along a creek.

The center offers interpretative nature hikes and programs (most require reservations) and features some small exhibits, such as bird nests and animal skins and a diorama of the foothills wildlife, and some hands-on exhibits, such as a bear cave to climb around in.

The naturalists at the center are very friendly and helpful and advised us to look for the huge mound of an anthill along the pathway. (The kids invested lots of time looking for it and were both excited and grossed out when we finally found it.) We also borrowed binoculars for a closer look at the numerous birds.

Many of the visitors appeared to be folks out for a stroll in the peaceful and pretty setting. We followed a short hike along the creek, and despite the nippy weather, the kids didn't hesitate to take off their socks and shoes and plunge in. To our delight, we also spotted three deer in the brush.

● The Broadmoor Hotel

1 Lake Avenue. (719) 634-7711. Rooms start at $290 during high season, May 1 to October 31; prices drop to $195, November 1 to April 30 (price includes up to four in a room); special packages (with perks such as "kids eat free") are available on some holidays. **All ages.**

The stately Broadmoor has been one of Colorado's premier resorts since it was built in 1918. Rising in all its pink splendor, it's the crown jewel of Colorado hotels.

Befitting the 1990s, it has become increasingly child-friendly through the years with programs to satisfy both kids and parents. Kids, ages 5 to 12, can participate in the B-Bunch, daytime and evening programs featuring hiking, swimming, paddleboating, or field trips to places such as the nearby Cheyenne Mountain Zoo (see entry). The program is held summers, daily, 9 A.M. to 4 P.M., and nightly, 6 to 10 P.M., and on holiday weekends between Thanksgiving and Christmas and at Easter.

Cost is $45 for the first child, $35 for the second, $30 for the third, $25 for the fourth (prices include lunch and a snack); evening B-Bunch, $35 per child (includes dinner and a snack). Three- and four-year-olds can participate in the Little B-Bunch, 9 A.M. to 2 P.M. only, $35 per child (includes lunch and a snack).

In addition to the organized programs, The Broadmoor has a movie theater on-site that plays only PG-13, PG, or G movies, horseback riding, hot-air ballooning, paddleboating, an arcade, two outdoor pools and an indoor pool, and an arcade.

● Cafe Michelle

122 North Tejon. (719) 633-5089. Summer: Monday to Saturday, 9 A.M. to midnight; Sunday, 10 A.M. to midnight. Winter: Sunday to Thursday, 9 A.M. to 11 P.M.; Friday and Saturday, 9 A.M. to midnight. **All ages.**

When you've been around since 1952, you must be doing something right, and so it is with Cafe Michelle, known locally as Michelle's, which has been serving food, ice cream, and chocolates for more than 40 years.

This comfortable family restaurant, a combination of ice cream parlor, dinette, and chocolate shop, is known for its homemade chocolates and lavish ice cream specialties. Try the Gold Strike, a "mother lode" of vanilla, chocolate, and strawberry ice creams with chocolate, pineapple, and raspberry toppings, whole pecans, chocolate sprinkles, sugar wafers, whipped cream, cherries, and chocolate candy. Or, how about the American Beauty: vanilla and strawberry ice cream covered with strawberries and banana chunks, and topped with chopped nuts, chocolate sprinkles, sugar wafers, whipped cream, and cherries?

The kid's menu has inexpensive food and scaled-down ice cream specialties. Michelle's, in the heart of downtown and easily accessible, is a good rest stop between Colorado Springs attractions.

● Cave of the Winds

Take Interstate 25 to exit 141, then head six miles west on Highway 24. (719) 685-5444. Winter, spring, and fall: daily, 10 A.M. to 5 P.M. May 1 to Labor Day: daily, 9 A.M. to 8 P.M. Adults, $10; ages 6 to 15, $5; under age 6, free. **Ages 5 and up.**

This is one of Colorado Springs' most promoted tourist attractions, so if you're in the Springs, there's no doubt you'll be wondering if Cave of the Winds is worth a stop. The answer is yes, but only if you can overlook the heavy-duty commercialization of the site.

The standard cave tour, featuring "delicate crystal flowers, giant stone columns," and "massive limestone canopies," as the brochure puts it, wends its way through 20 underground rooms, spread out through three-quarters of a mile. Unfortunately, the entrance to the cave is located at one end of the gift shop—the better to catch your child's eye on an overpriced bauble or two. Once the tour starts, you'll be asked to pose for a picture with your group (and wait while others have their pictures taken); and, no doubt you've guessed, once the tour ends, you'll be given the developed picture and asked whether you'd like to buy it. There are video games and the de rigeur snack shop in the lobby. The cave itself is a touch of kitsch, with colored lights that highlight various crystal formations and spots where vandals have left their mark.

On the plus side, kids will enjoy making their way through narrow passageways, up steep stairs, and around winding paths. After all, what child hasn't imagined his own secret hideout at one time or another? This is the ultimate—if you can ignore the scores of other visitors wending their way past your tour group.

The cave has more than 200 stairs, so if you have toddlers, be prepared to do a fair amount of carrying. And, although most of the tour is well-lit, the guides turn out all the lights at one point in the tour; parents with children who are afraid of the dark may be better off avoiding this attraction. The tour lasts approximately 45 minutes.

Cave of the Winds also features a nighttime laser show, projected onto spectacular Williams Canyon below the visitor's center. The show is at 9 P.M. from May 1 to Labor Day weekend. Adults, $6; ages 6 to 15, $3; under age 6, free.

● Cheyenne Mountain Zoo

4250 Cheyenne Mountain Zoo Road. (Take Interstate 25 south from Denver to exit 138, follow South Circle Drive west, which will turn into Lake Avenue, continue to the Broadmoor Hotel. Make a left at the stoplight to Lake Circle. Follow the road until you see the signs for the zoo.) (719) 475-9555. Memorial Day to Labor Day: daily, 9 A.M. to 6 P.M. (admission gate closes at 5 P.M.). Rest of year: daily, 9 A.M. to 5 P.M. (admission gate closes at 4 P.M.). Adults, $6.75; ages 3 to 11, $3.75; under age 3, free. Ticket price includes Will Rogers Shrine of the Sun. **All ages.**

Get out your hiking shoes. The Cheyenne Mountain Zoo, at 7,000 feet, runs straight up the side of the mountain, a real workout for anyone pushing a stroller. But take your time and enjoy the spectacular views at this unique zoo overlooking the Broadmoor Hotel (see entry) and, in the distance, Colorado Springs. The faint-of-heart can ride the tram, which stops throughout the park and is both wheelchair and stroller accessible ($1 for unlimited rides).

The zoo covers 75 acres and once housed the wild animal collection of Spencer Penrose, founder of the Broadmoor Hotel. Because the zoo winds up the mountain, you'll have a unique perspective looking down on many of the animals in their open-air cages. The zoo is home to more than 500 animals. Don't miss the rare okapi, animals that look like a cross between a zebra and a giraffe. The okapi lives next to the giraffe cages, which you can't miss because the kids will be clamoring to join the crowd feeding the tall animals ($1 for giraffe crackers that look suspiciously like human crackers).

On a recent trip, the monkey house was particularly active and a lot of fun with the monkeys chattering and shrieking. The nocturnal house with its chief attraction—bats—was also worth a stop. Even the peacocks wandering freely put on a show, spreading their feathers to the delight of the crowd. There's also a primate house to showcase the larger apes.

Because the zoo is so strenuous, you can easily spend a couple hours exploring the animals within a few yards of the entrance. If you hope to reach the petting zoo and carousel near the top (50 cents), you may want to take the tram and work your way down. The food at the zoo is standard-issue concession fare—hamburgers, fries, ice cream—although you'll find a couple alternatives such as fat-free yogurt. You may want to pack a lunch.

If you have some extra time, drive up to the Will Rogers Shrine of the Sun dedicated to humorist Will Rogers and Spencer Penrose, who's buried here. Climb the stairs of the shrine for a remarkable view of the area.

● The Children's Museum of Colorado Springs

750 Citadel Drive East, in the Citadel Mall next to J. C. Penney. (719) 574-0077. Summer: Monday to Saturday, 10 A.M. to 5 P.M.; Sunday, noon to 5 P.M. Winter: Monday, Friday, and Saturday, 10 A.M. to 5 P.M.; Tuesday to Thursday, 11:30 A.M. to 5 P.M. Adults and children, $3.50; ages 1 and under, free. Admission is half-price every Sunday. **Ages 2 to 9.**

The storefront of this museum in a mall is designed, with its columns and pediments, to look like a traditional, staid museum. But take a look through the glass windows and you'll see something entirely different: a lively place where children are active and engaged. Your children will leave the land of material needs behind when they enter here, enjoying the options of five educational galleries.

Here's the run-down: Health and Fitness offers insight into the human body, with its giant, human heart that children can climb through, stuffed dolls that double as "patients" for children to operate on, microscopes and more. In Recollections III, visitors walk into a dark room where a video camera captures the shadow of their image on a giant, colorful electronic screen. Cartwheels, playful jumping: it's all fodder for this live human art project. Small Wonders is dedicated to children under age 5, who can choose between sorting and stacking activities, puppets, a magnetic drawing board, and more. And Super Cool Science Stuff invites children to encase themselves in a giant bubble using a special bubble-making contraption, discover angular momentum in a gyro chair, and play with exhibits on light, laser, sound, and air pressure.

If that weren't enough, the museum also offers a changing gallery that features a different focus every six months. Past themes have included space exploration, complete with an "infinity tunnel" where children feel as if they are floating; and the environment, featuring a "green home," which shows children what it takes to run an environmentally conscious home.

The museum offers special programs from time to time; inquire about a schedule. The least busy hours, say staffers, are afternoons during the week, before older children are out of school.

● Colorado Springs Pioneers Museum ◆

215 South Tejon Street. (719) 578-6650. Tuesday to Saturday, 10 A.M. to 5 P.M.; May through October, also open Sunday, 1 to 5 P.M. Free. **Ages 5 and up.**

This museum, housed in the elegantly restored El Paso courthouse, has so little to do with pioneers that we're left to wonder why the name was chosen. The building has lovely terrazo floors and columns, spacious rooms, and corridors, and sweeping high ceilings, with exhibits that run the gamut from Indian artifacts to Civil War memorabilia to Van Briggle pottery. Perhaps the most fun is the toy exhibit on the lower floor. Not only does it include toys from the past but also from the present, so that today's kids can someday look back with the same nostalgia as their parents.

Take the old-fashioned Otis elevator upstairs, where you can look into three rooms reconstructed precisely from the home of Helen Hunt Jackson, a Colorado author best known for the popular book *Ramona*. Across from the Jackson rooms is the Native Origins display, with Native American artifacts such as bows and arrows and beaded mocassins. End this visit on a sweet note with a visit to the nearby Cafe Michelle or Josh and John's for ice cream (see entries).

● The Edward J. Peterson Air and Space Museum

U.S. Highway 24 east to the Peterson Air Force Base exit. (719) 556-4915. Tuesday to Saturday, 8:30 A.M. to 4:30 P.M. Free. **Ages 6 and up.**

What child wouldn't be impressed at the sight of the full-size aircraft and missiles that are anchored along the grounds just outside this museum?

Located on Peterson Air Force base, the Peterson Air and Space Museum features exhibits representing the space and aviation heritage of Colorado and Colorado Springs. Inside, the museum has a satellite, and numerous artifacts from past wars. But the real attraction is outside— the missiles and planes.

Although this is a no-touch place—with signs to remind you—our kids liked walking underneath the huge aircraft, looking for the places where weapons might have been carried during various wars.

● Flying W Ranch Authentic Chuckwagon Suppers

3330 Chuckwagon Road. (719) 598-4000. End of May to end of September: daily. Gates open at 4:30 P.M.; dinner is served at 7:15 P.M. (After Labor Day, gates open at 5 P.M. and dinner is served at 6:45 P.M.) Adults, $13; ages 8 and under, $7. Reservations required. **Ages 4 and up.**

The Flying W offers a solid slice of the Old West chuckwagon experience, from the hot biscuits that come out of the Dutch oven to the tepees and log cabins that dot the grounds. This is a working cattle and horse ranch, just north of Garden of the Gods (see entry), although visitors won't see any livestock on the grounds. Patrons are encouraged to arrive early to wander the grounds, which feature covered wagons here and there, a steep trail to a rocky mountain overlook (parents take note: this is extremely hard to manage with young children), a miniature train ride (for an extra fee), and plenty of cabins that are now mostly souvenir shops. It is, indeed, nice to leave time to look around—especially so your children can watch the "cooks" baking biscuits in an open hut near the front entrance; when the biscuits are done, they are handed out, piping hot and delicious. On the other hand, too much advance time will leave you at the mercy of the gift shops, and they are plentiful. Be forewarned.

When the bell sounds for dinner, patrons file to their assigned tables, which will be outside on nice evenings, inside during inclement weather. A folksy host then directs the proceedings as the immense crowd—1,400 strong—snakes its way through the food line, where barbecue beef, baked beans, biscuits, applesauce, and spice cake are spooned onto tin plates and coffee or lemonade are poured into tin cups. (Parents of toddlers may want to think twice about coming, as there is no one to help you carry your youngsters' plates; balancing your cup and plate, as well as theirs, can be a tricky proposition at best.) After dinner, a Western-style band takes over, with tunes and easy humor, that will round the evening out at about 9:30 P.M.

This can be a late evening for young ones, and the harmonious Western songs often act like lullabies. We saw many children nodding off during the latter half of the show—and some parents with young children left early. But for those who are in Colorado Springs and desire a Western experience, the Flying W provides a full evening with plenty of Old West flair.

● Garden of the Gods

Interstate 25 south from Denver to exit 146, Garden of the Gods road, follow the well-marked signs. (719) 634-6666. Park: summer, daily, 5 A.M. to 11 P.M.; winter, daily, 5 A.M. to 9 P.M. Visitor center: summer, daily, 8 A.M. to 9 P.M.; winter, 8:30 A.M. to 5:30 P.M. Free. **Ages 4 and up.**

One of the most famous sites in Colorado, Garden of the Gods is a 1,350-acre park with wondrous rock formations jutting and rising in every direction. The most well-known of these is Balanced Rock, where one rock rests on top of another, ready to topple.

Start at the visitor center to get oriented. Inside and directly outside the center are displays and a few hands-on exhibits to get the kids interested in what they might be seeing. There's a multimedia theater presentation, with a 12-minute movie on how the red rocks got there ($2 adults, $1 children ages 4 to 12, free under age 4). Magpies are common in the area, for instance, and the center displays one of their nests and identifying factors. The center also has a café, two gift shops, and rest rooms.

Balanced Rock and other sites may be tricky to find on your own; pick up a map at the visitor's center. Although you can drive through the park, we suggest walking to really appreciate the majesty of the site. Or, in the summer, there's a 30-minute round trip narrated bus tour from the visitor's center (adults, $3.75, children ages 4 to 12, $2.50, under age 4, free).

If you have small kids and you want to take just a short hike, walk from Garden of the Gods down to Rock Ledge Ranch (see entry) and explore the premises. The path is well-marked. Although the Rock Ledge Ranch doesn't operate in the winter, younger kids will probably enjoy walking along the duck pond at the ranch and looking for horses more than they'll be interested in the rock formations. In the summer, Rock Ledge Ranch (see entry) should be included as part of your trip to Garden of the Gods. Both activities will take the better part of a day and make a nice day trip from Denver.

● Ghost Town

400 South 21st Street. (719) 634-0696. June to August: Monday to Saturday, 9 A.M. to 6 P.M.; Sunday, noon to 6 P.M. September to May:

Monday to Saturday, 10 A.M. to 5 P.M., Sunday, noon to 5 P.M. (Closed some days around Christmas and New Year's.) Adults, $4.50; ages 6 to 16, $2; under age 6, free. **Ages 5 and up.**

Although it's called "Ghost Town," this is no ramshackle, tumble-weed-strewn site. It's an indoor, re-created ghost town, complete with player piano and stagecoach, offering a decent rainy day diversion. There's a general store, blacksmith shop, jail, newspaper office, saloon, barber shop, drug store, post office, and more. Children can walk into some of the shops and offices for a closer look at everything from old-fashioned typewriters to antique pinball, and view other rooms from a walkway. While this attraction is blatantly commercial—many of the features require a dime here, a quarter there—it's a lively, and educational re-creation of life in the horse and buggy days.

● Josh & John's Naturally Homemade Ice Creams
101 North Tejon, in downtown Colorado Springs. (719) 632-0299. Monday to Thursday, 11 A.M. to 11 P.M.; Friday and Saturday, 11 A.M. to midnight, Sunday, noon to 11 P.M. **All ages.**

See Denver entry for information.

● May Natural History Museum of the Tropics
Nine miles southwest of Colorado Springs on State Highway 115 or five miles southwest of Academy Boulevard and Highway 115 junction. (719) 576-0450. May 1 to September 30: hours vary seasonally, generally 9 A.M. to 5 P.M. July 1 to September 1: about 8 A.M. to 8 P.M. Ages 13 to 60, $4.50; ages 6 to 12, $2.50; seniors ages 60 and up, $3.50; under age 6, free. **Ages 4 and up.**

The giant beetle at the entrance to the May Museum is a tip-off. This truly unique museum houses mounted insects, a collection of 7,000 to 8,000 gathered in one room. Our kids were fascinated by the array of spiders, butterflies, scorpions, and beetles. We were fascinated by the silver butterfly; the kids loved the hairy tarantulas. The collection was started by James F. W. May and continued by his son, John. James May's granddaughters still handle the cash register and the questions.

● Memorial Park
Interstate 25 south to Bijou exit; turn right on Nevada, left on Pikes Peak one mile. Colorado Springs Park and Recreation Department: (719) 578-6640. Velodrome: (719) 634-8356. Aquatics and Fitness Center: (719) 578-6634. May to early November: daily, 5 A.M. to 11 P.M. Early November to end of April: daily, 5 A.M. to 9 P.M. Free. **All ages.**

The Memorial Park complex, near the U.S. Olympic Training Center (see entry), has an aquatic and fitness center with public hours, a playground for the younger set, picnic areas, tennis courts, an in-line skating trail, boat rental, swimming, and plenty of room to roam.

Our kids watched, fascinated, as a fisherman pulled out fish after fish from Prospect Lake in Memorial Park on a brisk day in early spring.

The park is unusual for its 7-11 Velodrome, an area for Olympic-caliber cycling and rollerskating athletes to practice. Currently, cycling races are held on Wednesday (7 to 10 P.M.) and Friday (7:30 to 11 P.M.) in the summer, and the public can watch from the grandstand. (Cycling race days and hours are subject to change, so you may want to call first.) The public can also watch the athletes practice during the day.

● Michael Garman's Magic Town and Gallery

2418 West Colorado Avenue, Old Colorado City. (719) 471-9391 or (800) 731-3908. Magic Town: daily, 10 A.M. to 5 P.M. Gallery: daily, 10 A.M. to 5:30 P.M. (Hours are subject to change and are extended into the evenings in summer; call first.) Magic Town: adults, $2; ages 7 to 12, $1; under age 6, free. **Ages 3 and up.**

Old Colorado City, a renovated stretch of shops and galleries in Colorado Springs, is the site of Magic Town by world-renowned sculptor Michael Garman. Garman, a Colorado Springs–based artist, has brought to life his sculptures in one darkened room in his gallery. Here, you'll find talking holograms and magically changing scenes in his doll-house-sized cityscape. Peer in a window and a woman is posing for an artist; look again, and the model has disappeared. Look in another window and a painter is painting; look again and a child is taking a piano lesson.

Although it is only one room in the small gallery, and pricey, children and adults will find Magic Town fascinating, and you can spend a good 20 minutes just looking through the changing windows.

Coupled with a few other stops in the Colorado Springs area, this would make a pleasant day trip from Denver.

● Monument Valley Park

Interstate 25 south to Uinta; follow Uinta east to Glen Road, make a right, then follow Glen Road into the park. Park is also flanked by Madison Avenue, Fontanero Street, and Columbia Street. Colorado Springs Park and Recreation Department: (719) 578-6640. Summer: May 1 to November 1, daily, 5 A.M. to 11 P.M.; 5 A.M. to 9 P.M. Free. **All ages.**

Near the American Numismatic Association Museum (see entry) and other downtown Colorado Springs spots, Monument Valley Park is known for its unusual shape—long and narrow—and its formal gardens. The park also has a duck pond, tennis courts, public pool, picnic grounds, walking trails, and a playground for the elementary and preschool set.

Because of its convenient locale, this is a good park for kids to blow off steam after a couple hours of sightseeing in the Colorado Springs area.

● North Pole/Santa's Workshop

Exit 141 off Interstate 25, then ten miles west on Highway 24. (719) 684-9432. Mid-May to May 31: Friday to Wednesday, 9:30 A.M. to 6 P.M. June 1 to Labor Day: daily, 9:30 A.M. to 6 P.M. Day after Labor Day to December 24: Friday to Tuesday, 10 A.M. to 5 P.M. Admission, including unlimited rides and other attractions, ages 2 to 59, $9.50; under age 2, free.
Ages 2 and up.

It's Christmas year-round at this outdoor amusement park, where the rides are dressed in holiday style (the candy cane slide, for example) and Santa is always happy to take a child on his lap and smile for a keepsake photo. It may seem odd, entering Christmas-land when the holiday is months away, but this is a fun place to spend the day at anytime of the year.

The rides are the main draw here, and there are plenty, from the automated cars that are sure-pleasers for the younger ones to an old-fashioned carousel and our personal favorite, "the world's highest ferris wheel" (if you've ever been stopped at the top of this monster, you won't doubt the claim!).

In between rides, you can shop in gift stores decorated for the yuletide season, catch one of the magic shows offered periodically throughout the day, or enjoy ice cream or hot chocolate—whatever the weather suggests—in the Ice Cream Parlor and Cafe.

Plan to spend a good part of a day. (Since the rides are unlimited, there's no need to rush.) Keep in mind, however, that the park is at a high elevation. Even in summer, it can be chilly here. Bring plenty of wraps for the kids—and when the weather is bad, call first. On particularly stormy days, the park closes down.

● Pikes Peak Highway

Ten miles west of Colorado Springs and a few miles up Ute Pass off U.S. 24. Follow signs from U.S. 24. (719) 684-9383. March to Memorial Day weekend: daily, 9 A.M. to 3 P.M. Saturday of Memorial Day weekend and through the summer: daily, 7 A.M. to 7 P.M. Tuesday after Labor Day weekend to January: daily, 9 A.M. to 3 P.M. January and February: Wednesday to Sunday, 9 A.M. to 3 P.M. All hours are weather permitting. Adults,

$6; ages 6 to 11, $3; ages 5 and under, free. Fishing pass: adults, $2; ages 15 and under, free. **Ages 5 and up.**

OK. So Katherine Lee Bates was so inspired by the view at the top of Pikes Peak that she wrote "America the Beautiful" in 1893. Does that mean the rest of us should schelpp up this hair-raising toll road, navigating 19 twisting miles (someone once counted 156 turns here) so steep in places you'll swear even mountain goats would turn back? Well. Let's put it this way: we're glad we did it—and we're also glad we don't have to do it again anytime soon!

On the plus side, the trip up this road, which is paved the first seven miles and becomes a groomed dirt road beyond that, offers some truly spectacular sights. You'll eventually be so high after climbing beyond timberline that even the clouds look small far below. On the minus side, once you get to the top, 6,710 feet higher than when you started, your only reward is an observation deck with viewing scopes and a view that isn't much better than the ones you had on the way up. In addition, your children won't want to get right back in the car to head down, which will leave you with time to kill and only a gift shop and snack bar in sight. (Pikes Peak T-shirts and $3.50 cheeseburgers anyone?)

Oh well, you'll likely only do this once. So buy a few souvenirs, relax, and comfort yourself with the knowledge that you've given your children valuable appreciation for their environment (not to mention a healthy fear of heights!). The trip takes 45 minutes to an hour each way. Bring coats: the weather at the top is always far different than down below and can be windy and cold, even in summer.

For those interested in fishing, Crystal Creek (at mile six), South Catamount, and North Catamount reservoirs are open and provide a scenic stopping point, even for those who are only there for the ride.

● ProRodeo Hall of Fame and Museum of the American Cowboy

101 Pro Rodeo Drive (exit 147 from I-25). (719) 528-4764. Daily, 9 A.M. to 5 P.M., except Thanksgiving, Christmas Day, Easter, December 31, and January 1. Adults, $6; ages 5 to 12, $3; under age 5, free. **Ages 9 and up.**

This is the West, so it's not surprising to find a museum dedicated to the folks who made cowboys a legend and the rodeo a competitive game. This is an impressive facility by anybody's standards, with two theaters showing short films about the rodeo, well-lit displays, and even a courtyard in back where live animals, including a retired champion bronco, are housed and kids can practice their lassoing on a small, iron bull head.

Museum officials encourage visitors to bring only older children, because they like you to go through the museum in an orderly fashion. The films, one on the history of rodeo and one on modern rodeo, are too long (more than 20 minutes combined) for younger kids, unless they have a keen interest in rodeo. There are displays of famous cowboys, including saddles, boots, and brief histories of cowboy hats through the ages, equipment, clothing, and sculptures. Even if your kids are not terribly familiar with rodeo, they will probably find enough of interest to warrant a stop on your way to the other attractions in Colorado Springs. The museum is very close to the U.S. Air Force Academy and the Western Museum of Mining & Industry (see entries).

Despite cautions to the contrary, the younger child we had in tow during our visit did find something of interest: a real live bull. Separated by only a fence, our 5-year-old decided that "it must be a girl" because of its curly hair. He wasn't all that interested in the museum, while he did ask to see the bull again the next day.

● Rock Ledge Ranch Historic Site

Gateway Road, just before the entrance to the Garden of the Gods. (719) 578-6777. Mid-June to Labor Day: Wednesday to Sunday, 10 A.M. to 5 P.M. September to December 24: Saturday, 10 A.M. to 4 P.M., and Sunday, noon to 4 P.M. Closed Christmas Day to mid-June. Adults, $3; ages 6 to 12, $1; under age 6, free; seniors ages 56 and up, $2. **Ages 4 and up.**

In the summer, the Rock Ledge Ranch, formerly the White House Ranch, a living history park, is alive with activity. Costumed interpreters, who will answer questions only about their historic period, reenact what it was like in the late-1860s homestead period, on an 1895 working ranch, and at a 1907 estate house. Visitors can wander the grounds at their own pace. Our kids were mesmerized by the working blacksmith shop and by the animals. They were least interested in the guided tour of the estate house, so take note if you're pressed for time.

In the winter, the grounds are open for exploring, although the ranch is quiet and the guides are gone. Follow the trail from Garden of the Gods (see entry) to the ranch. The two places, within shouting distance of each other, are a pleasant way to spend a day in the area.

● Seven Falls

From Interstate 25, take exit 140B. Turn south on Tejon Street, then west on Cheyenne Boulevard. Follow the signs to the park. (719) 632-0765. Daily: winter, 9 A.M. to 4 P.M.; summer, 8 A.M. to 11 P.M. (Hours vary during *transitional months of May and September, call first.) Adults, $6 before 5 P.M., $6.50 after 5 P.M.; ages 6 to 15, $3.50; under age 6, free.* **Ages 5 and up.**

A highly commercialized attraction in the Springs, Seven Falls features seven separate waterfalls that, together, drop 250 feet into a box canyon. Visitors can take an elevator to an observation deck for a good view of the falls, or walk up 185 steps to the same observation deck. In addition, another long staircase (265 steps) leads to a mile-long nature trail overlooking the city.

While adults will enjoy the scenery, don't count on the falls to enthrall your children for more than a few minutes. The kids are more likely to have fun tackling the challenge of the stairs and feeding the chipmunks that flock to the observation deck or the fish in the pond at the bottom of the falls. They will also enjoy spotting the rock formations that are marked on the way in and out of the park: look for a Mexican saddle, an alligator's head, a mouse's head, and more.

A souvenir shop contains a snack bar for moderately priced treats, and in the summer, the falls are lit at night, beginning around 8 P.M.

● Starr Kempf Sculptures

Evans and Pine Grove avenues. Follow the directions to Seven Falls (see entry above), and at the base of Seven Falls, turn left on Evans, following the sign to the Cheyenne Mountain Zoo. Free. **Ages 3 and up.**

This is one of those slam-on-the-brakes attractions that most people stumble across on their way to Seven Falls or to the back side of the Cheyenne Mountain Zoo.

The futuristic metal sculptures of prehistoric birds, rockets, and windmills dot the front yard of sculptor Starr Kempf's home like some kind of out-of-season Christmas display. There are eight metal sculptures, all painted silver and taller than the nearest trees, with parts that turn lazily in the wind. This is worth a stop because you will truly say, "I've never seen anything like it." Don't rear-end the driver in front of you, who just hit the brakes to stop and look.

● United States Air Force Academy

Interstate 25, on the outskirts of Colorado Springs; well-marked signs will direct you to the visitor's entrances, coming either from Denver or the Colorado Springs area. (719) 333-8723 (recording) or (719) 333-2025 (visitor center). Visitor center: Memorial Day to Labor Day, daily, 9 A.M. to 6 P.M.; Labor Day to Memorial Day, daily, 9 A.M. to 5 P.M. Academy grounds:

6 A.M. to sundown, year-round. Cadet Chapel: Memorial Day to Labor Day, Monday to Saturday, 9 A.M. to 6 P.M.; Sunday, 1 to 6 P.M.; Labor Day to Memorial Day, Monday to Saturday, 9 A.M. to 5 P.M.; Sunday, 1 to 5 P.M. Free. **Ages 6 and up.**

The Air Force Academy, training ground for future officers in the Air Force, is one of the top attractions in Colorado. We still get a thrill when the cadet salutes us at the guardhouse and when we spot the B-52 bomber that stands like a sentry nearby. The road to the visitor center winds through the grounds, and deer can sometimes be spotted along the road (be careful to drive accordingly). Stop at the visitor center (six miles, follow the signs) for a self-guiding tour map. The visitor center also has a display on the Air Force Academy, a snack bar, and rest rooms.

If you time your visit right, you can watch the cadets march en masse to the dining hall (11:35 A.M., Monday to Friday, August to May), an impressive sight. On some days, you can also watch from the Thunderbird Overlook (near the south entrance gate) as the cadets practice parachuting from planes.

And don't miss the Cadet Chapel with its 18 majestic spires, probably the most-visited spot at the academy. The public can attend Protestant and Catholic services there at 9 A.M. and 11 A.M. Sunday, or Jewish services at 8 P.M. Friday. Note that the chapel can be closed for special events from time to time.

During the summer, the academy has planetarium shows (ask for times at the visitor center or call the recording. (Generally, shows in the summer months are scheduled for Tuesday through Friday at 1, 2, and 3 P.M.) On the third Friday of every month, there's an hour-long evening show at 6:30 P.M. in the summer and 7:30 P.M. in the winter. The show is followed by an open house at the observatory where kids can view the night sky. There are also walking trails, but keep in mind that the altitude at the academy is more than 7,000 feet. If you're not used to it, you will tire quickly.

You can easily spend a couple hours or more touring the facility. This is a nice day trip from Denver, coupled with one other Colorado Springs activity. The academy is close to the ProRodeo Hall of Fame, White House Ranch, Garden of the Gods (see separate entries), and many other Colorado Springs attractions.

● U.S. Olympic Training Center

1750 Boulder Street. (719) 578-4618. Guided tours every half hour and every hour on the hour: Memorial Day weekend to Labor Day, Monday to

Saturday, 9 A.M. to 5 P.M.; Sunday, 10 A.M. to 5 P.M. Rest of year: guided tours every hour on the hour, Monday to Saturday, 9 A.M. to 4 P.M.; Sunday, noon to 4 P.M. Free. **Ages 8 and up.**

Countdown Japan. Countdown Australia. The giant clock at the U.S. Olympic Training Center is ticking away ever closer to the next Olympic games. This may be as close as some of us will ever get—and it's almost as thrilling. Athletes train year-round on this 37-acre site, practicing their skills in a number of arenas. The guided, one-hour walking tour takes you through the complex, where you'll view sports centers one and two, aquatics center, and the shooting arena. (The athletes train in another state for winter sports.) While we were there, gymnasts were honing their skills on the parallel bars.

The equipment is look, don't touch, and if the younger kids get restless, there are several points where it's easy to leave the tour.

The complex is close to Memorial Park (see entry) and other Springs attractions and is a special place to take elementary school kids and older—and a don't-miss tour for budding young athletes.

● Van Briggle Art Pottery Tour

600 South 21st Street. (719) 633-7729. Monday to Saturday, 8:30 A.M. to 4:30 P.M. (last tour at 4:15 P.M.). Free. **Ages 5 and up.**

This is one of the oldest active art potteries in the country—with one of the most famous names. Van Briggle pottery is synonymous with graceful lines and pure, colorful glazes, including its famous unique turquoise color. Here, you are invited to watch the pottery in progress. You'll see artists throwing clay on a potter's wheel and hundreds of molds drying before being readied for glaze.

The tour is short (ours was no more than 10 minutes), so children will have no time to be bored. But be aware that the tour ends up in the showroom—where hundreds of breakable pieces beckon tiny fingers. You'll want to usher small children out in a hurry. Also, we recommend this only if you're in the area. The tour is too short to be worth a special trip.

● Western Museum of Mining & Industry

1025 North Gate Road (take Interstate 25 to Exit 156A; go east on Gleneagle Drive). (719) 488-0880. Monday to Saturday, 9 A.M. to 4 P.M.; Sunday, noon to 4 P.M. December to February: call for winter hours. Guided tours at 10 A.M., 12:30 P.M., and 2:30 P.M. (except December to February, when tours are offered at 10 A.M. only). Adults, $5; ages 5 to 12, $2; students ages 13 and up and seniors ages 60 and up, $4; under age 5, free with paid adult. **Ages 4 and up.**

Nothing could sound more dry than a bunch of exhibits about mining—unless you've been to these exhibits, where hands-on is not just a catch-word but a credo. Children will see a steam engine in operation, pan for gold in a small trough, hold a steel rod while the tour guide demonstrates how holes were hammered into rock for dynamiting, and more. Wheels churn, displays move, old mining lamps are lit, all to children's delight.

Although you can tour the museum on your own, guided tours are offered that are well worth your time. Tours take about 1½ hours, but can last longer, depending on the interest of the group and the amount of questions it has for the guide. Tours are geared for the predominant age group and include an engaging 18-minute video featuring historic pictures of miners and mining towns.

Come early and plan to spend some time. Picnic tables on the 27-acre site offer a great place for a lunch break. You might couple a trip here with one to the nearby U.S. Air Force Academy (see entry).

● The World Figure Skating Museum and Hall of Fame
20 First Street (one block north of the Broadmoor Hotel off Lake Street). (719) 635-5200. Weekdays, 10 A.M. to 4 P.M. Also open Saturday, 10 A.M. to 4 P.M., June to August and first Saturday of the month, September to May, 10 A.M. to 4 P.M. Adults, $3; ages 6 to 12 and seniors ages 66 and up, $2; under age 6, free. **Ages 6 and up.**

Not surprisingly, this has been a popular place since the 1994 Winter Olympics. You'll find all the skating greats represented here through costumes, medals, and other paraphernalia.

There's a special tribute to hometown hero Scott Hamilton, with his gold medal shimmering behind glass. You can't come that close to the gold without feeling some of the thrill of the Olympics. Our kids also enjoyed the retrospective on skater/movie star Sonja Henie; the display includes two Sonja Henie dolls from the Madame Alexander collection. Don't miss the nearby portrait of Dorothy Hamill by Andy Warhol.

The costumes, which include outfits worn by such popular skaters as Debi Thomas and Peggy Fleming, are displayed on mannequins, instead of behind glass. Although the exhibits have a "do not touch" sign, the kids can get close enough to count the sequins and ooh and ahh.

MANITOU SPRINGS

● Iron Springs Chateau Melodrama Dinner Theater
444 Ruxton Avenue. (719) 685-5572 or 685-5104. Summer: Monday to Saturday. Winter: Friday and Saturday. Dinner reservations, every fifteen

minutes between 6 and 7 P.M. Theater seating, 8 P.M.; show starts at 8:30 P.M. Dinner and show: adults, $20; children, ages 4 to 10, $11; under age 4, free. Show only, Monday to Friday: adults, $10.50; children ages 4 to 10, $6.50; under age 4, free. Show only, Saturday night: all seats, $10.50. **Ages 6 and up.**

The entertainment at the Iron Springs Chateau begins with an all-you-can-eat dinner of chicken and ribs, served family style in two rustic dining rooms. Then it's upstairs to the theater for the sing-along, melo-drama, and olio, a bawdy set of skits and tunes served up vaudeville style. Our kids enjoyed booing the villain, cheering the heroine, and singing along to "Bye Bye Blackbird" and "Won't You Come Home Bill Bailey." We were concerned about the olio; as it turned out, our young children didn't really understand the bawdy parts, but they loved the vaudeville numbers. If you're concerned about exposing your kids to the olio, you can leave after the melodrama and sing-along and you'll still have gotten your money's worth.

Because of the lag time between the first seating at 6 P.M. and the actual show, around 8:30 P.M., it's wise to come as late as possible for dinner. Our kids were very restless in between with little to do.

Kids under five won't understand the plot of the melodrama or the olio, and with the show at two hours, it could be a very long evening for them.

● Manitou Cliff Dwellings Museum

West of Colorado Springs on Highway 24. (719) 685-5242 or (719) 685-5394. Daily, June to August, 9 A.M. to 8 P.M.; rest of year, 9 A.M. to 5 P.M. Adults, $6; seniors ages 60 and up, $5; ages 7 to 11, $4; ages 6 and under, free. **Ages 4 and up.**

The cliff dwellings that are the centerpiece of this outdoor museum were constructed in 1907 from the original stones of Indian dwellings and modeled after actual cliff dwellings that date to A.D. 1100. They look authentic, but offer one advantage over the real thing: while at most ruins sites visitors are implored not to climb on the dwellings, here guests are encouraged to explore.

Children will enjoy climbing the ladder to a tiny balcony on one of the dwellings, creeping through narrow passageways, and going in and out of doors cut in stone. In the summer, Indian dancers entertain visitors with periodic performances. And year-round, a small indoor museum features Southwestern Indian artifacts, including an interesting video on pottery making. Keep in mind that you'll likely spend most of your time at the cliff dwellings, so bring coats on cool days and don't forget the sunscreen.

One caveat: There's nothing like Mesa Verde for a true look at our Indian heritage (see entry under Durango, Southwest), and this can in no way compare. But if you can't make the long trip south, it's worth a stop at this museum.

● Miramont Castle

9 Capitol Hill Avenue. (719) 685-1011. Daily: Memorial Day to Labor Day, 10 A.M. to 5 P.M.; Labor Day to early January, 11 A.M. to 4 P.M.; early January to March or April (depending on the weather), noon to 3 P.M.; rest of year until Memorial Day, 11 A.M. to 4 P.M. Adults, ages 12 and over, $3; ages 6 to 11, $1; ages 5 and under, free; seniors ages 60 and older, $2.50. **Ages 6 and up.**

This rambling castle built by a Catholic priest combines nine styles of architecture and is famous for its nonsquare rooms, including the eight-sided chapel and six-sided conservatory.

Most of the castle is furnished in period pieces; the pamphlet provided at the start of the self-guided tour points out the highlights. Our kids were fascinated by a small glassed-off closet under the stairs that contains the original wallpaper made with a poison compound. As an added highlight, you start the tour in the International Museum of Miniatures—a collection of miniature dollhouses on the bottom floor of the castle; in the summer, you end the tour at the Golden Circle Model Railroad Museum in an adjacent building (the railroad museum is open Memorial Day to Labor Day and during Christmas holidays). The three weekends after Thanksgiving are devoted to a Victorian Christmas, with Victorian decorations, live entertainment, free cider and cookies, a bake sale and crafts table. A tea room, with an old-fashioned soda fountain, is open in the summer from 11 A.M. to 4 P.M.

Because it's self-guided, you can wander through at a pace suitable to your kids. Although this is a no-touch museum, kids will find plenty to see and explore.

● Pike's Peak Cog Railway

515 Ruxton Avenue. (719) 685-5401. May to October: daily, weather permitting, hours vary; call for schedule. Advance reservations are strongly suggested. Adults, $22.50; ages 5 to 11, $10.50; under age 5, free if held on lap. **Ages 6 and up.**

If you want to see the inspiration for "America the Beautiful," you have two choices: drive the Pike's Peak Highway (see entry in Colorado Springs) or take the train and leave the driving to someone else.

Billed as the world's highest cog railway, the train will take you through some of the most magnificent scenery Colorado has to offer. The spectacular view from the top—14,110 feet—will leave no doubt about the purple mountains' majesty.

However, as with most train rides, particularly one with scenery as the only draw, the novelty quickly wears off for kids. The trip takes three hours and 10 minutes round trip, including a 30- to 40-minute stop at the top to admire the view and hit the concession and gift shop before boarding your train again. Note that there are no rest room facilities on the train, although there are facilities both at the boarding station and at the peak.

If you'd like to make the trek, prepare as you would for a car trip. Food and drink are allowed on the train, so pack a picnic or lots of snacks and plenty to do. Because the train travels slowly, you might want to buy a disposable camera and let your little shutterbugs capture the memories along the way. (If you're lucky, you may see mountain goats.) Bring a jacket for the summit; it's likely to be cold and windy at such a high elevation. (The rule of thumb is the top is 30 to 40 degrees colder than the temperature at the station.)

Northwest

NOWHERE IS THE VARIETY of the state of Colorado more evident than in the northwest. You'll witness the majestic mountains as you ski Aspen and Vail and marvel at the canyonlands and near-desert of Dinosaur as you approach the Utah border. And just when you think you can't find scenery any prettier, you'll have to stop at Grand Lake and take a hike through Rocky Mountain National Park.

As you travel through this part of the state, be prepared for the weather. Swift changes from sun to snow to rain are possible, particularly in the mountains, where seasons are whimsical and a summer attraction can often be closed by snow. Also, take note that mountain ski towns virtually shut down between the end of ski season and mid-June and between Labor Day to the start of the new season. Two words of advice: call ahead.

ASPEN

● Ashcroft Ghost Town

Ten miles south of Aspen. Exit Highway 82 to Castle Creek Road. Look for parking lot on the left. (970) 925-3721 (Aspen Historical Society). Suggested admission: adults, $2; children under age 12, students, and seniors, $1. Guided tours available June, July, and August, Tuesday to Sunday, at 11 A.M. and 1 P.M. **Ages 5 and up.**

There's nothing like the sight of a smattering of log cabins and the sound of the wind whistling through trees to make you shiver a bit thinking of the way people lived a century ago. In this valley, you'll see boarded-up log cabins, most lining a main street that is now just a dirt trail leading, eventually, to a river and beyond. In its heyday in 1883, this silver mining town boasted 2,500 residents, two newspapers, a school, two sawmills, and 20 saloons—and was bigger than nearby Aspen.

This is a beautiful setting for a picnic; follow signs to the tables. In addition, guided tours at the times mentioned offer a bit of history, as well as information on the plant life of the area. Tours last from 30 to 45 minutes and are geared for ages 8 and up.

Plan to spend some time here exploring or just stop a moment to contemplate life in another era.

● Aspen Center for Environmental Studies (ACES)

100 Puppy Smith Street. (970) 925-5756. Monday to Saturday, 9 A.M. to 5 P.M. Adults, $2; ages 12 and under, 50 cents; members, free. **Ages 2 and up.**

If you aren't thinking about nature during a trip to Aspen, then you are missing the point. Take a few minutes to learn about the surroundings with a stop at ACES, located at Hallam Lake Wildlife Sanctuary. Inside the ACES building, children are invited to bird-watch, using the binoculars that line a large picture window. They can also handle items on the "touch table," including feathers, a beaver jaw, and a deer skull. In a back room, there are microscopes set up; a peek through the lenses reveals magnified insects and other surprises.

When you're ready to head outside, take the self-guided tour pamphlet, which will lead you, step by step, on a 30- to 45-minute hike past a golden eagle, great horned owls, beavers, and a host of interesting vegetation. Kids can also pick up a "Scavenger Hunt" sheet to bring along, which allows them to check off items that they see along the way ("a feather," "something prickly").

ACES also offers fun additional programs throughout the year, including snowshoe hikes, guided walks on top of Aspen Mountain, and seminars that zero in on a topic, such as hawks or bugs. The programs are geared for various age groups, and they can fill up fast during peak seasons, so call early and inquire about reservations.

● Aspen Ice Garden

233 West Hyman Avenue. (970) 920-5141. Daily, generally afternoon and some evening sessions; hours vary seasonally. Closed mid-April through early June. Adults, ages 18 and older, $4; ages 5 to 17, $3; ages 4 and under, $2. Skate rental, $2. **Ages 5 and up.**

You don't have to wait for winter at this almost year-round skating facility. Aspen Ice Garden, under the auspices of the Aspen Recreation Department, offers daily public sessions at its indoor rink. If your kids love to skate or the weather turns nasty, this is a good place to keep in mind to while away the nothing-to-do blues.

● Aspen Mountain Silver Queen Gondola ◆

At the base of Aspen Mountain. (970) 925-1220. Open part-time from late May to mid-June and September to early October (call for days and hours). Daily: first week in June to Labor Day, 10 A.M. to 4 P.M. (last ride down is 4:30 P.M.); also open Tuesday evenings until 7:30 P.M. (last ride down at 8 P.M.) On Tuesday evenings, there's a barbecue dinner at the top in the Sundeck restaurant, 5:30 to 7:30 P.M. One price includes dinner and gondola ride: adults, $25; ages 13 to 19, $22; ages 7 to 12, $11; ages 6 and under, $6. Free guided nature walks from the summit, mid-June to Labor Day, 11 A.M. to 3 P.M., every hour on the hour. Gondola ride: Adults, $18; ages 13 to 19, $12; ages 7 to 12, $6; ages 6 and under and 70 and older, free. Gondola/Maroon Bells Bus Tour package available (see Maroon Bells entry), $19 (buy ticket at Ruby Park Transit Center, Durant Avenue and Mill Street, or at the ticket office in the Gondola building). **Ages 3 and up.**

The Aspen Mountain Gondola can carry as many as six people for a smooth, scenic ride to the summit of Aspen Mountain, 11,212 feet, in 18 minutes.

When you get to the top, you'll find the naturalists from the Aspen Center for Environmental Studies waiting to guide you on a 45-minute loop along marked trails. (The hike is easy; however, don't discount the altitude.) The naturalist will explain the trees, plants, and wildlife, and point out remnants of a cabin with its pit of rusted cans left by miners a hundred years ago. The guide talks to children and engages them by having them count the levels of an alpine spruce, look for porcupine marks on the base of trees, and find gopher tunnels. The guide also has water and sunscreen available for everyone.

There are rest rooms and the Sundeck restaurant, cafeteria-style, open 11 A.M. to 3:30 P.M., at the summit. The scenery is beautiful and having a guide makes it an even more meaningful experience, especially for kids. If you can't time your visit with the guide, as with the Maroon Bells, the gondola ride and the beauty of the mountain are worth experiencing anyway.

● Aspen Music Festival

Located where West Fifth Street dead-ends into the parking lot of Aspen Meadows. (970) 925-3254. Late June to late August. Price varies; some concerts and all rehearsals, free. **All ages.**

The hills are alive with the sound of music every June, July, and August in Aspen. Under the tent—or in the nearby subterranean concert hall or Wheeler Opera House—operas, orchestral concerts, recitals, and chamber programs are presented daily by dozens of world-famous artists.

Many of the concerts are free, others are not, but you're allowed to bring a picnic and sit out on the lawn outside the tent and enjoy any concert or rehearsal for free. Don't worry, you won't be alone; this annual rite of summer draws throngs of picnickers. And, yes, you can hear the music coming from the tent.

Pick up a concert schedule at the Visitor Information Center, next to the Wheeler Opera House, at East Hyman Avenue and Mill Street. Many concerts are geared just for children. Recent summer events included storytelling and music for kids under age 8 and concerts of improvisatory music for kids ages 10 to 16, and *A Child's Midsummer Night's Dream,* a one-hour opera, based on the original play.

 ● **Boogies Diner**

534 East Cooper Avenue. (970) 925-6610. Daily, 11 A.M. to 10 P.M.
All ages.

You won't find a lot of restaurants in Aspen that cater to children, but Boogies is ready for families, with crayons for the kids and plenty of fifties paraphernalia on the walls for their baby-boomer parents. This is a happening spot, just upstairs from the Boogies' boutique, with a menu that runs the gamut from $6 burgers to $130 bottles of champagne. And yes, this is Aspen, so the menu points out that the meats are lean, the mayonnaise is cholesterol-free, and the food that is fried is done so in canola oil. The portions are large. For kids, we recommend splitting an order (Boogies' wait staff will be happy to bring it on separate plates to avoid any arguments)—and beware of the boutique below. The prices are steeper than the mountainous sandwiches and piles of fries on your plate.

 ● **Hard Rock Cafe Aspen**

210 S. Galena, (970) 920-1666. Open 11:30 A.M. to 11 P.M. (may close earlier in May and November). **All ages.**

The Hard Rock Cafe Aspen likes to boast that it's the smallest, the coolest, and the highest (in altitude) of all the Hard Rock Cafes in the world. About one-third the size of its Aspen neighbor Planet Hollywood (see entry), it has the same mix of celebrity memorabilia and hip packaging. Some of the local celebs are represented on the walls here, with treasures from the Eagles, Willie Nelson, and John Denver, along with ski memorabilia from Olympic champions such as Franz Klammer. The kids menu, $2.99 to $4.99, is a welcome sight—hamburgers, hot dogs, grilled cheese, chicken fingers, mac and cheese, with all the trimmings included in the price. That may sound cheap, but as you probably know, you'll never make it out of the restaurant without dropping more than a few bucks at the T-shirt counter so that everyone will know where you've been.

● Hyman Avenue Mall Fountain

Located at Mill and Hyman streets on the Hyman Avenue Mall in central Aspen. **Ages 2 to 12.**

On a hot day, bring a few beach towels to this spot in the midst of Aspen's popular outdoor mall and let your kids do what, well, kids will do when a source of water is nearby: get absolutely soaking wet. This fountain shoots streams of water skyward in random fashion. Children enjoy attempting a run through the fountain, in the hopes they'll make it to the other side without getting wet. Fat chance. But who's complaining? This is a great summertime diversion—and better yet, it's free!

● Independence Ghost Town

Take Highway 82 east of Aspen for 13.5 miles; watch for a scenic overlook sign. (970) 925-3721 (Aspen Historical Society). Suggested admission: Adults, $2; children, students, and seniors, $1. Guided tours available in June, July, and August, Tuesday to Sunday, 11 A.M. and 1 P.M. **Ages 5 and up.**

Established in the early 1880s, this town was doomed when nearby Aspen was named county seat for Pitkin County in 1881. Miners who had come in search of gold were eventually lured to the more prosperous Aspen, where the pay was better, the climate warmer, and the work more plentiful. Today, a handful of log cabins remain in this valley below Independence Pass; they make for a quick, interesting reminder of life in a very different era. As you head over Independence Pass, stop for a few moments to see what's left of the general store, a boarding house, stables, and more.

Guided tours, which last approximately a half hour to 45 minutes, are available in the summer and are geared to ages 8 and up.

● Maroon Bells Nature Tour at Maroon Lake ◆

Maroon Lake. (970) 925-5756 (for tour information). Mid-June to Labor Day: daily, 10 A.M. to 2 P.M.; tours on the hour. Free. Maroon Bells is closed to car traffic during most of the day and tourists must ride special buses (see below), except in early spring and late fall. Buses run every 20 minutes from Ruby Park Transit Center, located at Durant Avenue and Mill Street in Aspen, from 9 A.M. to 4:30 P.M. (970) 925-8484. Bus cost: adults, $5; ages 6 to 16 and seniors 65 and up, $3; ages 5 and under, free. Dogs on leash are allowed on the bus. Four bike racks on bus—first come, first served. Maroon Bells closes in winter, usually around mid-October (to check on road conditions and closures, call 970-925-3445). **Ages 3 and up.**

The peaks and valleys of Maroon Bells were once considered sacred by the Ute Indians. It is one of the most beautiful spots in Colorado—and one of the most popular. Because of the fragile ecosystem, cars are prohibited throughout much of the day.

When you get off the bus—a narrated ride, by the way—a naturalist is waiting with a telescope on a tripod to introduce visitors to the wildlife of Maroon Bells. Following that, the guide leads the group on a gentle 45-minute stroll along Maroon Lake, pointing out the wildflowers and the active beaver dam and explaining the history of the region.

Although it's pleasant to have someone explain the area, if you miss the naturalist, don't miss the experience. Trails are well-marked and you can easily navigate on your own. There are picnic tables, rest rooms, and water but no food concessions.

● Paradise Bakery

On the corner of South Galena Street and East Cooper Avenue. (970) 925-7585. Daily, 6:30 A.M. to midnight during peak seasons; 7 A.M. to 10 P.M. during off-seasons. **All ages.**

If you talk to Aspen regulars, they'll eventually talk about Paradise Bakery, waxing poetic about the gigantic, homemade muffins, the freshly baked cookies, the creamy, homemade ice cream. This is a good place to keep in mind for treats for the kids, or when you're packing a picnic to take to one of Aspen's many great getaway spots.

● Pitkin County Library

120 North Mill Street. (970) 925-4025. Monday to Thursday, 10 A.M. to 9 P.M.; Friday and Saturday, 10 A.M. to 6 P.M.; Sunday, noon to 6 P.M. Music room: Monday to Thursday, 10 A.M. to 9 P.M.; Friday, 10 A.M. to 6 P.M.; closed Saturday and Sunday, except during Aspen Music Festival, noon to 3 P.M. **Ages 2 and up.**

The Pitkin County Library has a Children's Library with its own entrance on Mill Street and a knowledgeable head children's librarian. The younger set can prowl among the books or listen to stories on tape on their own cassette players and headphones. The older set can head for the sophisticated Music Library down the hall.

The Music Library has 14,000 classical, jazz, pop, and folk recordings, as well as 5,300 tapes of the Aspen Music Festival (see entry).

● Planet Hollywood

312 South Galena Street. (970) 920-7817. Daily, 11 A.M. to 10 P.M. Hours extended in winter. Reservations accepted. Menu prices: $6.50 to $13.95. **All ages.**

Arnold Schwarzenegger, Bruce Willis, and Sylvester Stallone may own this popular eatery in Aspen, but there's nothing intimidating about it. Rather, the wait staff is pleasant, the prices are reasonable ($7.50 for a hamburger and fries), and the atmosphere is friendly.

For starters, there's a life-size model of Schwarzenegger as the Terminator revolving in the window. Once inside, you can roam among the three floors, looking at such diverse television and movie memorabilia as the "bomb" from the movie Batman, the Halloween costume from an episode of Roseanne, and a letter written by Bruce Lee. Then there's the wall of famous handprints where you can match your prints with those of the stars.

While you eat, movie and television screens drop down to show film clips—and not just those of the illustrious owners.

The menu features kid-pleasing items such as grilled cheese, pizza, pasta, and shakes. And yes, Arnold, "we'll be back."

● Silver Circle Skating

433 East Durant Avenue. (970) 925-6360. Late October to mid-April: daily, 10 A.M. to 10 P.M. 90-minute session, adults, $6; ages 16 and under, $4. Skate rental, $2.50. **Ages 3 and up.**

This privately owned outdoor ice rink, managed by Grand Aspen Hotel, operates during the winter season in the heart of Aspen. Although half the size of a standard rink—6,000 square feet—it's still big enough to spin, twirl, and glide to the music. Skate under the lights at night. A concession stand is on-site.

● Wagner Park Playground

At the west end of Hyman Avenue Mall in central Aspen. **Ages 2 to 10.**

After a few hours of shopping, the kids will be ready for a play break. Take them here and let them loose on the tire swings, slides, and jungle gym. You can keep an eye on the children, and since this is right off the mall, people-watch at the same time.

● Wheeler/Stallard House Museum

620 West Bleeker Street. (970) 925-3721. Mid-June to mid-September and January to Easter, Tuesday to Friday, 1 to 4 P.M. Adults, $3:50; ages 11 and under, 50 cents. **Ages 8 and up.**

Although Jerome Wheeler built this house in 1888, his wife refused to live here, and the family never moved in. In 1905, Edgar and Mary Ella Stallard moved in, living here for the next 40 years.

A self-guided tour takes you through rooms furnished mostly in period pieces. The children's room has an interesting collection of period toys, including an indoor croquet set, picture blocks, a doll with pierced ears and human hair, a hobby horse, and pictures of kids at play (circa 1900).

In addition, the museum recently added guided tours designed for elementary school age children. Museum docents offer insight into another era through the objects in the house. For example, our guide picked up a cup from an elegantly decorated dining table and explained to our children that it was a "mustache cup," designed so that a man's mustache wouldn't dip into the drink. This, of course, led to a short discussion about men's facial hair habits at that time. The tour will appeal to children who haven't previously visited a similar historic home, but seems to be loosely organized and dependent on staff availability any given day.

Whether you choose a guided tour or go it alone, be advised: this is very much a no-touch museum (signs are everywhere), and you would be wise to leave the little ones at home.

AVON

● Avon Recreation Center

Interstate 70 West to Avon, Beaver Creek exit, 0325 Benchmark Road (on the outskirts of Nottingham Park, at the east end of the lake). (970) 949-9191. Daily, all year round, except Christmas, New Year's Day, and Fourth of July: Monday to Friday, 6 A.M. to 9 P.M.; Saturday and Sunday, 8 A.M. to 9 P.M. Admission (includes use of pool): adults, $7.50; children, ages 3 to 17, $5; under age 3, free. Child care available for ages 6 months and up.
All ages.

When the weather outside is gloomy—and even when it's not—this new addition to Avon is the perfect way to spend a day or an evening. The recreation center is child friendly with plenty of swimming activities to take the chill off the gloomiest day. The aquatics center includes a lap pool; baby pool; diving pool with diving board; leisure pool with fountains, sprays, bubblers, and a kids' slide. In an adjacent pool, kids can slide down the 140-foot long water slide that empties them into the jet-propelled lazy river.

● Nottingham Park

Interstate 70 West to Avon, Beaver Creek exit. (970) 949-5648. Memorial Day to Labor Day: daily, 10 A.M. to 8 P.M. Paddleboats: two passengers, $4 per half hour; $6 per hour; four passengers, $6 per half hour, $8 per hour. Canoes: up to three people, $7.50 per hour; $15 for a half day. In-line skates rental and pads, $6 per hour. Croquet sets, footballs, basketballs, frisbees, soccer balls, $2 per hour. Mountain bikes (helmets included): adults, $6.50 per hour, $4.50 half hour; children, $6 per hour; $4 half hour. Kayak lessons (ages 13 and older), are offered through the Avon Recreation Center (see entry), (970) 949-9191. Ice skating starting around Christmas through first couple weeks of February (determined by ice conditions), daily, noon to 8 P.M., $4 per hour (includes skate rental). Call the Avon Recreation Center for exact opening. **All ages.**

This 48-acre park in the town of Avon, directly adjacent to Beaver Creek Resort, offers just about every outdoor activity you can think of. Nottingham Lake, within the park, is the center of activities from kayaking in the summer to ice skating in the winter.

The best news is that you can rent almost every piece of equipment you might want from the Log Cabin headquarters on the premises. Your kids can enjoy in-line skating, biking, croquet, and for the older kids, even kayaking. Concessions, open during both summer and winter, sell drinks, popcorn, candy, and the like.

BEAVER CREEK

● The Beaver Creek Children's Theatre and Sunday Family Showcase

Pedestrian Plaza and Covered Bridge, top of Main Village Road. (970) 426-7752. Informal performances, mid-June to early-September, Thursday, Friday, and Saturday, 11 A.M. to noon in the Pedestrian Plaza area; Sunday, 11 A.M. to noon at the Covered Bridge. Free. **Ages 2 to 12.**

A troupe of performers from the Beaver Creek Children's Theatre roam the plaza area every Thursday, Friday, and Saturday performing children's poems, fables, fairy tales, music, and magic.

On Sunday mornings, a variety of theatrical troupes from around Colorado entertain for an hour at the Covered Bridge in performances geared just for kids. Entertainers include regional theater companies, puppeteers, magicians, jugglers, and musical groups.

● Beaver Creek Wading Spot

To the left of the covered bridge at the entrance to Beaver Creek Ski Resort. Free. **Ages 2 and up.**

There's no official sign, no listing in the Beaver Creek brochures about this spot, just a few steps cut into the grass where gentle Beaver Creek rushes by. For a relaxing diversion, stop here for sunning and to let the children dip their toes into the cool creek. Young children love it, and you can't beat the price.

● Centennial Express Chairlift

At the base of Beaver Creek Ski Resort (behind the Hyatt Regency Beaver Creek). (970) 845-9090. Summer: Daily, 9:30 A.M. to 4:30 P.M. (last trip down: 5 P.M.). Winter: 8:30 A.M. to 4 P.M. Open weekends only, September. Closed late-September to start of ski season (around Thanksgiving) and mid-April to mid-June. Summer prices: free with voucher (available at any of the merchants in Beaver Creek and most hotels). Winter prices: Same for skiers and nonskiers; call for information.

The Centennial Express chairlift is a scenic, open-air ride to the top of the mountain. The chairs seat four and the ride takes about 11 minutes each way. Once at the top, you can walk around the replica of a ghost town (originally built for the pleasure of skiers); kids will like the mining shaft and fake tombstones. In the summer, there's a free Frisbee golf course. Bring your own Frisbee.

If you're interested in a bit of history with your scenery, stop at the Nature Center (9:30 A.M. to 4 P.M.) in the Spruce Saddle Lodge, also at the top. The Nature Center (970-845-5331) has interpretive displays and is the starting point for three free nature hikes, offered by the Forest Service rangers. On Tuesday, Wednesday, Thursday, Saturday, and Sunday, the 11 A.M. tour is an easy one-hour, one-mile loop, perfect for children. Also on the same days, the rangers offer a five-mile hike down the mountain, at 1 P.M. (ending around 4 P.M.), pointing out wildflowers, the history of the area, and wildlife. (This is not suggested for folks with knee or leg problems.)

On Mondays and Fridays, the rangers conduct a day trip, 10 A.M. to 4 P.M., a 6-mile round trip tour around Beaver Lake. Bring a picnic lunch and water. Note that the Beaver Lake hike is the most demanding because it's entirely uphill. Hike schedules are available at the Beaver Creek Resort concierge, in the middle of the Plaza, or at the Nature Center.

Around mid-June, the Spruce Saddle restaurant opens for summer trade. It offers lunch (11 A.M. to 3 P.M., featuring everything from hot dogs to barbecue beef) and has rest rooms and a place to rent mountain bikes for those who want to bike down, about a 45-minute ride, instead of taking the chairlift (970-845-5411; $11 first hour; $7 each additional hour). Although it's 4.8 miles to walk down the mountain, many people enjoy the scenic hike down.

BRECKENRIDGE

● Amaze 'N Breckenridge

Breckenridge Ski Area, at the base of Peak 8. (970) 453-7262. End of May: Friday, Saturday, Sunday, and Monday, 9 A.M. to 5 P.M.; Memorial Day

*weekend to first week in June: Friday, Saturday, and Sunday, 9 A.M. to 5
P.M.; Mid-June to September 1: daily, 9 A.M. to 5 P.M. First time, adults, $4;
ages 5 to 12, $3; ages 4 and under, free. Anytime thereafter, with first-time
pass, $2.* **Ages 4 and up.**

For a description of this human-size maze, see Amaze 'N Winter Park
entry under Winter Park.

● Breckenridge Recreation Center ◆

*880 Airport Road. (970) 453-1734. Monday to Friday, 6 A.M. to 10 P.M.;
Saturday, 7 A.M. to 10 P.M. and Sunday, 8 A.M. to 10 P.M. Admission:
Adults ages 18 to 59, $6.50; ages 13 to 17, $4; ages 3 to 12, $3.25;
seniors, ages 60 and up, $4; ages 3 and under, free.* **All ages.**

This outstanding facility includes the standard equipment of all recreation centers—tennis courts, swimming pools, basketball courts, weight
rooms, hot tubs—with some added features that make it a paradise for
kids of all ages.

Outside, the facility has a free skateboard park. Inside, it has two
rock-climbing walls, a water slide, and a rope swing that drops the swim-
mer into the pool.

To use the rock-climbing walls, you must take one class—repeated
several times a week—on the basics. The class is $10 and includes rental
of shoes, helmet, harness, and other equipment. Minimum orientation
time is 20 minutes. Once certified, you can practice climbing any time.
On Mondays through Saturdays, from 6 P.M. to 9 P.M., kids ages 6 to 12
may reserve belay rides, where an instructor harnesses them and oversees
their climbing. A 15-minute session is $5. (It's advisable to call ahead and
make a reservation.)

The water slide feeds into a separate pool, with a graduated depth up
to 3½ feet. It's open most of the day and into the evening. The rope swing
is part of the 25-yard, four-lane swimming pool and is open only an hour
during the day and an hour on some evenings. Public pool hours, water
slide, and rope swing times vary seasonally; call for current information.

If you're planning to be in the Breckenridge/Frisco/Dillon area for
even a short time, this is a great place to satisfy even the most ornery
young traveler.

● Breckenridge Super Slide

*Breckenridge Ski Resort. (970) 453-5000. End of May: Friday, Saturday,
Sunday, and Monday, 9 A.M. to 5 P.M. Memorial Day weekend to first week
in June: Friday, Saturday, and Sunday, 9 A.M. to 5 P.M. Mid-June to
September 1, daily, 9 A.M. to 5 P.M. One ride: adults, $8; ages 7 to 12, $7;
ages 2 to 6, free. Discounts for multiple rides.* **Ages 2 and up.**

Yes, this is a pricey outing, considering the whole event will be over in less than an hour. But a ride down this alpine slide is worth it for the adrenalin rush alone. Simply board the chairlift that takes you to the top of Peak 8. Then position yourself in a sled at the top of the track, point it downhill, and take off. You control your own speed with the center-mounted control lever. Sleds are big enough for an adult and child, and children ages 2 to 6 must ride with an adult. Children under 2 are not allowed on the slide.

● Country Boy Mine

0542 French Gulch Road, two miles from downtown Breckenridge. (970) 453-4405. Memorial Day to mid-October: daily, 10 A.M. to 5 P.M. Thanksgiving Day to mid-April, Tuesday to Sunday, 11 A.M. to 4 P.M. At the beginning and end of each season, mine may open for reservations only; call first. Adults, $10; ages 4 to 12, $5; under age 4, free. Gold panning included. Guided tour, every hour on the hour. **Ages 4 and up.**

From 1948 to 1990, the Country Boy Mine was closed and rock slides and nature did their work. Now the mine is up and running and miners work daily to clear the tunnels and open new passages. Although there is an estimated $30 to $35 million in precious metals still inside, the owners say they have no intentions of going for the gold, a procedure that would prove costlier than the metals in the end.

The tour combines the thrill of the underground mine with gold panning, always a surefire hit with kids. During the 45-minute tour, the guides run the drills, contrast mining then and now, and discuss the history of the region as you take an easy walk underground. Of special interest to kids: the cave-ins where the miners are hard at work cleaning up.

After the tour, you get to pan for the gold in the creek. (You can also pan for gold, without taking the mine tour, $3 a person.) Everyone leaves with gold and, yes, they sell little vials of water, 75 cents, to magnify your new possession.

From Memorial Day to Labor Day, the owners offer evening hayrides (daily, except Wednesday and Friday, 6 P.M.), complete with campfire, marshmallows, hot chocolate, and burros roaming about. Admission is the same as for the mine, but reservations are required. If you want to cap off your day in Breckenridge, come for the last tour and stay on for the hayride. (**Note:** You will be charged for both mine and hayride.)

● Lomax Placer Gulch Tour

Ski Hill Road. (970) 453-9022. June through September: Hours and days to be determined. Tickets for the tour may be purchased at the Breckenridge

Information Center, 309 North Main Street, across from the fire station.
Ages 8 and up.

This 90-minute guided tour, sponsored by the Summit Historical Society, talks about hydraulic mining and takes you through a miner's cabin. (If you're in search of an underground mine, take the Washington Gold Mine Tour—see entry.)

After a 45-minute talk, which includes a short slide show, the guide shows everyone how to pan for gold. Then the real fun begins. Each visitor, from youngest to oldest, is handed a pan prefilled with dirt to wash away in search of the precious metal. Gold fever quickly takes over as everyone eagerly dips their pan in water and swirls and swirls in search of the precious metal. Almost everyone finds a speck or two, which can be placed in a vial of water (50 cents) that magnifies the gold for the folks back home.

● Maggie Pond

535 South Park Avenue, behind the Bell Tower Mall in the Village at Breckenridge. (970) 453-2000. Ice skating: daily, once the lake freezes over, 10 A.M. to 10 P.M. Skate rental, 10 A.M. to 9 P.M. Ice pass (good for all day): adults, $5; children, $2. Skate rental: all ages, $3 an hour for the first hour, $1 after that. Sled rental: $5 an hour. Summer activities: paddleboats, $7 for a half hour; kayaks, $9 for a half hour (higher on festival weekends: $5 every 15 minutes). **Ages 3 and up.**

This is skating the way it used to be done, when kids flocked to the nearest frozen lake, twirled and tumbled, then headed home for a cup of hot chocolate. You'll find a small warming hut near the steps that lead down to the lake. You can stash your things here and rent skates in adult to toddler sizes. Sleds are available for those with babies or toddlers and the energy to pull them along behind. As for the hot chocolate, try one of the many cafés that border the lake.

In the summer, this is a beautiful setting for taking a paddleboat out for a spin.

● Washington Gold Mine Tour

Illinois Gulch Road. (970) 453-9022. Mid-June to mid-fall (depending on the weather): hours and days vary. Tickets for the tour may be purchased at the Breckenridge Information Center, 309 North Main Street, across from the fire station. **Ages 8 and up.**

This is an in-depth look at mining, with a guided tour through two shafthouses and the anteroom of the Washington Gold Mine, a once-active mine. The kids get to handle some of the artifacts of mining life and don hard hats for their quick trip into the mine. At one point, the guide simulates a dynamite blast with accompanying sound effects.

The tour guide from the Summit County Historical Society is very knowledgeable, and this is an excellent way to learn in detail about this important industry. Although the tour is 90 minutes—too long for some children—our younger kids were fired up by the idea of gold and were content to explore among the rocks, just outside the shafthouses, seeking their own treasures.

CENTRAL CITY

● Teller House Museum and Opera House Tours

120 Eureka Street. (303) 582-3200. Daily, tours on the half hour, 10 A.M. to 4 P.M. Tours of Teller House and Opera House, adults, $3 for each tour; ages 11 and under, free. Opera House may be closed during performances.
Ages 12 and older.

The Teller House has long been famous as the grand ole hotel of a once-booming mining town. President Grant slept here; so did numerous other luminaries of the late 1800s.

Even though it is a casino now, the Teller House has maintained much of its past lustre and is still well known for its *Face on the Barroom Floor,* a painting that is, indeed, on the barroom floor.

A tour guide in period dress greets you in the lobby of the Teller House and takes you on a 15- to 20-minute tour of the premises, including the presidential bedroom and guests' parlors, which are off-limits to gamblers. Our guide made a point of trying to interest the kids with some of the special features of the rooms, such as the mirrors made of diamond dust.

After the Teller House tour, the guide will walk with you to the Opera House—if you want to continue the tour—little more than a stone's throw away. If your kids are restless on the Teller House tour, you'll probably want to stop there.

For those who continue, the Opera House, built in 1878, is still operating, with performances June through August. With its carved red velveteen chairs, painted cherubs, and crystal chandeliers, you'll feel as if you've slipped into some long-ago era.

COPPER MOUNTAIN

● Copper Mountain Summer Activities

Exit 195, off I-70, (800) 458-8386, extension 2. Mid-June to Labor Day. Most activities, free or nominal charge. **All ages.**

This ski area is undergoing extensive renovations and expects to expand both its winter and its summer activites over the next few years. The summer season kicks in around mid-June and lasts through Labor Day, with many special activities. The resort offers free pony rides for children under 7; paddleboating (four to a boat), $1 an hour; and free fishing at the well-stocked West Lake for children ages 12 and under. (Kids may catch two trout; then it's catch and release; ask for fishing poles at the Copper Resort activities desk.) The resort also conducts free fly fishing clinics, for anyone over age 12, on selected days.

A paved bike path connects all of Summit County and you can rent in-line skates and bikes at retail outlets in the resort. You can also take the kids for a free chairlift ride (the lift seats four) to Solitude Station at mid-mountain. There, U.S. Forest Service personnel conduct kid-friendly hikes twice a day, 11 A.M. and 1:30 P.M.

CRAIG

● Craig Swimming Complex

605 Washington Street. (970) 824-3015. Early June to end of August: Monday to Friday, 1 to 8 P.M.; Saturday and Sunday, 1 to 6 P.M. Adults, ages 18 and up, $3; ages 12 to 17, $2.50; ages 4 to 11, $2; ages 3 and under, free with a paying adult. **All ages.**

In your kids' eyes, this small town will be notable for one thing: having the latest sensation in swimming, the wave pool. Every 10 minutes, the waves rear up in the otherwise placid swimming pool, rising as high as six feet, and kids can ride them out on rubber rafts ($1.50 rental with 25 cent refund) or bob up and down, jumping them as they would at any seashore.

In addition to the wave pool, this outdoor swimming complex also has a standard-size pool with a small water tube and low diving board. There are lockers, changing rooms, and concessions, but bring your own suits and towels. There is a playground just outside the pool complex.

Craig is about 4½ hours from Denver, and about an hour from Steamboat Springs. If you're traveling to Dinosaur National Monument (see entry under Dinosaur), you might choose to spend a couple hours here.

DILLON

● Dillon Reservoir Recreation Area

Interstate 70 West to Silverthorne, Dillon exit 205. (970) 468-5100 (Dillon Marina). Dillon Marina: Memorial Day to end of June, daily;

weekdays in August and during the month of September to first week in
October, 9 A.M. to 6 P.M.; July, daily, and weekends in August, 8 A.M. to
7:30 P.M. Marina closed in winter. **All ages.**

This popular recreational spot is centered around Dillon Reservoir,
a 3,300-acre lake with a mountain backdrop. Most people come here to
boat, and you can rent a pontoon, fishing boat, runabout, kayak, or a
sailing boat (if you have experience) from the Dillon Marina (follow the
signs). The marina also has information on the area.

For those with no boating experience, a pontoon is a family favorite.
This flat boat seats six to nine with walking-around room and maneuvers
somewhat like a car (two hours, $80 plus fuel). Even if you don't take a
boat out, your children will enjoy watching the other skippers, playing
along the water's edge, and walking out on the boat ramp.

Overlooking the lake near the marina are covered picnic grounds, a
sandy area for sandbox play, a concession stand (opens July 4), and rest
rooms. There are other picnic grounds in the area as well. No swimming
or water skiing are allowed in the lake.

Hikers can choose from the many trails, including a paved one that's
part of the 44-mile Summit County Recreational Trail, which connects
Dillon, Silverthorne, Frisco, Keystone, Breckenridge, Copper Mountain,
and Vail.

DINOSAUR

● **Dinosaur National Monument**
Two miles east of Dinosaur, Colorado, just off U.S. 40. (970) 374-3000
(for information on both Colorado and Utah attractions) or (801) 789-
2115. Monument Headquarters Visitor Center (in Colorado): summer, late
May to August, daily, 8 A.M. to 4:30 P.M.; winter, Monday to Friday,
8 A.M. to 4:30 P.M. Dinosaur Quarry Visitor Center, seven miles north of
Jensen, Utah, via State Route 149. Summer: late May to early September,
daily, 8 A.M. to 7 P.M. Winter: daily, 8 A.M. to 4:30 P.M. Colorado side, free.
Utah side, $10 per vehicle. Closed Thanksgiving Day, Christmas Day, and
New Year's Day. **Ages 5 and up.**

Dinosaur National Monument covers more than 300 square miles,
spilling across the border between Colorado and Utah. Most people stay
overnight in Vernal, Utah, because it has most of the accommodations and
it's closest to the real drawing card of the monument: the quarry building
where the dinosaur bones are on display. In fact, big signs on the Colorado
side alert you that there are no dinosaur bones to be found there. Whether
you're in Colorado or Utah, the climate can be very hot and dry in the

summer in this corner of the state, so get an early start to the day. And wear insect repellant, if possible. The mosquitoes are unrelenting.

Here's a look at what you'll see on both sides. The entrances are about 31 miles apart.

Dinosaur National Monument, Colorado. This side boasts beautiful scenery and spectacular canyon views. From the Monument Headquarters, you can take a self-guided driving tour that includes numerous overlooks. If you have limited time, follow the tour to Plug Hat Butte, about two miles (pick up a map at the visitor center). Here you can walk an easy quarter-mile loop along a sandy path that borders the canyon. The views are great and the topography, with gnarly, scruffy trees, has its own charm.

Dinosaur National Monument, Utah. The monument is famous because of the treasure that was uncovered in 1909—dinosaur bones. Earl Douglass, a paleontologist from the Carnegie Museum in Pittsburgh, Pennsylvania, came to Colorado to hunt for dinosaur remains. He was rewarded by spotting eight of the tail bones of a brontosaurus, which are preserved in their exact position embedded in the ridge.

Thousands of bones have come from the quarry site, which became a national monument in 1915. When you arrive at the quarry in the summer, open-air shuttle buses drive you from the lower parking lot the short distance to the Dinosaur Quarry Visitor Center. Here you'll find a number of dinosaur bone exhibits, a working lab (you can peer through the glass), and the main attraction: the quarry wall. One side of the building is the authentic stone face where fossil bones were found but not removed, and you can see the bones just as they were preserved by nature. During the summer, rangers give talks at the Quarry.

Although an impressive sight, the museum is at least an eight-hour drive from Denver, and we spent only about 45 minutes there. If you're going to make the trip, we suggest you also incorporate a few other attractions. You can pick up the brochure (50 cents at the gift shop) for the Tour of the Tilted Rocks, a self-guided auto tour to see Indian petroglyphs (carved designs) and pictographs (paintings) within the park. At the very least, follow the tour for the first mile, where you can walk right up to the side of a cave-like shelter to examine the drawings. Continue on the Tour of the Tilted Rocks and you'll wind up at Josie Morris cabin, home of a turn-of-the-century woman who ranched alone. You can't enter the cabin; however, there is an easy walking trail into the canyon, where you can see plant life and the sheer canyon walls. And it's cool. On the driving tour at points 3, 4, and 5, you can see Split Mountain, where the Green River cut through the rocks, one of the highpoints of the drive.

Also worth noting: the **Utah Field House of Natural History & Dinosaur Garden,** 235 East Main Street in Vernal, Utah (801) 789-3799. The museum has 18 life-size prehistoric animals that look so authentic in the outdoor gardens that the younger ones—and even older children— will be enthralled. The kids are issued a dinosaur hunting license as a souvenir. Summer: Memorial Day to Labor Day, daily, 8 A.M. to 9 P.M. Winter: daily, 9 A.M. to 5 P.M. Adults and children, ages 6 and up, $2; under age 6, free. Family price, $5. (Fees are subject to change; call ahead.)

ESTES PARK

● Aerial Tramway
420 East Riverside Drive. (970) 586-3675. Daily, two weeks before Memorial Day to one week after Labor Day, 9 A.M. to 6:30 P.M. (weeks before Memorial Day and after Labor Day, open only until 5:30 P.M.). Adults, $8; ages 6 to 11, $4; under age 6 free if accompanied by an adult; seniors age 60 and up, $7. **Ages 2 and up.**

For a quick fix of splendid mountain vistas without taking the time to drive into Rocky Mountain National Park (see entry), try the Aerial Tramway. Simply pile into a small gondola car with other visitors and you'll be whisked to the top of Prospect Mountain, where you can practically reach out and touch Longs Peak and the mountains of the Continental Divide. Picnic tables are available, and if you don't have time to pack a lunch, you can buy food at the snack bar. Children will enjoy feeding peanuts (available in the snack bar) to the chipmunks and hiking along the easy mountain trails. Unfortunately, the conveniences are also the drawbacks here, as the concessions and the mechanical trappings of the tramway tend to detract from the beauty of the surroundings. As we said, this is a quick fix. For a purer experience, head for the park.

● Enos Mills Cabin and Nature Trail
Eight miles south of Estes Park on Highway 7. (970) 586-4706. Memorial Day to Labor Day, Tuesday to Sunday, 11 A.M. to 4 P.M. In winter, by appointment only. (Call 970-586-1016.) Free. **Ages 6 and up.**

You may not know the name Enos Mills, but if you've been to Rocky Mountain National Park and enjoyed the unspoiled views, you owe this man the credit. Known as the "Father of Rocky Mountain National Park," Mills lobbied for the government to set aside park land, and was successful here in 1915. He also helped organize lobbying efforts in other areas where parks were under consideration. When he wasn't busy fighting for the rights of nature, he lived in peaceful awe of his surroundings. Mills spent 20 years using this one-room cabin as home base, from which he photographed nature scenes, wrote his observations in journals that were later widely read as published books, and traveled to places beyond.

Visitors are invited to tour Mills's cabin accompantied by his daughter, Enda, who has preserved his personal effects. Now in her 70s, Enda lives nearby and is happy to lead groups down a short nature trail—where vegetation is labeled to educate visitors—to the cabin her father built at age 14. Inside the tiny house, you'll see photographs taken by Mills, as well as snowshoes, boots, and other items from his days in the cabin. Posted in spots outside the house are quotes from Mills, such as this one: "This is a beautiful world, and all who go out under the open sky feel the gentle influences of nature."

Make a quick stop here for a slice of history as well as some restful contemplation. The best tours, we are told, are those led by Enda, although other relatives also take turns showing visitors around.

● Fun City/Fun Trax

375 Moraine Avenue. (970) 586-2070. Mid-May to Labor Day (weather permiting): daily, 10 A.M. to 10 P.M. After Labor Day, open as weather permits; call ahead. Park closes around October for the year. Tickets, $1 each. Slide, one ticket; bumper cars, two tickets; miniature golf, $4; go-carts, $5, riders under 56 inches tall, $1. (Ticket discounts available if buying 30 or more.) **Ages 3 and up.**

The main attraction here is the slide, which is likely to catch your child's eye from the road. It's 42 feet high, with a few savage dips, yet still gentle enough for a tot riding on a parent's lap. When the novelty wears off, kids can play video games in the small arcade, ride on the bumper cars, or play a round of miniature golf. They can also jump on go-carts that takes them around two loops and beneath three underpasses. Fun City closes down in bad weather, so call before coming on questionable days.

● MacGregor Ranch Museum

North on MacGregor Avenue until it turns into Devil's Gulch; go straight until you see the sign. (970) 586-3749. June, July, and August: Tuesday to Friday, 10 A.M. to 4 P.M. Free; donations requested. **Ages 5 and up.**

Step inside the manor house here and enter the early 1920s, when one quart of milk cost 13 cents, starched white dresses and shirts were always hanging in the closet, and the organ stood ready for duty in the front parlor. MacGregor Ranch was homesteaded in 1873; the home, now a museum, was built in 1896. More than a century later, the rooms look much like they did then, with clothes, household utensils, china, photographs, and more displayed in every room. Visitors are invited to walk through the house and tour the surrounding grounds, which include a milk house, root cellar, blacksmith shop, smoke house, and corral.

The acreage remains a working ranch, supporting about 60 head of cattle on approximately 1,200 acres. On a good day, you'll see horses in the corral, and an occasional authentic cowboy, complete with spurs and chaps.

● Ride-A-Kart Family Amusement Park and Cascade Creek Mini-Golf

Two miles east of Estes Park on Highway 34. Memorial Day to Labor Day: daily, 9:30 A.M. to 10 P.M.; reduced hours the rest of May and September. (970) 586-6495. Train ride, 50 cents; bumper cars, $2.50; bumper boats, $3.50; go-carts, $4; toddler golf (ages 5 and under), $2; child golf (ages 9 and under), $4; adult golf, $5. Discounts available for packets of tickets.
Ages 2 and up.

This amusement park offers something for everyone: a train ride for tots that goes around the park, bumper cars and other rides for the bigger kids, and great scenery for the adults paying the bill. It isn't a large park, but the kids will keep busy on the go-cart track, the bumper cars, and the bumper boats. The miniature golf course is one of the best in town, and when it's time to take a break, there's a snack cart with hot dogs, burritos, soft drinks, and more and a video arcade. One warning: adults will have to accompany small children on most of the rides. Be prepared to get plenty wet on the bumper boats. And, as at any amusement park, the cost can add up.

● Rocky Mountain National Park ◆

U.S. 34 or 36 or Colorado Highway 7 from Estes Park. (970) 586-1206. (West entrance to park is from Grand Lake, see entry there.) Open every day, year round, 24 hours a day. $10 per vehicle; $5 per hiker, motorcyclist, or bicyclist. **All ages.**

At 65 miles northwest of Denver, Rocky Mountain National Park is the most popular park in the state. The park covers 415 square miles, and has 355 miles of hikes and 78 peaks, which reach more than 12,000 feet. More than 3.1 million visitors arrive every year to sample its unparalleled beauty. In 1994, Emperor Hirohito of Japan made this one of his few stopping points on his U.S. tour.

There are five visitor centers in the park. The closest is Park Head-
quarters/Visitor Center, 2.5 miles west of Estes Park on U.S. Highway 36.
It's open in the summer from 8 A.M. to 9 P.M. and in the fall, winter, and
spring from 8 A.M. to 5 P.M. Stop at the headquarters for brochures and
information on the rest of the park.

The park offers everything from snowmobiling to ice fishing to rock
climbing to hiking. Many hikes are well-suited to children, easy strolls
around mirror-clear lakes. Two suggested hikes:

Sprague Lake. Take Highway 36 past the visitor center, turn left on
Bear Lake Road, and continue for about 15 minutes. Follow the sign for
Sprague Lake. The hiking path is a half mile loop around the lake and is
wheelchair (and stroller) accessible.

Bear Lake. Take Highway 36, go past the visitor center, turn left on
Bear Lake Road, and follow Bear Lake Road to the end. The walk around
Bear Lake is a half mile loop and is only partially wheelchair (and stroller)
accessible.

There are also a number of ranger-led, age-appropriate programs just
for kids, including evening campfire programs in the summer. On Saturday nights year round, the Park Headquarters/Visitor Center offers an
evening program. Children can become Junior Rangers and can pick up a
book of activities ($1) at the visitor centers that will help them earn Jun-
ior Ranger status. Programs and times change year to year; inquire at the
Park Headquarters/Visitor Center.

In addition, don't miss a drive along **Trail Ridge Road,** the highest
continuous road in the U.S. The 50-mile stretch goes beyond timberline,
offering stark yet striking scenery (open according to weather, so call
ahead; generally closed mid-October to the end of May).

Although summer is peak season at the park, fall is also a special time
of the year. In early October, the elk mate, and crowds of visitors line the
roadway to watch the herds and listen for their eerie mating call, known
as bugling. If you can plan a trip to the park mid-September into early
October, this is a not-to-be-missed rite of fall.

● Estes Park Center YMCA of the Rockies ◆

*Located 65 miles northwest of Denver, five miles southwest of the town of Estes
Park (from Denver, take Interstate 25 north to Highway 36; go west on
Highway 36 through Boulder and Lyons to Estes Park; drive through town,
staying on Highway 36 until highway divides at town limits; veer left to
Highway 66; drive about two miles until you see the sign). (970) 586-3341
or (303) 448-1616 (if calling from Denver metro area). Open year-round.*

Prices range from $46 for a room in the lodge ($32 in the off-season) to $216 for a four-bedroom cabin. **All ages.**

If you liked camp as a child, you'll love the YMCA Estes Park Center. It is chockful of camp atmosphere—without a 5 A.M. wake-up time, nagging counselors, and watery "bug juice"! You can choose between more than 200 cabins, each with kitchen and phone (while some come outfitted complete with coffee makers and TV, others are extremely rustic, so be sure and ask for details when you book your reservations). Once settled in, peruse the long list of activities detailed in a packet of information you'll receive at the front desk. Most of your choices will be free, and you can participate in them as a family or send the children off on their own.

In the summer, the resort offers hiking, horseback riding, hay rides, crafts, swimming in an indoor pool, minigolf, and more. You might even attend a campfire, complete with s'mores! Winter activities include ice skating, sledding, indoor swimming, snowshoeing, roller skating, and volleyball.

Besides the endless list of things to do, plenty of amenities help families enjoy a vacation, including babysitting, several dining rooms, from sit-down to cafeteria-style, and recreational equipment visitors are welcome to borrow. In addition, Rocky Mountain National Park is nearby, with its own allure.

Don't be scared off by its religious affiliation. This may be a Young Men's Christian Association center, but all denominations are welcome. It's easy to avoid religion altogther, if you're not interested. And if you are, there are regular worship services and fellowship.

But be forewarned: the rooms book early—and procrastinators are sure to be out of luck, especially in the busy summer season. Priority goes to those who have donated money for cabins on the premises, followed by members, all of whom receive reservation information months before the season begins. Those who do not belong can submit their requests, which are processed for summer dates in April and for winter dates in October. (The summer/fall season is from June 1 to November 30; winter/spring season is from December 1 to May 31.) Nonmembers will be asked to pay a small membership fee, valid only for the duration of their stay ($5 per family or $3 per single adult). Phone early for reservation applications.

In addition, once you arrive, be sure to study the list of activities immediately and sign up for events that seem inviting. Like the cabins, these, too, book early in summer. Sign-up begins two days in advance of the activity.

What you miss in spontaneity, you'll make up for down the road. We guarantee your visit will be well worth the advance planning!

Note that the YMCA of the Rockies offers a similar center in Winter Park, called the Snow Mountain Ranch. Both are approximately the same distance from Denver, and offer generally the same programs. However, there are some distinctions that may be important to you. See Snow Mountain Ranch YMCA entry under Winter Park.

EVERGREEN

● Evergreen Lake

Take Interstate 70 to Evergreen Parkway exit; drive eight miles southwest on Highway 74. (303) 512-9300. Ice skating: starts mid-to-end of December and continues as long as the ice remains frozen. Hours: Monday, 1 to 7 P.M.; Wednesday, 4 to 7 P.M.; Friday, 4 to 9 P.M.; Saturday, 9 A.M. to 9 P.M. and Sunday, 9 A.M. to 7 P.M. During three-week Christmas holiday season: daily, 8 A.M. to 7 P.M. All hours weather permitting. Adults, $2.50; ages 13 to 18, $2.25; ages 12 and under and seniors, $2. Skate rental, $2 per hour. Summer: Open weekends only in May and September, 10 A.M. to 4 P.M. (last boat rental at 3 P.M.); early June to mid-August: daily, 10 A.M. to 7 P.M. (last boat rented at 6 P.M.). Canoes, $5 per hour; paddleboats, $5 per half hour. $5 deposit and picture ID required to rent either. Lifejackets free with rental. **Ages 2 and up.**

This 55-acre reservoir, about 20 minutes from Denver, provides ample recreation year-round. In the winter, the lake features $4\frac{1}{2}$ acres of groomed ice, including five smaller rinks for private rental and hockey or broomball games. (Renting a smaller rink for an hour is a great idea for a birthday party. The cost is $15 to $35 an hour, depending on the number of partygoers.)

If you don't have skates of your own, stop in the lodge at the edge of the lake, where you can rent skates, buy snacks, and duck inside when the weather becomes too biting. The concessions are moderately priced and sell hot and cold drinks, hot dogs, pretzels, and other snack items. (In summer, concessions sell only soft drinks and candy.)

This is skating in the great outdoors, so remember that conditions here may be different from those in Denver or other outlying areas. And those conditions can mean the difference between a fun or a miserable outing. When it's windy, skaters have been known to "blow across the ice like so much tumbleweed," in the words of one spokeswoman. By contrast, when it's over 45 to 50 degrees, the ice begins to melt and the lake is closed to skating. The moral? Always call before coming to be sure the lake is open for skating; the recorded message you will reach is updated daily. On good weather days, mornings are the best time to come (if the lake is open at this time), as the ice may begin to soften in midday.

In the summer, visitors can enjoy boating (canoes and paddleboats are available for rental) or fishing in this scenic area.

● Hiwan Homestead Museum

4208 South Timbervale Drive. (303) 674-6262. Winter: Tuesday to Sunday, noon to 5 P.M. Summer: Tuesday to Sunday, 11 A.M. to 5 P.M. Free.
Ages 6 and up.

This is the site of a 17-room log cabin built in the 1880s and kept meticulously with furnishings of that era. (The term "cabin" is somewhat of a misnomer; this is a large house, not a tiny bungalow in the woods.) The home is steeped in history and boasts beautiful architectural detail at every turn. Guides will take you through the house, offering stories of the families who once lived here as well as of the man who built the cabin with such care.

While some children may become impatient with the abundance of information offered during the tour, there are plenty of hands-on items to keep them in the game: from animal pelts on the wall that children can touch to fluffy wool ready for spinning. The guide who led our tour made it a point to address much of his talk to the kids and held their interest well.

The site also offers an easy nature trail, a one-room cabin that boasts a rock display, and another building housing an exhibit on the man who built Hiwan Homestead, as well as old tools and an antique printing press. But you may find the biggest hit of the trip are the two covered wagons out front: children are welcome to climb in and out of these "museum" pieces—and they do, with abandon.

FAIRPLAY

● South Park City Museum

4th and Front streets. (719) 836-2387. May 15 to Memorial Day and Labor Day to October 15: daily, 9 A.M. to 5 P.M. (ticket window closes at 4 P.M.); Memorial Day to Labor Day: daily, 9 A.M. to 7 P.M. (ticket window closes at 6 P.M.) Adults, $5; ages 6 to 12, $2; seniors, ages 62 and over, $4; ages 5 and under, free. **Ages 4 and up.**

This reconstructed mining town, circa 1870 to 1900, will give you a pretty authentic look at life in a boom town. The 35 buildings—all of them original, many moved here from other sites—have more than 60,000 artifacts inside. The period pieces include everything from toys to schoolhouse desks to scales for weighing gold.

There are no tour guides, and visitors may explore at their own pace, making it suitable for kids of any age. Visitors walk on planked sidewalks throughout the town and can stop in at the various places: a one-room schoolhouse, a trapper's log cabin, a bank, a drugstore, a dentist office, a general store, even the old brewery where South Park Lager was once made. A train is parked permanently at the station; visitors can scramble aboard the caboose for a look around.

This is one of the best and least commercial of Colorado's re-created "Western towns." Fairplay is 85 miles from Denver on Route 285; it makes a nice day trip. Stop at the nearby Fairplay Hotel, circa 1873, a cozy and child-friendly place for lunch. One other note: Fairplay is located at an altitude of almost 10,000 feet, and the weather can turn cloudy and cold very quickly. On a summer outing from Denver, where it was 85 degrees, Fairplay was a very chilly 50 degrees. In addition, the buildings are not heated. You'd be wise to wear long pants and have warm sweaters or jackets at the ready.

FRASER

● Tubing Hill at Fraser ◆
Near Winter Park, half mile behind the Safeway complex in Fraser. (970) 726-5954. Season begins around Thanksgiving and usually continues until Easter, but will vary with the snowfall. Weekends, 10 A.M. to 10 P.M.; holidays and holiday seasons, 10 A.M. to 11 P.M.; weekdays, 4 to 10 P.M. Admission (includes rubber tube): $10 per hour per tube until 6 P.M.; $11 per hour after 6 P.M.; small discount for families; children ages 3 to 6, free (because they share a tube with adults); seniors, ages 60 plus, free. **Ages 5 and up.**

Truly a Colorado experience, you fly down the well-groomed hill on these rubber inner tubes. Once you get to the bottom, a minilift jettisons you to the top (you lie on the tube and grab a moving handle).

Children under 3 are not allowed on the hill. Children ages 3 to 6 must share a larger tube with an adult. Older children and more daring younger kids will have a blast. The facility is efficiently run with a warming house and hot drinks available. Bring gloves, hats, and snowpants (or a change of clothes). Although the tubes have seats, you're likely to get wet from the spray as you zoom down the hill.

FRISCO

● Frisco Historical Park
120 Main Street. (970) 668-3428. Winter: Tuesday to Saturday, 11 A.M. to 4 P.M. Summer: Tuesday to Sunday, 11 A.M. to 4 P.M. Donations requested. **Ages 5 and up.**

This small site (less than half a block long) is packed with historic buildings, all originally built in Frisco, but later moved to the park for easy viewing. You will enter a schoolhouse (built in the 1890s as a saloon), complete with school bell on top, where glass display cases house old-time clothes, miners' equipment, photographs, and more. In the back of the room, school desks and small blackboards show children what a school room might have looked like years ago.

The site also contains an austere old jail house (closed in the winter); a furnished turn-of-the-century, middle-class home; a relatively recently built (1943) log chapel; a trapper's cabin, complete with animal pelts; and a few other buildings that house craft and gift shops. Visitors are invited to walk in and out of the buildings at their own pace.

If you're in the area, this offers a nice change of pace from the usual outdoor activities. In the summer, the park hosts musical concerts as well as workshops on panning for gold, and arts and crafts festivals. Call for details.

FRUITA

● Devil's Canyon Science and Learning Center

550 Jurassic Court (just south of Interstate 70's Exit 19 on Highway 340). (800) 344-3466. Daily, Monday to Saturday, 9 A.M. to 5 P.M., Sunday, 10 A.M. to 5 P.M. Adults, $5; ages 3 to 12 and seniors ages 55 and up, $3.50; ages 2 and under, free. **Ages 3 and up.**

A velociraptor grips another dinosaur's bloody head in its mouth; baby dinosaurs hatch from large, wiggling eggs; a dilophosaurus spits at visitors who dare to get too close. Sound ominous? Nah. It's just good old Jurassic-style fun. This $2 million project offers seven robotic dinosaur exhibits and plenty of hands-on activities, all housed in one giant room. Children will learn about the weather and geology as well as fossils as they are invited to whip up a sandstorm in one exhibit; stand on a moving floor plate that simulates the feel of an earthquake; uncover "fossils" by brushing sand away until the discovery is made and more.

This is the kind of place you can let your children loose without worry that they will disrupt things; they are free to roam, with only their individual interest to guide them. When they're through, a stop in the gift shop is fun, if only to see the huge number of dinosaur-related items one could buy! (Of course, as always, beware of the ever-shrinking wallet.)

Some tour books will tell you this is a not-to-be-missed attraction, even if you have to drive out of your way to get here. We tend to disagree. It's a wonderful diversion if you're in the areaa, but other museums offer similar experiences and your stay is likely to last less than two hours. Plan accordingly.

GEORGETOWN

● Georgetown Loop Railroad

Board at Silver Plume, near exit 226 on Interstate 70, or Devil's Gate, near exit 228 on Interstate 70. (800) 691-4386 or (303) 670-1686 (from Denver area). Open daily from last weekend in May through first week in October. Call for times. Round-trip fare: adults, $11.95; ages 3 to 15, $7.50; ages 2 and under, free. Lebanon Silver Mine Tour, an optional stop during the train ride, same operating days. Adults, $4 (in addition to train fare); ages 3 to 15, $2; ages 2 and under free. **Ages 3 and up.**

This railroad served the mining camps between Denver and Silver Plume in the late 1800s and early 1900s. Today, it serves tourists instead, who enjoy the scenery and the sheer pleasure of a train ride complete with whistle and steam. The train covers 4¼ miles of track that rise 600 feet in elevation. You'll see foliage, a rushing river, and, unfortunately, the highway during parts of the trip. Oh well. It's not perfect, but kids love the ride, which—at an hour and 20 minutes round-trip—is one of the more palatable train adventures in the state when you're traveling with young children and their notoriously short attention spans.

A few warnings: The railroad cars are open, so the ride can be a chilly one on cool days. Bring coats or windbreakers. You may also want to wear long pants, even in summer. And don't forget the sunscreen—your kids will be soaking up the sun along with the scenery.

For those who have time, the optional stop at the Lebanon Silver Mine Tour is well worth the hour-and-20-minute detour. You'll put on hard hats, see a mineral vein, step into an area where miners used to eat their meals, and more. This is not recommended, however, for pre-schoolers, who will likely be bored with the long explanatory segments of the tour. The mine is 44 degrees, so, again, bring coats and comfortable walking shoes.

● Georgetown Viewing Station

West on Interstate 70; take Georgetown exit 228; left on Alvarado Road; ¾ of a mile to the viewing area. Open year-round. 25 cents for use of viewing scopes. **Ages 5 and up.**

This small station off the highway is set up with viewing scopes and informational signs. For a quarter, you can scan the mountainside with a scope, looking for some of the 150-plus Rocky Mountain bighorn sheep who make their home near Georgetown. The best time to stop is during winter months, when the sheep are at a lower elevation and easier to see. In addition, volunteers staff the station on winter weekends, 10 A.M. to 3 P.M., and can answer questions.

From November to January, you may get an even bigger payoff: this is the time of year males butt horns as they try to establish dominance over the herd; the crack of their clashes echoes through the valley, an awesome, if eerie, sound.

A stop here may not always prove fruitful, but the station is a quick detour off the highway and well worth the trouble for the chance to spot these majestic animals.

● **Hamill House**
305 Argentine Street. (303) 569-2840. Memorial Day to September 30: daily, 10 A.M. to 4 P.M. Rest of year: Saturday and Sunday, noon to 4 P.M. Adults, $5; students, ages 5 through college, and seniors ages 55 and up, $3; under age 6, free. **Ages 8 and up.**

The Hamills, who made their fortune in silver mining, built this home, which was luxurious for its time, and expanded it between 1867 to 1885. Historic Georgetown, Inc., began to restore the house to its glory years in 1971.

A tour guide takes you on the 20- to 25-minute tour through the house and shows you the points of interest. Hamill made some noteworthy additions through the years, particularly the solarium with its indoor fountain, bay windows, and walnut woodwork. In 1974, a fire gutted the rear of the house. The dining room has been restored, right down to the hand-painted wallpaper; the kitchen is still sparse. Noteworthy outside the house is a six-seat privy with separate sides for the family and its servants.

The Hamill House recently opened the laundry building and the carriage house, complete with carriages and a sleigh. If you're lucky, you may hit the tour on one of the occasions when horses are housed there. Nevertheless, because the tour is no-touch, it's really better suited for the more mature child.

● **Hotel De Paris**
409 6th Street. (303) 569-2311. June 1 to end of September: daily, 10 A.M. to 5 P.M. October to June 1: weekends only, noon to 4 P.M. Adults, $3.50; seniors, ages 60 and older, $2.50; children, ages 6 to 16, $1.50; under age 6, free. **Ages 8 and up.**

The Hotel De Paris is distinguished by having many of the original pieces from the hotel's heyday in the 1870s and 1880s. Founded by Frenchman Louis Dupuy, it was famous for its many decorative and luxury features, including steam heat, hot and cold running water, and a fine wine cellar.

Older children, particularly those fond of history, will have some interest in the guided tour, around 30 minutes. The cellar in particular, a somewhat spooky place, is fun to visit. Tour guides are tuned into those traveling with younger children and will adjust the tour accordingly during the slower season.

GLENWOOD SPRINGS

● Doc Holliday's Grave

Trailhead at 12th Street and Bennett Avenue. Free. **Ages 3 and up.**

Doc Holliday, renowned Old West gunman, was put to rest in a cemetery located at the top of a hill overlooking Glenwood Springs. You'll see a sign at the trailhead explaining Holliday's life, and that of the townspeople. You'll then be directed up a path, approximately half a mile long, to the cemetery. The incline is relatively steep on this short hike, and you're likely to hear a few complaints from the little ones on the way up. Even so, this is an enjoyable outing for the fresh air, the view at the top of the hill, and the gravestones dating back to the 1800s, including Holliday's, which is etched in one corner with a poker hand and, in the other, with a trusty six-shooter. The headstones tell a tale of hardship better than any history book; we spent a good deal of time searching for anyone who might have lived beyond 20 and 30 years of age (there weren't many). Remember to bring water or other drinks on your outing—your children will be asking for it by the time you reach the top.

● Frontier Historical Museum

1001 Colorado Avenue. (970) 945-4448. May to September: Monday to Saturday, 11 A.M. to 4 P.M. October to April: Monday and Thursday to Saturday, 1 to 4 P.M. Adults and children ages 12 and up, $3; under age 12, free; seniors, ages 60 and up, $2. **Ages 6 and up.**

Built in 1905, this lovely home was eventually donated to the Frontier Historical Society for use as a museum. In addition to early 1900s furnishings and rooms set up as though still in use (complete with mannequins dressed in period clothing), the museum includes Native American artifacts; a mining exhibit, with photos of miners, equipment, and informational dioramas; a timeline of important events in Glenwood Springs; and last but not least, an authentic saddle once owned by Teddy Roosevelt.

● Hanging Lake

If heading west on Interstate 70, take exit 121 and follow the signs, which will direct you to double-back east on Interstate 70 for approximately four miles; take exit 125 and follow signs to trailhead. If heading east on Interstate 70, take exit 125; follow signs to trailhead. **Ages 6 and up.**

Just outside of the town of Glenwood Springs and up a rocky trail about 1,000 feet high is a tiny jewel called Hanging Lake. Here, waterfalls cascade into a crystal, emerald lake; trout swim in the water; in summer, columbines, asters, and other wildflowers provide gorgeous bursts of color. In short, it's a wonderul, idyllic spot. And that's the good news.

The bad news is that you'll have to work to get here; this is a strenuous hike, approximately 1.2 miles that stretch relentlessly upward, sometimes in a steep, 15 percent grade. The trail is rocky, and often you will find yourself picking your way up the hill with extra care. On the plus side, it is heavily wooded, so at least you are often shaded from the sun while you're working your way to the top.

Can kids handle this tough little hike? The question on our outing seemed to be: can the parents? Our 6-year-old sprinted up like a mountain goat, barely stopping to look back as we wheezed and huffed to the top; on the other hand, our 10-year-old complained most of the way up. We saw 3- and 4-year-olds on their way down; their parents indicated the tots enjoyed the climb. Gauge your own kids' style. And if you go, be prepared. Bring water and ponchos; afternoon showers—and they can be violent—are always a threat.

● Hot Springs Pool ◆

Adjacent to Interstate 70 at Exit 116, 160 miles west of Denver. (800) 537-SWIM or (970) 945-7131 (pool area). Daily: winter, 9 A.M. to 10 P.M.; summer, 7:30 A.M. to 10 P.M. Adults and teens, $7.25; ages 3 to 12, $4.75; ages 2 and under, free. Water slide: $3 for four rides; $4 for eight rides. Miniature golf: adults and teens, $4; ages 12 and under, $3. Pool is closed the second Wednesday of September, in January, March, and May and three days in November. **All ages.**

Welcome to Glenwood Springs' star attraction. This oasis is billed as "the world's largest outdoor hot springs pool," and with the main pool more than two blocks long, that's probably no exaggeration. Children will love this pool extravaganza, where they can swim all day and never find themselves shivering from cold. The main pool is kept at 90 degrees. A smaller pool, dubbed the "therapy pool" for its restorative powers, stays at 104 degrees. In the summer, children can take a turn on the huge twisting water slide (for an extra fee); they can dive from boards at one end of the main pool or stand comfortably at the shallow end. Adults, more than children, tend to congregate in the therapy pool, where the water quickly turns tense muscles to mush. There are even whirlpool-like chairs you can turn on for a quarter for an ultra-luxurious soak. In the winter, ease your ski-weary body into the pool and watch the snowflakes dissolve as they fall through the steam.

The extensive facility includes miniature golf, a dining room, lodging, and locker rooms. If you are in need, you can rent swimsuits ($2.50) and towels ($1.50).

GRAND JUNCTION

● Colorado National Monument ◆

From Grand Junction, follow the signs on Highway 340 to the east entrance. From Fruita, take Interstate 70 to exit 19 (Highway 340) and go south for three miles to the west entrance. (970) 858-3617, ext. 360. Daily, winter, 8 A.M. to 4:30 P.M.; summer, 8 A.M. to 6 P.M. Seven-day vehicle pass, $4; 7-day individual pass, $2; campground fee, $9. **Ages 5 and up.**

After touring the expansive Colorado National Monument, with its sweeping vistas and dramatic rock formations, we have only one thing to say: who needs the Grand Canyon? These 32 square miles offer splendid views, and you and your children will have fun recognizing shapes in the plethora of interesting jutting rocks. Look for the Kissing Couple, the Praying Hands, the Sentinel Spire, and more, all detailed in the brochure you can receive at each entrance. The park offers plenty of camping sites that are rarely crowded, we're told. Other activities include hiking (check the brochure for a list of trails and their level of difficulty), horseback riding, cross-country skiing, rock climbing, and bicycling. The visitor center offers a small educational display of animals in the park, as well as pottery fragments from the Freemont Indians, who used to inhabit the area. A slide show depicts vegetation and shows off the park's many stunning views.

● Cross Orchards Historic Site ◆

3073 F (Patterson) Road. (970) 434-9814. April 1 to September 30: Monday to Saturday, 9 A.M. to 5 P.M.; Sunday, noon to 4 P.M. October, November, December: Tuesday to Saturday, 10 A.M. to 4 P.M. Closed January,

February, and March. Adults, $4; ages 3 to 12, $2; ages 2 and under, free; seniors ages 60 and up, $3.50. **Ages 4 and up.**

Cross Orchards was founded in 1896 by the wealthy Cross family— owners of Red Cross shoes—from Massachusetts. Boasting more than 22,000 apple trees, the farm was one of the largest orchards in the state until an infestation of coddling moths began causing extensive damage and eventually forced the family to divide the land and sell it in 1923. Today, the site is a wonderful outdoor museum where children can see, touch, and feel what life was like in an orchard in those early years.

First, pick up a brochure to guide you through the stops. The tour, aided by guides dressed in period costumes posted along the way, takes you through a gazebo that served as a summer house used by the Cross family and their friends during visits from the East, a ranch house where you're likely to be greeted by the smell of freshly baked cookies (on our tour, the lady of the house offered us hot cookies, then speared some apples on an old-fashioned apple peeler and corer, turned the crank, and in minutes, offered us freshly peeled apples), a packing shed where you'll learn how fruit was sorted and boxed, a bunkhouse, a carpentry shop, and more. The museum also includes a barn filled with old-time construction equipment and a railway exhibit.

The guides are terrific at explaining life on the ranch, and real animals—geese, hens, cows—add to the fun for the kids. Watch for special events throughout the year, including Easter egg hunts, ice cream socials, children's woodworking workshops, and apple jubilees.

● Dinosaur Valley

Fourth and Main streets. (970) 242-0971. April 1 to September 30, Monday to Saturday, 9 A.M. to 5 P.M., Sunday, 9 A.M. to 4 P.M. October 1 to March 31, Tuesday to Sunday, 10 A.M. to 4 P.M. (Last admission is a half hour before closing.) Adults, $4; seniors age 60 and up, $3.50; ages 3 to 12, $2; ages 2 and under, free. **Ages 3 and up.**

This is a sure-hit for children struck with dinosaurmania. In this museum, they'll see several robotic dinosaurs: a stegosaurus whose tail wags, an apatosaurus (your children will tell you that's the same thing as a brontosaurus) whose head bobs, a triceratops whose eyes blink and feet stomp. In addition to the moving, howling dinosaur replicas—which are half the size of the real things—your children will see actual dinosaur skeletons, foot tracks, and other fossils. One of the best features of the museum is a paleontological lab, where children can watch workers chipping away at rock to free actual bones that have been dug from nearby quarries. The workers, volunteers at the museum, are happy to answer questions and explain what they are doing. When we visited, we saw volunteers working to free a brontosaurus bone that was 140 million years old. A worker gave a chip of rock to our 6-year-old, who held onto it as if it were gold for the rest of the day.

● Doo Zoo

635 Main Street. (970) 241-5225. Monday to Saturday, 10 A.M. to 5 P.M. Adults, ages 18 and up, $1; ages 2 to 12, $3; ages 13 to 18, $1.50; under 2, free. **Ages 2 and up.**

Surely, there are more innovative children's museums. And yes, the Doo Zoo is in need of some attention. But it would be hard to match this space for sheer friendliness and accessibility. Think of it as the best basement around, with puppets, toy cars, a fire engine, dress-up clothes, and a pretend post office, bank, and grocery store. The museum has space devoted to an art project and face painting, an old-fashioned switchboard, and more. This is the kind of place where children will play "let's pretend," rather than indulge in the more structured educational activities of many children's museums. But in today's high-tech world, such old-fashioned fun is a joy to watch. This is a fine place to park yourself for awhile and let the kids get to work—at their play.

● Lincoln Park

12th Street and North Avenue. (970) 244-1548. Pool open Memorial Day to Labor Day: daily, 1:30 to 8 P.M. (except Wednesday, when hours are 9:30 A.M. to noon, 1:30 to 4:30 P.M., and 5 to 8 P.M.). Adults, $3; ages 3 to 17 and seniors ages 60 and up, $2.25; ages 2 and under, 50 cents. Water slide: Monday, Tuesday, Thursday, and Friday, 10 A.M. to 1 P.M. and during pool hours. Wading pool: Monday, Tuesday, Thursday, and Friday, 9:30 A.M. to 1 P.M. Water slide, an additional $1.50. Wading pool, 50 cents per child. Family admission, $8 after 5 P.M. and all day Sunday. Free for ages 17 and under on Wednesday (evening hours excluded). **All ages.**

On a hot summer day, this is the perfect spot to find relief. The park boasts three swimming areas: a kiddie pool, beginning area, and deep section. Children will be thrilled with the 351-foot water slide, and for a faster ride down the slide, tubes are available. Keep in mind that the pool is generally occupied with swimming lessons in the morning, although those interested in the water slide or wading pool can pay for those attractions only during these times. In addition, you'll find lighted tennis courts, playgrounds, picnic areas, and a nine-hole golf course in the park.

● Museum of Western Colorado

*248 Fourth Street. (970) 242-0971. Winter: Monday to Saturday,
10 A.M. to 5 P.M.; Sunday, noon to 5 P.M. Adults, $2; ages 2 to 17, $1.*
Ages 6 and up.

You've heard about notorious outlaws like Butch Cassidy and Kid
Curry. You know the legend of Annie Oakley. This is where you can see,
among other things, the weapons (or models of weapons) they brandished
and read about their exploits. This museum's room of historic firearms
may not be politically correct in this age of concern about guns and vio-
lence, but it's interesting, nonetheless, to see a Winchester rifle used by
Tom McCarty, who was implicated in robberies with Butch Cassidy and
the Wild Bunch, or a 45.70 caliber carbine used at the Battle of Little
Bighorn. And who can resist a "Wanted" poster of Curry that describes
his occupation as "cowboy, train robber, horse and cattle thief, holdup
man and murderer"? It's just one step removed from an Old West movie.

The museum also features a Pioneer Room, with artifacts of life in
Grand Junction from the 1800s on up, including photos of the Palisade
Peach Queen of 1921, an old top hat and cane, and an admonition from
a program of the Park Opera House that "Gentlemen Do Not Spit on the
Floor."

The East Wing Gallery features Indian items, a butterfly collection,
a mineral display, and a timeline that starts in 1880 and goes through
1950. Here, again, you'll see items of everyday life—such as a child's
construction set, beaded purses, ice tongs, and more—that were once the
latest must-have purchases and now something to explain to the kids.
("See that Kodak Brownie camera? Mommy used to have one just like
it. . . ."!)

● Rabbit Valley Research Natural Area and Trail Through Time

Twenty-five miles west of Grand Junction on Interstate 70 at Exit 2. Free.
Ages 6 and up.

Children will enjoy exploring this desolate spot, once lush forest
and swampland where diplodocus, brachiosaurus, allosaurus, and other
dinosaurs roamed the land and then died, leaving their bones as evidence.
You'll need to pick up a brochure at the Dinosaur Valley Museum (see
entry) before heading out to this quarry, approximately 30 minutes from
town, where you'll walk 1½ miles during a self-guided tour. The brochure will point the way past dinosaur vertebrae still embedded in rock,
points of geological interest, plant fossils, and finally, the vertebrae, partial ribs, and femur of a young diplodocus.

The trail is moderately steep at points (but pays off with some great views), and the brochure notes that the hike will take approximately 90 minutes, although we finished in an hour. If you are short of time (or energy), we recommend going to stop number 2 (the camarasaurus vertebrae) and turning back, or starting at the end of the trail and hiking to stop number 11 (the diplodocus skeleton). These are the points that will most interest children. Some of the other stops feature more obscure items that can be hard to spot, even with the helpful brochure. Still, this is a wonderful, educational diversion, as well as a vigorous walk.

Rabbit Valley offers a special kids day in July, where children can dig for fossil replicas, watch a real excavation and learn about the surrounding geography for a nominal fee. Call Dinosaur Valley Museum for details.

GRAND LAKE

● Amaze 'N Grand Lake
1120 Grand Avenue. (970) 627-9320. Memorial Day to Labor Day: daily, 10 A.M. to 8 P.M. (but can vary according to the weather; call first). Open weekends through September. First time: adults, $4; ages 12 and under, $3; ages 4 and under, free. Anytime thereafter, with first-time pass, adults and children, $2. For a description of this human-size maze, see Amaze 'N Winter Park entry under Winter Park. **Ages 4 and up.**

● Rocky Mountain National Park and Grand Lake
Interstate 70 to Highway 40 to the junction of Highway 34 and Highway 40, 15 miles north on Highway 34. Kawuneeche Visitor Center (970) 627-3471. Memorial Day to Labor Day, 7 A.M. to 7 P.M. Rest of year, daily, 8 A.M. to 5 P.M. Entrance to Rocky Mountain National Park: $10 per car. **All ages.**

The town of Grand Lake, about six blocks long, is the western gateway to Rocky Mountain National Park. The town derives its name from the beautiful lake at its center, the largest natural lake in the state. In the summer, you can take your kids on easy hikes along the water where they can watch people fishing and skip stones. Or you can rent a pontoon, canoe, or bumper boats at one of two marinas at lakeside. Grand Lake has a sandy beach; although the water is usually too cold for swimming, kids will certainly want to dip their toes.

In the winter, Grand Lake becomes the "snowmobile capitol" of Colorado with at least a hundred miles of trails. The town also has a 24-hour outdoor skating rink, not connected with the lake. (Skate rental is available for a nominal charge.)

The west entrance to Rocky Mountain National Park is about 1½ miles from town. You'll want to stop at Kawuneeche Visitor Center (before you get to the pay station at the park), which has dioramas and hands-on exhibits where you touch the animal skin or feel the antlers. You can also inquire there about ranger-led interpretative hikes during the summer. Also, inquire about the participatory ranger-led programs for kids, ages 6 to 12, on topics as diverse as fly fishing; maps and compasses; and birds. On Wednesday and Saturday nights, the center sponsors programs, usually a film and question-and-answer session on topics such as beavers and the antler kingdom, from 7 to 8 P.M.

In the fall, the aspen leaves turn golden and Grand Lake becomes even more spectacular. Less crowded than the Estes Park side of Rocky Mountain National Park, the Grand Lake side is also a good spot to view elk in the fall.

IDAHO SPRINGS

● Mount Evans and Echo Lake

Interstate 70 West to Idaho Springs, exit 240, south on Highway 103, 14 miles to Echo Lake. At Echo Lake, make a right on Highway 5 and follow the signs to Mount Evans. Just past Echo Lake, pay station, $6. **All ages.**

Although Pike's Peak gets all the glory, Mount Evans can boast that it's closer to Denver, and at 14,300 feet, somewhat higher than its more famous cousin. The views are spectacular and you may even glimpse a mountain goat or two. However, the mountain road is winding and steep, and as you wind toward the top, there are no guardrails. Most people make it as far as Echo Lake, a natural stopping point about halfway to the summit. Echo Lake has picnic facilities and hiking and fishing (bring your own equipment). In the summer, Echo Lake Lodge (303-567-2138) offers food and rest rooms.

Just after the lodge, you'll spot the turn-off that will take you to Summit Lake, another nine miles, and on to Mount Evans, 14 miles from Summit Lake. The road is open in summer only. About three miles up this road, you'll come to Mount Goliath, a parking area where you can get out of your car for a closer look at the vistas, the mountain run-off, the lingering snow, and the stunted trees that have survived the altitude and weather. The topography is unforgettable, even for the kids.

Beyond Mount Goliath, the road becomes edge-of-the-world frightening, with no guardrails and sheer drops. Frankly, even our kids were scared and asked us to turn back.

However, if you're an experienced mountain driver or undaunted by such things, continue to Summit Lake (no facilities) and on to the top, where you'll be looking down on the mountains with the same rush that mountain climbers must feel when they finally reach the peak.

● St. Mary's Glacier

Interstate 70 West to Fall River Road, exit 238 (follow the signs). Daily. Free. **Ages 6 and up.**

There aren't many places where you can see a real honest-to-goodness glacier. However, to get to this glacier, you have to walk about three-quarters of a mile up a steep, boulder-and-rock-strewn path, the kind of path that's so demanding to hike that everyone you pass on your way down will stop to ask you how much farther to the top.

Nevertheless, the pay-off is great. Once at the top, you come to the picturesque St. Mary's Lake with the glacier as backdrop. There are numerous run-offs to wade through, and our 5-year-old ran back and forth across a small creek that had strategically placed stones. You can hike along the lake or up to the glacier or stop and picnic in this picture-postcard setting. If you decide to walk or play on the glacier, beware that people have gotten seriously hurt, falling or sliding. Watch your children and warn teens in particular: It's easy to find yourself slipping quickly downhill with no means to stop and sharp rocks at the bottom.

Take the hike slow and easy, and rest frequently. It's particularly tough going for those not used to this altitude and younger than about age 6. Wear closed-toed shoes suitable for hiking, and bring a water bottle. Definitely consider a backpack carrier if you plan to bring a toddler. You might also consider long jeans for the preschool set, to avoid scrapes and cuts if they trip on the numerous stones. Once you reach the half mile mark or so, the path levels out and the walk gets easier.

For such a popular place, the actual entrance to St. Mary's is poorly marked. You'll know you've come to it when you see a lot of cars pulled off to the side of the road and shortly after you've passed the only gift/concession/horseback riding place in the area.

You can easily spend a half-day here. To round out a day trip from Denver—if you're not too tired—you may want to visit Georgetown or stop in Idaho Springs for an ice cream treat.

KEYSTONE

● Keystone Gondola

In the River Run Village. Take Highway 6 to Montezuma Road; turn south and follow the signs. (970) 468-4130 or (800) 451-5930. End of June to early September: Monday to Thursday, 9:30 A.M. to 3:30 P.M.; Friday to

Sunday, 9:30 A.M. to 7:30 P.M. Adults, $10; ages 6 to 14, $6; under 6, free. Bike transport, $5 extra. **Ages 3 and up.**

Take in the view two miles high as you are whisked to the top of Keystone Mountain via the gondola. Children will enjoy the novelty of the ride, and once at the top, you can grab lunch at the Outpost, hike, or if you brought along a bike, ride down the many designated trails.

● Keystone Ice Arena

At Keystone Lake, in the center of Keystone Village, Keystone Resort. (970) 468-4130 or (800) 451-5930. Daily, 10 A.M. to 10 P.M., as long as the lake remains frozen. Adults, $8.50; ages 13 to 17, $7.25; ages 5 to 12, $5.25; ages 4 and under, $1. Skate rental: adults, $6.25; ages 13 to 17, $5.25; ages 5 to 12, $2.25. Sled rental, $4.75 per hour. Hockey stick rental, $2.25 per day. Hockey pucks (for sale only), $4.50. **Ages 2 and up.**

This is a great spot for skating, which gets underway, generally, around Thanksgiving, when the lake has frozen over, and closes around mid-March, when it begins to thaw. Two machines clear the ice periodically, and a section of the lake is set aside for hockey. Enter the building at the west end of the lake. Here, you can store your things and rent skates as well as hockey sticks. Sleds are also available for rental for those who prefer to pull their toddlers behind them. The only drawback here, as with most outdoor rinks, is that there are no rails to hold onto. But a helping hand is good enough for most kids, who have a blast slip slidin' the time away. Lessons are available by reservation and can be taken on a one-time basis. Cost is $30 for a half-hour private lesson; $9.25 for a half hour group lesson.

Be sure to call before coming, as hours can vary according to the weather. In the summer, this is the spot for paddleboating and other lake activities. See SportShaq entry for details.

● Keystone Stables' Petting Farm

On Highway 6, turn south at the main stoplight in Keystone (Keystone Road), veer left, then turn right on Soda Ridge Road. (970) 468-4130 or (800) 451-5930. Mid-June to Labor Day: daily, 8 A.M. to 4 P.M. Free. **Ages 2 to 10.**

One of many places you can go horseback riding in the mountains, Keystone Stables also offers an alternative for the younger kids: a petting farm, complete with sheeps, pigs, goats, calves, and chickens. Children can walk in the pens and see the animals up close. Be sure to take the kids around the horse stables to the back of the facility, where they can peek at the giant draft horses that are also housed here. They will be thrilled at the size of these animals. Pony rides are also available at the stables for children ages 3 to 7; at $5 for a 15-minute ride and $10 for a half hour, however, they are quite pricey.

● Rocky Mountain Nature Walks

Organized at the Activities & Dining Center in Keystone Village. (970) 468-4130 or (800) 451-5930. Summer (days and times vary). Adults, $10.50; ages 5 to 12, $8.75. Not recommended for young children. **Ages 9 and up.**

Guided hikes of varying difficulty are offered through Keystone Resort nearly every day, generally in the mornings before the typical Colorado afternoon rain showers. Hikers explore Colorado high country, wildflowers, or beaver habitats during the treks, which generally last two hours. Organizers recommend that children be at least age 9 to understand the guide's talk along the way.

For young children, the most popular hike by far is the Beaver Prowl (usually from 8 to 10 P.M.). On this walk, children learn what it feels like to be a beaver as hikers are chosen to don mitts (to simulate a beaver's webbed feet), opaque goggles (to simulate the film beavers have over their eyes), buck teeth, ear flaps, and a tail. (If hikers feel silly, at least they can take these impediments off, unlike their furry friends!) The hike winds up at a beaver pond, where there is a 50 percent chance, say organizers, of seeing the animals.

All hikes leave from the SportShaq and include juice, a snack bar, and ponchos in case of rain. Reservations at least one day in advance are recommended.

● SportShaq

Southeast end of Keystone Lake in Keystone Village. (970) 468-4130 or (800) 451-5930. Early summer and late fall, hours vary; call for times. Memorial Day to Labor Day: 9 A.M. to 8 P.M. Paddleboats, $10 per half hour; one-person kayaks, $8 per half hour; two-person kayaks, $9.75 per half hour; canoes, $9.75 per half hour; regular bikes, $6.75 per hour; mountain bikes, $9.25 per hour; kid's bikes, $5.75 per hour; kids' trailers for bikes, $9.50 per hour (discounts for half- and full-day bike rental); in-line skates, $8.25 per two hours. Prices are discounted early summer and late fall. Volleyball, horseshoes, tetherball, ping-pong: free. **All ages.**

The SportShaq is the recreational activity headquarters for all Keystone busybodies. Here, you'll find paddleboats, kayaks, and canoes for rent, as well as many styles of bikes. And if you're just looking for a volleyball or some ping-pong paddles to try your luck at the nearby net or table, just ask. The staff will be happy to loan the equipment free of charge.

The SportShaq is located at the southeast end of Keystone Lake. To the side of the building, there's a small, sandy playground (ask for loaner toys, including shovels and buckets, at the SportShaq). You'll also find a volleyball net setup as well as horseshoe courts and a ping-pong table.

Bike trails run past the building and along a nearby creek, for those who like to stick close to home. But you can also take a bike on the Keystone Gondola (see entry) for more difficult and remote mountain terrain.

Boating is a fine option here, and children will especially enjoy a spin out on a paddleboat. Each paddleboat seats four adults or two adults and four children; lifejackets are provided. We recommend buying a bag of duck and fish food for $1 to take along on the ride; children will delight in watching the ducks follow the boat as the birds gobble up their moveable feast.

Or, if you just want to spend a quiet hour or so in this lovely setting, why not buy a few bags of duck and fish food and let your children sprinkle the pellets over the water from the pier? They will love watching the variety of fish surface for mealtime. Meanwhile, you can lay back for a wonderful respite.

LEADVILLE

● Healy House

912 Harrison Avenue. (719) 486-0487. Memorial Day to Labor Day: daily, 10 A.M. to 4:30 P.M. Adults, $3; ages 6 to 16, $2; ages 6 and under, free. **Ages 10 and up.**

A knowledgeable volunteer greets you at the door of the Healy House and gives you its brief history—it was predominantly a boarding house—before sending you on your self-guided tour. You will also receive a children's self-guided tour leaflet with items they can spot along the way, such as musical instruments used for entertaining friends and the least-identified item on the tour: a pencil sharpener in the smoking room. You'll see some beautiful treasures, such as the mahogany desk that was given to Colorado Governor and Leadville Mayor Jesse McDonald in the early 1900s and a collection of turn-of-the-century toys. Note, however, that most of the rooms are cordoned off so that you can peer inside but not enter.

● Leadville, Colorado & Southern Railroad

326 East 7th Street. (719) 486-3936. End of May to mid-June, daily, 1 P.M. Mid-June to early September: daily, 10 A.M. and 2 P.M. Early

*September to early October: daily, 1 P.M. Adults, $22.50; ages 4 to 12,
$12.50; under 4, free.* **Ages 5 and up.**

There's nothing quite as exciting as a conductor calling "All aboard"
and the giant engine of the train hisses and roars to life. The Leadville,
Colorado & Southern Railroad takes you on a 2½-hour, scenic roundtrip
ride from Leadville to the Climax Mine, once a major player in the mining
game. The train stops once for a 15-minute break at the French Gulch
water tower where you can get off, look around, and stretch your legs.
The trip is narrated, and the conductor will point out old telegraph wires,
wildlife, and other points of interest.

This is a very child-friendly trip—there are rest rooms and a conces-
sion/gift shop on board, and you can move from seat to seat and car to car
(there are open-air, semi-enclosed, and all-weather cars). Railroad personnel are friendly and helpful. Take note, though, that the trip is on the
long side and the novelty may wear off long before the ride is over. Nevertheless, this is a good way to sample a quickly vanishing piece of Americana and enjoy some beautiful mountain scenery to boot. You might want
to bring a sweater or jacket because the weather can be cool.

● Leadville Heritage Museum and Gallery
*9th Street and Harrison Avenue. (719) 486-1878. Early May to October:
daily, 10 A.M. to 6 P.M. Adults, $2.50; ages 6 to 16, $1.50; ages 6 and
under, free.* **Ages 10 and up.**

This museum chronicles Leadville's history with artifacts and
dioramas—similar to those at the National Mining Hall of Fame &
Museum (see entry), and changing exhibits. The second floor has a model-
size replica of Leadville's famed Ice Palace, a skating rink and dance hall
that was constructed completely of ice around the turn-of-the-century.
Unusually warm weather caused the palace to melt prematurely a few
months after construction.

● The Matchless Mine Cabin
*One mile east from Harrison Avenue (Highway 24) on East 7th Street.
(719) 486-3900. Memorial Day to Labor Day: daily, 8 A.M. to 5 P.M.
Closed the rest of the year. Adults, $3 ; ages 6 to 12, $1; ages 5 and under,
free.* **Ages 5 and up.**

In 1899, Senator H. A. W. Tabor's last words to his wife, Baby Doe,
were "hang onto the Matchless." In the richest silver strike in the state,
Tabor had made his fortune from the Matchless Mine only to lose it in the
Silver Panic of 1893. Taking him at his word, Baby Doe lived the rest of

her life in a one-room cabin adjacent to the worthless mine. She was found frozen to death—some say in the shape of a cross—in the cabin in 1935.

The cabin, little more than a shack, hauntingly illustrates the riches-to-rags epic of the colorful Tabors, once prominent members of Denver's society. Their life is chronicled through old newspaper clips and photographs in the sparsely furnished room. Kids can also peer into the mine shaft and adjacent mining shed in this picturesque locale, which is an eerie contrast to the stark cabin. Baby Doe and the Tabor name are such an important part of Denver lore that a trip to Leadville would not be complete without a stop here.

● The National Mining Hall of Fame & Museum

120 West 9th Street. (719) 486-1229. First of May to end of October: daily, 9 A.M. to 5 P.M. November to April: Monday to Friday, 10 A.M. to 2 P.M. Adults, $3.50; ages 6 to 12, $2; under age 6, free; seniors ages 61 and up, $3. **Ages 3 and up.**

Despite a stuffy name, this is a child-friendly museum, with educational hands-on exhibits, some interesting collections of minerals and precious metals, and a replica of a hard-rock mine, a coal mine, and a cave.

The museum, in a restored Victorian schoolhouse, has numerous rooms to wander through, named according to the treasures kept there. Hence, the Scale Room has a variety of scales—including one that's five feet tall—used to weigh metals. The Fluorescent Room has black lights to bring out the colors in the rocks. The Diorama Room features 22 hand-carved dioramas depicting the history of gold mining. Of most interest to kids is the replica of the hard-rock mine next to the Diorama Room. A quick walk through will give you a real feel for what the miners endured working in the dark. You can also walk through the coal mine and the prospector's cave, which has a quartz wall, a wooden bridge, and running water. For the younger set, there are Etch-a-Sketches to play with under a display sign, Design Your Own Mine.

Although kids groan at the idea of educational exhibits, the hands-on ones here are fun and informative. One exhibit asks where we find certain minerals in the home; press the button on a particular mineral and a button lights up in the home to show you. One exhibit gives the names of minerals found in common household items, challenging you to figure out which minerals are found in toothpaste, the toaster, an alarm clock, the shower. One room of the museum is called the Magic Room of Industrial Minerals, a walk through a miniature house that depicts where you'll find minerals on a large scale. We found it intriguing; so did the kids. Plan on spending 45 minutes to an hour here, possibly longer if you're with older children.

REDSTONE

● Redstone

13 miles south of Carbondale on Highway 133. (970) 963-1890 (Carbondale Chamber of Commerce). **All ages.**

Known as the "Ruby of the Rockies," Redstone is a small town—basically one block of shops and quaint houses—nestled in a valley surrounded by daunting red cliffs. The Crystal River runs beside the town and, in winter, with the snow falling and sleigh rides operating, you'll feel as if you took a giant step back in time. In short, it's a nice, idyllic setting if you don't mind a rather out-of-the-way diversion as you travel between Glenwood Springs and Aspen.

Visitors can browse through the gift shops and art gallery here, let the young ones loose on a small playground, or enjoy a picnic at one of the public picnic tables overlooking the river. There's a general store with a limited selection of food; this is also a great place to stop for an ice cream cone. If you're looking for more active endeavors, the usual mountain fare is also available, including mountain biking, horseback riding, and camping.

Visitors might be tempted to take a tour of the historic Cleveholm Manor Redstone Castle, built by the founder of Redstone, industrialist John Cleveland Osgood. The 42-room Tudor mansion situated on a hillside just past the main strip of town serves as a bed-and-breakfast inn and is often the site of special events, such as weddings. Tours are offered daily throughout the summer and on weekends during winter; inquire in town for tickets and times. But one word of warning: tours are lengthy (about an hour and a half) and kids under age 10, in particular, will quickly lose interest.

SNOWMASS

● Anderson Ranch Arts Center

5263 Owl Creek Road. (970) 923-3181. Self-guided tours: summer, Monday to Friday, anytime after 4 P.M.; Saturday and Sunday, anytime; winter, 9 A.M. to 5 P.M. weekdays. Guided tours: summer, 4 P.M.; other times by reservation. Free. **Ages 6 and up.**

If your children are the least bit interested in art and the process of turning raw materials into something others love to behold, it's well worth making a stop here. Artists flock to this beautiful spot in the mountains to participate in visiting artist programs, residency programs, workshops, and lectures. They ply their crafts on these four acres, where various cabins house studios of nearly every discipline, including photography, painting, ceramics, and woodworking. Visitors are invited to tour the facilities and, when artists are inclined (and they often are), chat with those at work. From the sterilelike photo studio to the clay-spattered ceramics room packed with bowls and cups waiting to be fired in the kiln, your children will enjoy seeing art in progress and having a chance to speak with real-life artists. (One caveat: The formal artist programs take place from June to August and from October to May. If you are visiting in late September or May, the studios are likely to be empty.) Such tours are on an entirely informal basis and the hours listed are somewhat arbitrary. Visitors are welcome to stop by at almost any time and inquire about touring the grounds.

If you are in Aspen for an extended period of time, check out Anderson Ranch's catalog of classes. During the summer, the center offers many workshops for children, ages 6 to 8 or 9 to 12, which can range from weaving and Native American art to photography.

In addition, lectures on various disciplines are offered in a large tent regularly throughout the summer. Surprisingly, the lectures, where colorful slides are flashed on a large screen, tend to captivate even young children. And when the kids get restless, there's a playground just outside the tent—put there for just that purpose.

● Krabloonik Kennels

Follow Brush Creek Road to Divide Road, turn right, and follow to the end of the pavement. (970) 923-4342. Tours: Mid-June to Labor Day, Wednesday to Monday, 11 A.M. and 2:30 P.M. Tour is one hour. Adults, $4.50; ages 10 and under, $4. Winter dog sledding: adults, $185; children, ages 3 to 8, $120 (includes gourmet lunch). No kids under age 3 on sleds. **Ages 3 and up.**

Krabloonik Kennels is actually a dog-sledding facility, featuring one-day, 10-mile dogsled trips with 12 dogs harnessed to a sled.

During the off-season, the kennels will introduce you to the sport with an educational tour on the subject. The tour includes a five-minute video on dogsledding and a demonstration of sled-building. Kids can pet the huskies—all 220 of them—at the end of the presentation.

Dog-loving kids will find this a change of pace from the outdoor activities so popular here. However, it can be unnerving to have so many dogs barking at once; younger kids or those who don't like the animals may be frightened. Wear sunscreen and sunglasses to protect you from the bright sun. Note that the approach to the kennels is somewhat of a steep climb up and down stairs and may leave you somewhat breathless at this altitude.

● Snowmass Rodeo

Snowmass Stables, Brush Creek Road (the main road into Snowmass). (970) 923-4433. Starts at the end of June and runs approximately 10 weeks, Saturday and Wednesday nights only, 7 P.M. Barbecue dinner, 5 P.M. Rodeo only, adults, $15; ages 3 to 10, $9; under age 3, free. Dinner: adults, $12.95; ages 3 to 10, $7.95; under age 3, free. **Ages 3 and up.**

Colorado cowgirls and cowboys compete each week at this local rodeo in Snowmass, which is fast-paced and fun. Visitors are invited to arrive at 5 P.M. for a barbeque dinner, but even those who don't wish to pay the extra fee for a meal are welcome to enter the grounds and enjoy the activities. Children can pan for "gold" (actually coins that are hidden in a trough filled with dirt and gravel); enjoy a Western skit; sit on a saddle, or ride a mechanical bull. All of this, the owner tells us, is free of charge even to those who don't plan to attend the rodeo.

But it would be a shame to miss such fun. Kids will delight in watching real-life, dust-raising, bronco-busting in this intimate setting. The rodeo, which begins at 7 P.M., features bull riding, barrel racing, and more. Spectators will also see another Western shoot-em-up skit, and children are invited to participate in a calf-scramble. In this event, children congregate in the arena as a host of calves are let in; those who are lucky enough to grab a yellow tag from a calf's tail win a prize.

For those who didn't eat barbecue first, concessions sell reasonably priced burgers, hot dogs, pretzels, and the like. And when the rodeo is over, visitors are encouraged to toast marshmallows in a big bonfire just outside the arena, where a few cowboy crooners are singing and strumming guitars.

Amidst the sometimes overwhelming glitz of Aspen and Snowmass, this is a sweet evening of old-fashioned fun. As an unexpected bonus to the outing, it's also a wonderful place to watch a glorious mountain sunset.

STEAMBOAT SPRINGS

● Amaze 'N Steamboat

1255 S. Lincoln. (970) 870-8682. Memorial Day to Labor Day: daily, 10 A.M. to 9 P.M.; open weekends in September, hours vary. Maze, first time: adults, $5; ages 5 to 12, $4; ages 4 and under, free. Anytime thereafter, with *first-time pass, $2. Miniature golf, first time: adults, $6; ages 5 to 12, $5; ages 4 and under, free. Anytime thereafter, with first-time pass, $3. Maze and miniature golf: adults, $8; ages 5 to 12, $7.* **Ages 3 and up.**

For a description of the human-size maze, see Amaze 'N Winter Park entry under Winter Park. This attraction also offers an 18-hole miniature golf course.

● Fish Creek Falls

North on 3rd Street from Lincoln Avenue, continue to Oak Street and follow the signs. Upper parking lot (paved and handicap accessible) $3 per car; lower parking lot, free. **Ages 3 and up.**

This is a not-to-be-missed Steamboat attraction. A short scenic walk—about 200 yards—brings you from the parking lot to the base of the spectacular 283-foot waterfall where townspeople once gathered to catch fish for the winter. Visitors can view the waterfall from the wooden footbridge at the base. Wear closed-toed shoes; the path is pebbly. (There is also a wheelchair-accessible path.)

More ambitious hikers can continue up the trail about seven miles to Long Lake, which feeds the waterfall. It's not a loop trail, which means a 14-mile round-trip hike. There are a few small waterfalls along the way to make the hike interesting, but it's a long trek and the power of the water-fall is easily enjoyed from the base. If you do take the longer hike, you might want to bring a picnic.

● Howelsen Park and Howelsen Hill

Take Route 40 into downtown Steamboat, turn left at 5th Street, then go two blocks and cross the bridge, make a right in front of the rodeo, and you'll arrive at the lodge. Howelsen Hill information: (970) 879-4300. Indoor ice skating information: October 1 to May 31 (970) 879-0341; ice skating admission: $3.50; ages 5 and under, free. Skate rental: $2. Summer activities, including rodeo: mid-June to mid-August. **All ages.**

The Howelsen Hill complex is best known for its ski-jumping facili-ties, which are the training grounds for Olympic ski jumpers and numer-ous international and national competitors. During the winter, visitors can often catch the jumpers at practice, loosely from 1 to 6 P.M., Monday to Friday. Usually weekends find some sort of competition from Nordic Combined World Cup to National Championships to alpine slalom racing to cross country racing; spectators are welcome. Every other Wednesday and Thursday night, from 6 P.M. until 9 P.M., spectators can also come and watch professional competitions. Call the Steamboat Springs Winter Sports Club, (970) 879-0695, for information on any competitions at Howelsen Hill.

For those of us who won't be flying down the ski jumps, Howelson Hill, with its tame slopes, is a good place for beginning skiers to practice—a lift ticket costs only $5 for children (ages 12 and under) and $10 for adults. There's also a free tow line for beginners, and cross-country skiers will find the slopes just right.

The complex also includes an indoor ice-skating rink.

From mid-June to mid-August, the area switches to summer activities. Within Howelsen Park, you'll find mountain biking, horseback riding (Steamboat Stables, 970-879-2306), hiking, a playground, batting cages, tennis courts, basketball hoops, a skateboard, an in-line skating park (bring your own equipment; helmet required), and a **BMX** course (helmet and protective gear required; bring your own equipment).

On Friday and Saturday nights, the Steamboat Springs Pro Rodeo series rounds 'em up at 7:30 P.M. (Adults: $10; ages 12 and under with adults, free). At 6:30 P.M., before the rodeo, there's entertainment and a barbecue priced separately (dinner is ordered from a menu).

● Jack Schwall Memorial Park Playground
Amethyst Drive, next to Strawberry Park Elementary School. Follow the signs to Strawberry Park from 7th Street, turn left on Amethyst Drive. Free.
Ages 2 to 10.

Is it a castle or a fortress? This engaging playground structure that looks like either is a favorite of locals and the perfect outlet for the boundless energy of tots to preteens. Designed by architect Bob Leathers and built by the community, the wooden structure is sturdy enough to hold adults, who can scramble with their children across swinging bridges and up and down planked stairs. Kids can swing, slide, and climb in and out of the wall of tires. A short drive or bike ride (there's a bike trail) from town, the playground is a perfect way to cap off a day kid-style.

A second castle/fortress playground is behind the Soda Creek Elementary School at Del & Doris Scott Memorial Park. Follow 8th Street to Pawintah Street where the playground will be visible. Despite the names, neither of the playgrounds is connected to a park per se; rather, they are part of the elementary schools. There are no public rest rooms or other facilities.

● Steamboat Smokehouse
Thiesen Mall, 9th Street and Lincoln Avenue (look for the green awning). (970) 879-5570. Daily, 11:30 A.M. to 11 P.M. (serving stops at 10 P.M.).
All ages.

From the moment you're given a basket of peanuts, you're home-free at this restaurant. Younger kids will be busy all through the meal shucking peanuts and tossing the shells on the wooden floors. And that's the kind of casualness that sums up this popular Steamboat restaurant.

To add to the informality, the food is served in baskets. Barbecue is the specialty—ribs, beef—as well as "road kill specials" like buffalo roast. Kids' meals, priced around $3.95, run the gamut from chicken strips to peanut butter and jelly. If you don't want to wait, choose off-hours to dine, before 6:30 or after 8:30 P.M. for dinner. No reservations are accepted.

● Steamboat Springs Health and Recreation Association ◆

136 Lincoln Avenue. (970) 879-1828. Daily: summer and winter, 7 A.M. to 10 P.M.; fall and spring, 7 A.M. to 10 P.M. Adults, ages 18 and up, $5; ages 13 to 17, $3.50; ages 3 to 12 and seniors ages 62 and up, $2. Water slide: summer, daily, noon to 6 P.M.; winter, daily, 4 to 8 P.M. Ten rides, $3.50 plus pool admission. **All ages.**

No matter what the temperature of the outdoor air, you'll find people bathing in these outdoor mineral pools (water temperatures run 98 to 102 degrees) and the Olympic-size lap pool (82 degrees) at this popular place in downtown Steamboat Springs.

There are four pools in all: the lap pool, two smaller soaking pools, and a standard-size swimming pool. The largest pool has a shallow end for the youngest kids and a deep end with a diving board for the more advanced swimmers. Of course, the big drawing card for the kids is the enclosed water slide. Lifeguards are on duty at all times.

You can rent bathing suits and towels here, and there is a concession stand in the summer. When the younger kids grow tired of swimming, there's also outdoor playground equipment and on-site child care ($2.50 an hour). The kids will want to spend the day; plan on two to three hours minimum.

● Strawberry Park Hot Springs ◆

From Lincoln Avenue, turn right on 7th Avenue, and follow the signs. (970) 879-0342. Daily, 10 A.M. to midnight (no one admitted after 11 P.M.). Adults, $5 ($10, Friday, Saturday and Sunday); under age 12, $2. Sunday to Thursday evenings after 5 P.M.: Adults, $7; under age 12, $2 ; Friday and Saturday evenings, after 5 P.M.: Adults, $10; under age 12, $2. Children under 18 are not allowed in the springs after dark. **All ages.**

Wind up the narrow path by car or bike (for those who are used to biking) to the secluded Strawberry Park Hot Springs, seven miles north of Steamboat.

Once owned by the city, Strawberry Park Hot Springs is now privately owned, and the springs have been tamed into two large soaking pools enclosed by natural rock. The hot springs water flowing from the hill mingles with the creek water, keeping the temperature comfortably warm. The water is four feet deep throughout, so bring inner tubes or floating devices for the smaller kids. There are no lifeguards. Bathing suits and towels are available for rental, and changing facilities are on-site, along with picnic facilities. There are no concession stands, but there is bottled water and some soda pop available. In winter, driving can be tricky. You might want to consider taking a bus or van that goes to the hot springs. Check with the Chamber of Commerce or your hotel for transportation information.

● Tread of Pioneers Museum

8th and Oak streets. (970) 879-2214. Hours, year-round, 11 A.M. to 5 P.M. June to Labor Day: daily. Labor Day to Thanksgiving: Tuesday to Saturday. Thanksgiving to mid-April: Monday to Saturday. Mid-April to June: Tuesday to Saturday. Adults, $2.50; ages 6 to 12, $1; under age 6, free; seniors ages 63 and up, $2. **Ages 6 and up.**

A refurbished turn-of-the-century house, this museum has many points of interest: a toy exhibit from the 1900s, turn-of-the-century furnishings, local historical exhibits, and a ski collection from before the turn of the century to the forties, a Ute Indian exhibit, a cowboy exhibit, and a mining exhibit. Plan to spend around 30 minutes.

● Walking Tour of the Springs of Steamboat

Pick up a self-guided tour map at the Chamber of Commerce, 1255 S. Lincoln Avenue, across from Sundance Plaza. (970) 879-0882. Free. **Ages 3 and up.**

Kids will get a big kick out of the sights and smells of the various springs that seem to well up all over town. With a self-guided tour map, you can walk past the sites of seven springs, a tour that takes about two hours.

You can also drive to the more interesting ones, among them Steamboat Spring, which once chugged like a steamboat and gave the town its name, or Black Sulphur Spring, which has the distinctive odor of sulphur. The latter two springs are well-marked and are adjacent to each other on 13th Street, just across from the Depot Art Center.

● Yampa River Park

Just south of 3rd Street and Lincoln Avenue. Free. **All ages.**

Yampa River Park has scenic pathways for strolling or biking along the Yampa River. If you feel you can do that anywhere, then this is the place to try a popular water sport—inner tubing. Several companies in the vicinity of the park will take you up the river by van and let you float back by inner tube (rental is around $7 a day). Wear a bathing suit if you don't want your clothes soaked. The Yampa River is also suitable for kayaking and even has a kayaking course.

For the less adventurous, Yampa River Park has another surprise. Tucked inside the park is a small natural hot springs wading pool encircled by rocks and literally a stone's throw from the Yampa River. Parents can picnic or sunbathe while their kids kick up their heels in the warm water. The pool is fed by run-off from the Steamboat Springs Health and Recreation Center pool across the road.

To find the pool, enter next to the Rabbit Ears Motel on Lincoln Avenue and walk across the grassy knoll and toward the Yampa River.

VAIL

● Betty Ford Alpine Gardens
In Ford Park ($^1/_4$ mile east of main village, next to the Gerald R. Ford Amphitheatre). (970) 476-0103. Open snowmelt to snowfall, dawn to dusk. Donations welcome. **All ages.**

The brochure for this wonderful spot quotes William Blake: "To see the world in a grain of sand/And a heaven in a wild flower/Hold infinity in the palm of your hand/And eternity in an hour." All quite appropriate here. This is a taste of heaven. It's one of the highest alpine gardens in the world, according to promoters, and surely one of the prettiest. Three small gardens, each with a different theme, make up this burst of color, featuring nearly 2,000 varieties of plants. An Alpine Rock Garden and Education Center are planned for the future. This is within walking distance of the Vail Nature Center (see entry) and makes a nice complement to that visit.

● Colorado Ski Museum/Ski Hall of Fame
231 South Frontage Road East in the Vail Village Transportation Center. (970) 476-1876. Tuesday to Sunday, 10 A.M. to 5 P.M. (Closed during May and October; call for an appointment to visit during these months.) Free. **Ages 8 and up.**

In the beginning, there were snowshoes to help people travel in winter. Then, thanks to Norwegian miners who passed on a new mode of transportation to their American friends, there was skiing. It all began in the 1800s in Colorado—but no need to turn history into a dry subject. Drop in at the museum in Vail Village and see it all illustrated in pictures and paraphernalia. You'll see photos of men in bloomer pants, knee-high stockings, and beret hats (not a Gortex parka among them!) and women in long skirts and fedoras, posing atop their extra-long skis. You'll see old equipment and chairlifts—and if you have the time, you can watch a video of the history of skiing in Colorado. A stop here (most kids will remain interested for about 30 minutes) will make you appreciate modern, lightweight equipment, down-filled snowsuits, and the pluckiness of the people who got it all started.

● Dobson Ice Arena

Across from the Public Library on West Meadow Drive. (970) 479-2270 or (970) 479-2271. Call for public skating times, which vary daily. Closed mid-May to mid-June. Adults and children, ages 13 and up, $5; ages 5 to 12, $4; ages 4 and under, $2. Ice skating rental, $3; sizes start at a child's 6. **Ages 4 and up.**

Although skiing is the primary sport of Vail, skating is a popular alternative, especially if the weather is rainy or too warm for skiing. This indoor arena offers public skating in a large facility in between local hockey games and other special events. Make sure you call for skating times; the schedule varies because of hockey and other special events.

● Ford Park and Gore Creek School

One-quarter mile east of main village, near the Gerald R. Ford Amphitheater. Free. **All ages.**

After a stroll in the Betty Ford Alpine Gardens (see entry), your children will no doubt trot off to the playground in this adjacent park. It's a great spot to take a break, let your kids run around, and enjoy the scenery. The park offers a beautiful setting, and the playground has all the requisite kid needs, including a tire swing and fort-like structures. Don't miss a peek at the old school house at the south end of the park. Built in 1922, it offers a view of school at the turn of the century, when one room was more than enough to get the job done.

● Eagle Bahn Gondola and Adventure Ridge

In the center of the village at Lionshead. (970) 476-9090. Memorial Day to mid-June: weekends only. Mid-June to mid-September: daily. Mid-September to end of month: weekends only. Hours: 10 A.M. to 4:30 P.M. when operating. Adults, $11; ages 12 and under, $8; seniors ages 70 and older, free; family pass (two adults and one child), $27; additional child with family pass, $5.

Bike transport, $6 extra. During ski season, nonskiing passenger, $17; children, $12. **Ages 3 and up.**

There are two reasons to ride the gondola: to get to the top of the mountain to hike or bike down, or to enjoy the scenery and experience a gondola ride if you haven't had the opportunity before. Both are good excuses to pile into these cars (each can hold up to six people) and relax as you're lifted more than a mile up the mountain. You'll see some great vistas as you travel, and kids will feel as if they're on an amusement park ride (without the screams!).

For those who plan to hike or bike, it's best to pick up a brochure at the gondola building at the base of the mountain. It will detail your options (and indicate the level of difficulty for bikers). Take a look at the informational board at the gondola building as well, which will list which trails are closed on that day.

Once at the top of the mountain, now known as the Adventure Ridge complex, you'll find several features of interest, including:

Restaurants and picnic tables.

The Vail Wildlife Center, a small hut directly in front of the gondola exit, which features several interactive displays on wildlife and local flowers. Sponsored by Vail Associates, in conjunction with the U.S. Forest Service and the Colorado Division of Wildlife, the center also offers guided tours twice a day, generally from 11 A.M. to noon and 1 to 2 P.M. The hikes are relatively easy, but guides will talk about local history, and so on, and children with short attention spans are best left behind. (Rangers recommend a minimum age of 6 or 7.)

Eagle's Nest Deck, an observation deck complete with viewing scopes and overlooking awesome vistas.

The trailhead for two self-guided hikes that feature interpretive signs: Eagle's View and Lower Fireweed. These are great trails for kids, who can walk at their own pace and enjoy the stop-look-and-listen messages along the way. (Those who hike on Lower Fireweed will end up at the top of the Vista Bahn chairlift and can take the lift to the bottom of the mountain on their gondola ticket.)

Whatever your purpose, the gondola ride is a fun diversion that could take anywhere from less than an hour, round-trip, to the better part of a day.

When winter rolls around, other activities are also available at Adventure Ridge. Beginning around early November, they include:

Tubing. Noon to 10 P.M. Adult, $12 an hour, including tube; ages 12 and under, $8 an hour, including tube.

Ice skating. Noon to 10 P.M. $4 an hour; $8 an hour, including skates.

Snowmobiling. 4 to 7:45 P.M. $40 an hour for one rider; $55 for double rider; $50, adult with youth.

Sledding. Noon to 10 P.M. $4 an hour.

Snowshoeing. Noon to 10 P.M. $4 an hour; discounts for multiple hours.

Snowboard park and half-pipes. 8:30 A.M. to 10 P.M.; rent equipment at base and inquire about lessons; these must be arranged during the daytime.

● Piney River Ranch

Interstate 70 to the main Vail exit (176); take the North Frontage Road west one mile to Red Sandstone Road, turn right onto Red Sandstone and at the third switchback, go straight onto Forest Service Road Number 700. Follow the signs to Piney Lake. (970) 476-3941. Mid-June to Labor Day: daily. After Labor Day: call for possible activities such as snowmobiling. Hours of summer activities vary; generally, 10 A.M. to 5 or 6 P.M. Archery, $8; boating, $12 per hour; fishing gear rental, $5 per hour; crafts tepees, $6. Horseshoes, volleyball, playground, petting farm, fly-casting clinics, interpretive forest service talks, free. Round-trip transportation from Vail Transportation Center, free. **Ages 3 and up.**

About 14 miles north of Vail, Piney River Ranch is a mecca of activity in a beautiful setting. You'll find a secluded, 60-acre lake (40 of the acres are actually on ranch property) with the dramatic Gore Range as backdrop. Visitors might take a boat out for a spin (rowboats and canoes are available for rent); the lake is stocked for fishing (and children's gear can be rented); and the ranch is at the trailhead of more than a hundred miles of maintained trails leading into the Eagle's Nest Wilderness Area.

That's not to mention the archery range, petting farm, mechanical roping horse, and lunch and dinner options, including a Western barbecue and Saturday night country swing dance instruction.

One of the most popular activities is Thursday Family Night Out, featuring a Western-style barbecue dinner theater, with J. B. Tucker and the Buckaroo Bonanza Bunch, who spin tales of the Wild West and play lively music. The two-hour show is $20 for adults; $17.50 for ages 12 and under.

For those who don't want to make the ride from Vail on their own, the ranch offers free bus service to and from the Vail Transportation Center. You may want to take advantage of this service; the 14-mile drive is along a winding road, has no guard rails, and can take close to an hour.

Because of the inaccessibility of the road, the ranch generally closes in early spring until mid-June.

● Pirate Ship Park
At the base of the Vista Bahn ski lift. **Ages 2 to 10.**

Located just yards from the eclectic shops in Vail Village, this is a great playground for a summertime break. Let your kids play in and around a structure built like an old ship, complete with watchtower. And when they're done, head back to the village for an ice cream treat.

● Vail Nature Center
831 Vail Valley Drive. (970) 479-2291. End of May to September 30: daily, 9 A.M. to 5 P.M. $1 donation requested; Vail residents free. **Ages 5 and up.**

The Vail Nature Center features a small museum that includes animal pelts children can feel, bird nests, a board to test your nature knowledge (with bulbs that light up to indicate if you're right or wrong), stuffed birds, and butterfly displays. Children will enjoy watching birds peck at feeders near a window, then checking their identity against a display chart nearby. But the best part about the center is the easy hiking trails outside, leading past informative plaques and along a gurgling river. Wear comfortable walking shoes and take your time; the hikes are short. Don't forget to ask about the center's special programs, including the beaver pond walk ($5 adults, $2 children), the flower walk, and the bird walk.

● Vail Public Library
292 West Meadow Drive. (970) 479-2185. Monday to Thursday, 10 A.M. to 8 P.M.; Friday, 10 A.M. to 6 P.M.; Saturday and Sunday, 11 A.M. to 6 P.M.; toddler story hour, Tuesday and Wednesday, 10 A.M.; preschool story hour, Tuesday and Wednesday, 11 A.M. **Toddlers and up.**

Never underestimate the power of the library, especially when it's raining in the mountains or when you have a great set-up for kids like this one. Vail Library has a separate glass-enclosed room with play equipment, such as a Brio train set for toddlers and a cozy reading house for elementary school kids. Just outside the room are sophisticated color computers, with games and connections to the Internet. Special children's programs, such as puppet making, are offered from time to time.

● Vista Bahn and Wildwood Express Chairlifts
The Vista Bahn chairlift begins at the base of the mountain in Vail Village; the Wildwood Express chairlift begins mid-mountain near the top of the Vista

Bahn lift. (970) 476-9090. First weekend in July through first week of September: daily, 10 A.M. to 4:30 P.M. Adults, $12; ages 12 and under, $5; seniors ages 65 to 69, $6; seniors ages 70 and over, free. Bike transport, $7 extra. **Ages 4 and up.**

The Vista Bahn provides a high-speed ride halfway up Vail Mountain. From there, you can catch the Wildwood Express lift to the top. Bring your bike along (for an extra fee), plan a hike, or simply take a round-trip ride for the scenery. Those interested in hiking or biking will want to grab a brochure that details trails and their levels of difficulty at one of the many information booths around town. For an easy, self-guided hike, try Lower Fireweed at mid-mountain, a one-mile trail that features fun, interpretive signs along the route. The Wildwood Restaurant & Smokehouse is open for lunch at the top of the mountain.

WINTER PARK

● Amaze 'N Winter Park
At the base of Winter Park Resort, off of Highway 40. (970) 726-0214. Memorial Day to Labor Day, daily, 10 A.M. to 6 P.M. Mid-June to Labor Day: 10 A.M. to 6 P.M. (Also open weekends only in early June through September.) First time: adults, $4; ages 6 to 13, $3; ages 5 and under, free. Anytime thereafter, with first-time pass, adults and children, $2. **Ages 4 and up.**

Picture a maze made of wooden walls, yourself or your children as the confused mice, and your family and friends as passionate observers, screaming at you from a deck above the maze to go this way or that. Fun, eh? Well, if you don't have a blast, at least you can sympathize with the plight of the research rat. And we promise, everyone gets out. Sooner or later. Prizes are given to those with the fastest times.

● Cozens Ranch House Restoration/Museum
On Highway 40 between Winter Park and Fraser. (970) 726-5488. Memorial Day to the end of September: Monday to Saturday, 10 A.M. to 5 P.M.; Sunday, noon to 5 P.M. Mid-December to late April: Tuesday to Saturday, 11 A.M. to 4 P.M.; Sunday, noon to 4 P.M. Closed end of September to mid-December and late April to Memorial Day. Adults, $3; ages 6 to 12, $1; under age 6, free; seniors ages 62 and up, $2. **Ages 6 and up.**

Children will discover life in the late 1800s as they tour this stage stop and post office dating to 1876. The building was the home of William Z. Cozens and family and is all that's left of a family ranch that originally covered 700 acres and contained many other structures. You'll learn how difficult the simplest chores could be: cooking on a wood stove, bathing in an old metal tub, ironing and keeping food refrigerated. The house also contains several rooms devoted to the unique people in Fraser's history: "Doc Susie," whose medical paraphernalia takes up one room, the Ute Indians, and the loggers of Fraser's early years. Staffers are wonderful at explaining the items in each room to children and involving them in the tour. They are happy to give visitors a personal tour, as long as the museum isn't too crowded.

● Snow Mountain Ranch YMCA of the Rockies ◆

Take Interstate 70 to Highway 40, continue past Fraser 10 miles, then take a left on County Road 53. (970) 887-2152 or (303) 443-4743 (from Denver area). Open year-round. Prices range from $54 for a Pinewood Lodge room to $146 for a five-bedroom cabin. **All ages.**

Snow Mountain Ranch is very similar to the YMCA's Estes Park Center (see entry under Estes Park): it offers a camplike atmosphere for families who come to stay overnight and partake in the endless list of activities provided. Situated on 5,100 acres of land about 30 minutes from Rocky Mountain National Park, the facility serves about 50,000 visitors each year, who enjoy hiking, swimming in an indoor pool, hayrack rides, biking, and the many other activities.

While the setup of both places is more alike than different, there are noted distinctions. Here are a few things that make Snow Mountain different:

Unlike the Estes Park Center, which is just outside the tourist-oriented Estes Park, Snow Mountain Ranch is far from any hustle and bustle. If you prefer a more isolated, wooded location, this is the facility to choose. In addition, Snow Mountain serves far fewer people than the Estes Park facility. While the Estes Park Center feels like its own city, "Snow Mountain feels like a very small village," said Dave Thomas, director of communications for YMCA of the Rockies.

Snow Mountain has 54 summer campsites, ranging from those with no amenities to others with electricity, water, and sewer hook-ups. The sites are open from Memorial Day weekend to Labor Day weekend. (Estes Park Center has no campsites.)

While both facilities offer cross-country skiing, Snow Mountain Ranch generally receives more snowfall and features a much more extensive program, with more than a hundred kilometers of groomed trails, a Nordic Center, and a wide variety of skis for rent. In the past, the area has been a training site for the U.S. Olympic Biathlon team.

Estes Park offers mainly ungroomed wilderness trails and only basic skis for rent.

As with Estes Park Center, Snow Mountain Ranch is highly recommended, a guaranteed good time for families looking for time together and away from it all. The reservation process here is the same as it is at the Estes Park Center. Be sure to read that entry for details.

● Winter Park Resort Summer Activities

Winter Park Resort. Off of Highway 40; follow the signs. (970) 726-5514. Mid-June to Labor Day: daily, 10 A.M. to 6 P.M. (Weekends only in early June and September.) Alpine slide: adults, $6; children, $5. Zephryr chairlift: adults, $5; children, $4. Minigolf: adults, $5; children, $4. All-day and half-day activity passes available. In above prices, children are defined as ages 6 to 13; ages 5 and under and seniors ages 70 and over, free. Bicyclists riding the Zephyr Express need a $6 ticket for one-time bicycle transport. **Ages 2 and up.**

If you're looking for one-stop shopping when it comes to summertime activity, look no more. This is where the action is, a no-miss pleaser for travel-weary kids. At the base and on the mountains of Winter Park Ski Resort, you'll find an alpine slide, miniature golf, two playgrounds—one specifically geared to toddlers, another for the older kids—a mini-museum, mountain bike trails, snacks, and more. The only question is, where to begin?

If speed is your vice, try the alpine slide for a fun adrenalin rush. Take a chairlift to the top of the mountain, then clickety-clack down on a cement track in easy-to-control sleds. Children too young to pilot their own sled are welcome to sit in your lap—and they, too, love the thrill of it.

Mountain bikers—and their bikes—can take the Zephyr chairlift to the top of the mountain, where they can choose from 44 miles of trails that fan out over the area's three ski mountains. The trails are graded for difficulty. Bikes are available to rent for those who come without.

The less adventuresome will find plenty to do at the bottom of the mountain, where a minigolf course awaits, as well as the playgrounds. Also at the base, visitors can tackle Amaze 'N Winter Park, a human maze that is privately run and requires separate admission fees (see entry).

For more information on the area, peek into the Caboose Museum and Visitor Information Center. The 1945 vintage Rio Grand caboose houses pictures and plaques that tell the story of the ski area—and brochures that offer information on other activities in the region.

WOLCOTT

● 4 Eagle Ranch

Interstate 70 west to exit 157 (Wolcott exit). Follow the signs to Highway 131 north (toward Steamboat Springs). The ranch is at the four-mile marker on Highway 131. (970) 926-3372. Horseback riding: daily, 9 A.M. to 4 P.M. (970-926-1234); must be 6 years old and up to ride; no doubling up on horses. Other seasonal activities: pony rides; hayrides, sleigh ride dinners, live entertainment and Western barbecues, raft trips, and cattle round-ups. Horseback riding, $20 to $35 per person, depending on length of ride. Family discount on some activities. Reservations advised for hayrides, horseback riding, cattle round-ups, sleigh rides, sleigh ride dinners, and rafting. Cattle round-up on ranch (must be at least age 12, 9 A.M. to noon, Tuesday, Thursday, Saturday), generally June to mid-September. **All ages.**

If you have a hankering for horseback riding or a taste for Western adventure, this friendly ranch not too far from Vail and Beaver Creek offers horseback riding and a myriad of other activities year-round.

After we trotted across some lovely pastureland on horseback for an hour or so on a chilly afternoon, our guide offered steaming cups of cider to warm our hands back at the ranch. In the summer, the guide will offer lemonade. We also got to watch as the guide released the animals to run from pen to pasture for feeding time, a fairly thrilling experience for city folk. In the winter, visitors can take a sleigh ride, $10 a person, or an "animal feeding midday sleigh ride" on most Tuesdays and Thursdays, where hay is carried in the sleigh and dropped to feed the horses who follow behind.

Unless there's a private party afoot, visitors with children are welcome to mosey around this rustic place and see the animals (no charge), notably Reject, the buffalo adopted by the ranch. Pony rides, where the parent leads the child on the pony around the corral, are offered in the summer for children ages 6 and under for $5.

Lunch is offered daily in the summer from 11:30 to 2:30 P.M., featuring such items as grilled hamburgers, grilled chicken, and buffalo bratwurst, priced from $3.95 to $6.95 and including a complimentary hayride during the lunch hour. The ranch also has special Western family nights, 5 to 9 P.M., several times each summer (call for schedule).

From November through March, the ranch offers a combo platter: horse-drawn sleigh or wagon rides (depending on snow conditions) and a dinner of grilled sirloin, chicken, baked potato, Caesar salad, cornbread,

fruit cobbler and brownies, in the 1890s cabin. The entertainment includes a singer/guitarist and unlimited sleigh or wagon rides during the
evening. The price, $52.95 for adults; $29.95 for children ages 3 to 12;
$10 for children ages 3 and under, also includes transportation to the
ranch and back from most locations in Vail and Beaver Creek.

Southwest

ENTER THE LAND OF the Old West, where Indians found healing qualities in the natural hot springs, pioneers found rugged adventure in towns that sprouted overnight, and miners discovered that hardship—not riches—was the price they often paid for hope. You'll find what remains of their dreams here in the Southwest, in the form of historical museums, old mines now open to tourists, archeological sites, and more. From the dramatic ruins of Mesa Verde to the quaint mining towns of Silverton and Ouray, you can take your children back to another era.

Whatever your ultimate destination—be it the town of Durango, with its reknowned Silverton & Durango Narrow Gauge Railroad, Gunnison, with its spectacular Black Canyon of the Gunnison, or Mesa Verde, with its dramatic cliff dwellings of the Anasazi Indians, you'll find plenty of awe-inspiring scenery along the way. Some may argue, but we think Colorado's most rugged peaks and best drop-dead vistas are in this part of the state. Simply traveling around a curve in the road can bring you face to face with unforgettable sights.

There is ample recreational activity here, including boating, fishing, and some of the state's best whitewater rafting. And don't miss the many hot springs that dot the area. You'll find that the Indians were right: after a day of heavy outdoor activity, or traveling by car, these waters do have healing qualities.

ALAMOSA

● Great Sand Dunes ◆

Thirty-eight miles northeast of Alamosa off Highway 150. (719) 378-2312. Open year-round. Visitor center: open year-round, except winter holidays, daily, 8 A.M. to 4:30 P.M.; extended hours from Memorial Day to Labor Day. $3 per person, ages 17 and older; ages 16 and under, free. **All ages.**

If we had to name the seven wonders of Colorado, this would be right up there at the top of the list. The Great Sand Dunes, at the base of the Sangre de Cristo mountains, are a magnificent work of nature, rising nearly 700 feet at some points and covering a distance of 39 miles. The dunes were formed over thousands of years as eroded bits and pieces of rock and sediment were unable to blow over the mountains.

Visitors can climb the many swells; kids will delight in rolling down the sand hills, leaving their handprints and building castles in this open-ended sandbox. On one trip in August, a shallow creek had formed near the base of the sand and our kids waded and splashed as if they really were at the beach. On another visit in late October, the creek was nowhere to be found, but that didn't detract from the excitement of climbing up and down the dunes as if we had stumbled onto an Arabian desert. The older kids liked the idea of walking to the end of the dunes, a nearly impossible feat. But that didn't deter them from seeing just how far they could get.

As always, stop at the visitor center to get your bearings and watch the 15-minute movie on this spectacular sight before setting out. In the summer, kids ages 6 to 12 can participate in the Junior Ranger program. Ask at the visitor center.

● San Luis Valley Alligator Farm

Highway 17 north from Alamosa, two miles north of the Great Sand Dunes exit. (719) 378-2612. Daily, summer, 7 A.M. to 7 P.M.; winter (early September to May), 10 A.M. to 3 P.M. Adults, ages 13 to 79, $4; ages 6 to 12, $2; ages 5 and under, free. **Ages 2 and up.**

It hardly seems possible that you'd find alligators in the midst of Colorado, but here they are—80 plus, almost close enough to touch. The real business of the alligator farm is raising Rocky Mountain white tilapia, a fish sold in area grocery stores. The alligators were originally brought in to dispose of the waste from the fish processing; now they've become a major draw.

As you wander around the premises on the self-guided tour, you'll find the the alligator pond, a reptile barn with alligator eggs in incubators, boa constrictors, iguanas, and so forth, a petting zoo and a building that houses baby alligators. Our kids loved watching the gators in the pond—we spent a good deal of time trying to count them as they slid under the water or stood still enough to be mistaken for a rock or a log. Needless to say, the kids were impressed at finding alligators in such an unexpected place.

ANTONITO

● Cumbres & Toltec Scenic Railroad

Board at Antonito depot, at the corner of Highway 285 and Highway 17
West, or Chama, New Mexico, depot, 500 Terrace Avenue. (719) 376-5483
(Antonito) or (505) 756-2151 (Chama). Departs Memorial Day weekend to
mid-October, daily, 10 A.M. from Antonito or 10:30 A.M. from Chama.
Round-trip to and from Osier: adults, $34; ages 11 and under, $17. Through
trip to Antonito or Chama by train, return by van: adults, $52; ages 11 and
under, $27. Through trip to Antonito or Chama, return via your own
transportation: adults, $45; ages 11 and under, $21. **Ages 6 and up.**

Founded in 1880 as an extension of the Denver & Rio Grande, this
railroad was built to serve the mining camps in the San Juan Mountains.
Today, its 64 miles of track offer a scenic journey that, when boarded in
Colorado, climbs through rolling high country and into the San Juan
Mountain range. A trip on one of these narrow-gauge, coal-burning trains
peaks at the top of 10,015-foot Cumbres Pass, then drops into Chama,
New Mexico. You'll see beautiful mountain meadows dotted with wildflowers as well as awesome views of the Toltec Gorge during this popular
ride, which attracts more than 50,000 passengers annually.

The train offers many ride options, detailed above. Basically, you
can ride approximately 2½ hours to Osier, the halfway point, and return
by train. Or you can ride through to Chama (approximately two more
hours) and return to Antonito by van. Either way, you'll finish around
5 P.M. This makes for a long day. While all children can enjoy the
experience of an old-fashioned train ride, it's probably best to leave the
young ones at home; toddlers and preschoolers are likely to become cranky
and restless during the ride. For older children, be sure to bring books,
games, cards, and the like. There are snacks and rest rooms available on
board; hot lunches are available at Osier, or passengers can bring picnic
lunches.

It's also wise to bring sweaters, coats, and jackets, as the changes in
elevation can bring changes in temperature. In addition, the train offers a
combination of fully enclosed and semi-enclosed cars. All "through trip"
passengers will be seated in the fully enclosed cars; others are seated there
on a first-come, first-served basis only. The semi-enclosed cars, naturally,
can be cool.

For truly spectacular scenery, we recommend taking this ride in the
fall, when the leaves are in full glory.

BUENA VISTA

● Gilson Custom Leather Products

236 South Highway 24. (719) 395-6430. Summer: daily, 10 A.M. to 5 P.M. Winter: Monday to Friday and some Saturdays, 9 A.M. to 5 P.M. Hours may vary. **Ages 5 and up.**

You can't miss this shop, which is known for the antlers heaped in large piles outside on the sidewalk. Inside, you'll find all kinds of kitschy goods reminiscent of a trading post, from Indian "dreamcatchers"—a web of beads that you hang over your bed for sweet dreams—to animal skin boots and leather goods.

Buena Vista is a large recreational area, not far from Salida and Monarch Pass. The store is as much fun to browse as a museum—and you might even take home a prized pair of antlers.

● St. Elmo Ghost Town

Fifteen miles southwest of Buena Vista on County Road 162. **All ages.**

This block of ramshackle buildings offers a glimpse of life during the days when miners threw up towns as fast as they pulled on their boots. You'll view most of the wooden structures left here from the sidewalk, but there's a general store—complete with a cloth man hanging by a noose out front—that's open for business.

Surprisingly, one of the biggest attractions here for children is the community of chipmunks that has made its home across from the general store. Kids can buy food for the critters from the store, and the animals eat happily from their hands.

CANON CITY

● Buckskin Joe Park & Railway

Eight miles west of Canon City, off U.S. 50. Park (719) 275-5149: Memorial Day to Labor Day, 9 A.M. to 6:30 P.M. Also open early May and late September; hours vary. Railway (719) 275-5485: Memorial Day to Labor Day, 8 A.M. to 8 P.M. Also open March to Memorial Day and Labor Day to mid-November; shorter hours; call first. Park and railway (includes horse-drawn trolley ride): adults, $13; ages 4 to 11, $11; under age 4, free. Park only: adults, $7; ages 4 to 11, $5; under age 4, free. Horseback riding at Buckskin Joe: 30-minute, one-hour and two-hour rides available. Prices range from $3 for pony rides to $25 for a two-hour horseback ride. **Ages 3 and up.**

Just before you arrive at the Royal Gorge, you'll see the sign for Royal Gorge Country, the entrance to Buckskin Joe Park & Railway. Buckskin Joe was a Colorado mining town; here the town has been reassembled with authentically restored buildings to give the feel of the Old West. The theme park has been used in filming numerous movies and TV shows. (There are loads of signs pointing out exactly where such memorable flicks as *The Duchess and the Dirtwater Fox* were made and even a movie building with photos of the stars.)

The entertainment is kid-pleasing: gunfight skits staged throughout the day in the center of the town, "hangings," and a not-to-be-missed magic show that our kids were still talking about some time later. There's also a human maze to explore. However, much of the town is devoted to gift shops and souvenirs, and many of the attractions, notably the gold-panning (which is unsupervised) and the very short horse-drawn carriage ride fall wide of the mark.

The railway is a pleasant 15-minute ride in an open-car miniature train to and from an overlook above Royal Gorge and—here's a surprise— you exit through a gift shop. If you're planning to go on to Royal Gorge, the train may seem a bit redundant. However, we recommend taking the package deal to avoid being nickeled-and-dimed to death. As for whether to couple this with Royal Gorge or bypass one in favor of the other—hey, you might as well do it all while you're in the area.

At night when Buckskin Joe closes, there's a chuckwagon dinner and Western show by Everywhere West. The shows are offered nightly May 30 to Labor Day. Seating is at 7 P.M. Reservations are required; call (719) 275-3020. Adults, $14; ages 4 to 10, $6.50; ages 3 and under, free.

● Colorado Territorial Prison Museum

1st Street and Macon Avenue. (719) 269-3015. Early May to end of August: daily, 8:30 A.M. to 6 P.M. Winter: Friday, Saturday, and Sunday, 10 A.M. to 5 P.M. Adults, $3.50; ages 6 to 12, $2; under age 6, free; seniors ages 65 and up, $3. **Ages 6 and up.**

Not just the same old museum, the Territorial Prison Museum graphically illustrates life behind bars. The Territorial Prison Museum opened in Canon City in 1871 and is now also a minimum-security facility; the museum is housed on the other side of the wall from the real prisoners in Cell House 4.

Each of the displays is set up in a cell on the second floor; the kids can wander from cell to cell to gawk at everything from an actual hangman's noose to confiscated weapons. They can peer into an isolation cell and sit in a gas chamber chair. Newspaper clippings describe some of the notorious clientele, including 11-year-old murderer Anton Woods. The gift shop consists of items made by the inmates at several prison facilities. Some of the displays will make your hair stand on end; the setup is haunting and different from most museums—and well worth a stop as you make your way to Royal Gorge.

● Royal Gorge Bridge

Eight miles west of Canon City, off Highway 50. (Note that the first gate you come to on the road says "Royal Gorge Country," which is actually the entrance to Buckskin Joe Park & Railway; see entry. Continue up the hill to the Royal Gorge entrance.) (719) 275-7507. Daily, 9 A.M. to 7 P.M.; in winter, park closes at dusk. Summer: adults, $12; ages 4 to 11 and seniors ages 60 and up, $9; ages 4 and under, free. (Admission includes all attractions.) Winter (end of October to beginning of May): adults, $8.50; ages 4 to 11 and seniors ages 60 and up, $6.50; ages 4 and under, free. **Ages 2 and up.**

Royal Gorge Bridge, one of Colorado's most popular places, is an entertainment center these days. In addition to the original attraction—the world's highest suspension bridge—Royal Gorge is now laid out like an amusement park with an aerial tram, an incline railway, costumed characters (summer only), a minitrain, a carousel, a trolley (the train, carousel, and trolley are closed in the winter), a theater, and that delightful Colorado touch—live deer. The deer are so friendly at Royal Gorge that you can buy deer food in the souvenir shops. The animals are everywhere in the vicinity, even in the parking lot, and they'll eat right out of your hands.

Once you enter the gates, here's a look at what you'll find:

Royal Gorge Bridge. The bridge spans Royal Gorge more than a thousand feet above the Arkansas River. Although wide enough for cars to drive across, most people prefer to walk. The bridge is made of thick planks with small spaces between, making crossing both fun and scary. About halfway across, a sign marks the place where someone once bungee jumped for a television show.

Aerial tram. The aerial tram gently and quickly slides back and forth 1,200 feet above the Arkansas River. It holds 35 people at a time, so the wait to get on can be long. We suggest walking one way across the bridge and taking the tram the other way. On the far side of the bridge, the tram station is an uphill walk and can be somewhat taxing for those not used to this altitude.

Incline railway. The incline railway is something like an open-air elevator ride to the gorge, where you can see the Arkansas River in front of you and the bridge high above you. The incline returns every 10 minutes, long enough to walk along the observation path alongside the river and spot the icicles still clinging to the steep canyon walls.

Playground equipment. On the far side of the bridge are a few playground pieces for younger kids.

If you want to avoid the crowds, the best times to visit Royal Gorge are fall and spring. Plan on spending at least two hours here at any time of the year. If you have to make choices because of the crowds, skip the aerial tram in favor of the incline railway.

CORTEZ

● Anasazi Heritage Center

27501 Highway 184 (10 miles north of Cortez or 3 miles west of Dolores). (970) 882-4811. Daily, 9 A.M. to 5 P.M. November to February, 9 A.M. to 4 P.M. Ruins open daily, 8 A.M. to 5 P.M., weather permitting. Free. **Ages 3 and up.**

If you are planning a visit to Mesa Verde, this museum will seem a bit superfluous, housing the same kind of artifacts you can see at the park in a much more interesting setting. If not, however, the Heritage Center offers attractive displays of Anasazi life, including arrowheads, baskets, pottery, and tools. Children will enjoy seeing the re-created pit house and will also, no doubt, spend a fair amount of time in the corner devoted to interactive exhibits: here they can grind corn with a stone, practice weaving on a set-up loom, study pieces of rock and other items under a microscope, and more.

One of the nicest features of this museum is a half-mile paved trail that leads to some hilltop ruins and a wonderful view of McPhee Lake, Mesa Verde National Park, and other southwest Colorado vistas. The hike is easy (our 3-year-old managed it well), with signs describing interesting plants and how the Indians used them along the way. The hike takes about 40 minutes, round-trip. All told, plan to spend about two hours here if you're hiking; otherwise, an hour would be sufficient.

● Indian Dancing at Cortez CU Center Museum and Cultural Park

25 North Market Street. (970) 565-1151. Memorial Day to Labor Day: Monday to Thursday, 7:30 P.M. at the museum; Friday and Saturday,

7:30 P.M. at City Park in Cortez, on Main Street in the center of town. Donations accepted. **Ages 3 and up** *for dancing;* **ages 7 and up** *for the cultural program.*

Every night except Sundays through the summer, Cortez offers authentic Indian dancing. Weeknights, the event takes place in the square adjacent to the musuem. Visitors sit on the steps surrounding the square to watch the informal, hour-long program featuring young dancers in full Indian dress who perform to the beat of a drum and the chants of their colleagues. Weekends, the dancing takes place in Cortez City Park. While these performances lack the polish of a professional show, their casualness is also part of the charm, and children are likely to enjoy the setting and the colorful costumes. Afterward, visitors are invited back to the museum for a demonstration or lecture on native crafts and lifestyles (subjects change nightly). This also lasts an hour and may not hold the interest of young ones, but it's easy to leave if your children become restless.

CREEDE

● Creede Underground Firehouse

Just off Highway 149 at the north end of Main Street. (719) 658-2374 or (800) 327-2102 or (719) 658-0811. Tour is given in conjunction with Mining Museum (check with Mining Museum or Chamber of Commerce to make arrangements to see the firehouse). **Ages 6 and up.**

Next to the Creede Underground Mining Museum (see entry), the Creede Underground Firehouse was likewise hewn from the mountain by volunteer labor. It houses nine firefighting vehicles and operates at a small yearly cost of $2,000, since it lacks exterior walls and a roof to maintain. Kids will get a kick out of seeing a firehouse unlike any they've ever seen before.

● Creede Underground Mining Museum

Just off Highway 149, at the north end of Main Street. (719) 658-2374 or (800) 327-2102 or (719) 658-0811. Memorial Day to mid-September: daily, 10 A.M. to 4 P.M. Winter: Monday to Friday, 10 A.M. to noon and 1 to 3 P.M. (Hours tend to vary in the winter; call for information.) Adults, $5; ages 6 to 16, $3; seniors ages 60 and up, $4; ages 5 and under, free. **Ages 6 and up.**

Tour guides will take you through this museum about underground mining; often director Chuck Fairchild will take you on a tour of his "baby." Fairchild and a friend lovingly carved the museum from the side of a mountain, giving it the feel of a real mine—without the claustrophic narrow spaces. The museum has equipment—drills, ore cars—actually used in Creede between 1890 and the present. Artifacts are strategically placed throughout the "mine" as if you were really entering the realm of the miner.

The project is continually being updated; Fairchild shares his wealth of knowledge on both the museum and its artifacts, gearing his talk to entertain the adults and kids. At the end of the tour, kids can paw through an ore cart to find a huge rock sample (minimal charge) to take home. The guided tour takes about one hour; if you have children under the age of 6, take a self-guided tour. Also, bring jackets or sweaters (the museum has a few jackets to lend). The mine is a cool 51 degrees.

● The Old Creede Cemetery

Off of Highway 149, just above the town (follow the signs). Daily. Free.
Ages 6 and up.

We couldn't find the original grave site of Bob Ford, who killed Jesse James, but we did find plenty of interest in this open hillside cemetery. Worth a quick stop, the "Boot Hill" cemetery conjures up gunslingers and the Wild West. The kids found it interesting to read the dates on the headstones, most of which attest to the hard lives of the early settlers, and to read the special inscriptions, characteristic of another age.

CRIPPLE CREEK

● Carriage rides

On Bennett Avenue (the main street in town, right off of Highway 67). Free (tips suggested). Summer only. **Ages 3 and up.**

Few diversions in casino-ladened Cripple Creek offer such risk-free payoff as the carriage rides up and down Bennett Avenue. Sponsored by the casinos as a way to promote their businesses, carriages are ready to be hailed anywhere along the street. Simply hop on board and take a jaunt down the road. Children will enjoy the novelty—and parents get off cheap; the rides are free, but it's customary to tip the driver a dollar or so.

● Chamber of Commerce

337 East Bennett Avenue. (719) 689-2169 or (800) 526-8777. Monday to Friday, 8 A.M. to 5 P.M.; Saturday and Sunday, 10 A.M. to 6 P.M.

If you're planning on gambling in the casinos and have children in tow, you'll need to know which casinos admit children (many don't) and which offer attractions for them. Several casinos here feature video arcades, which can provide welcome entertainment for the younger set. Check with the information booth here for a complete list.

● Classic Victorian Melodrama and Olio

Imperial Hotel, 123 North Third Street. (719) 689-2922. Memorial Day to Labor Day: Wednesday to Sunday, 2 P.M. and Friday and Saturday, 7:30 P.M. (All times subject to change; call for current information.) Fall and winter holiday programs (call for information). Adults, $10 to $14; ages 12 and under, half price. **Ages 6 and up.**

This classy hotel, built in 1896 and furnished in the period, hosts a melodrama and olio, a comedy/musical show. The show lasts about 2 hours, but your kids won't have any trouble sitting through a matinee as they boo, hiss, clap, and sing along.

● Cripple Creek & Victor Narrow Gauge Railroad

At the Old Midland Terminal Depot at the top of Bennett Avenue. (719) 689-2640. Memorial Day weekend to the second weekend in October: daily, 10 A.M. to around 5 P.M. Adults, $7.50; ages 3 to 12, $3.75; ages 3 and under, free; seniors ages 66 and up, $6.75. **Ages 2 and up.**

You'll see the train engineer stoke the engine with fiery hot coals, hear the whistle blow, and watch the steam rise on this four-mile journey through the Cripple Creek mountainside. As the train slowly chugs past abandoned cabins and mines, the engineer will offer nuggets of information about the town's illustrious past at the turn of the century, when it was the second-largest city in the state, next to Denver, and $450 million worth of gold was mined from its mountains. This is a great ride for young children as it is fairly short (45 minutes round-trip). And children of any age will enjoy the quick stop at "Echo Valley," where the engineer slows the train, blows the whistle, and asks passengers to count how many times the sound echoes through the canyon.

Keep in mind that some of the cars used on the train may be open, so the ride can be a chilly one. Bring jackets, and don't forget the sunscreen.

● Cripple Creek District Museum

Next to the Cripple Creek & Victor Narrow Gauge Railroad depot, at the top of Bennett Avenue. (719) 689-2634. Memorial Day to September: daily, 10 A.M. to 5 P.M. May, October: daily, noon to 4 P.M. Weekends only the rest of the year, noon to 4 P.M. (main building and gift shop only). Adults, $2.25; ages 7 to 12, 50 cents; ages 7 and under, free. **Ages 7 and up.**

This museum, housed mainly in an old railroad depot, offers three floors of mining-related displays. You'll see rocks and minerals, old hammers and chisels, mining helmets, and other tools of the trade. In addition, the museum offers a view of everyday life in Cripple Creek during mining days, boasting mannequins dressed in period clothing, a carriage, some old slot machines, and, especially engaging for kids, several re-created rooms on the upper level that are meant to show what an elegant early home might have looked like.

In the summer, visitors can also tour the Assay Office next door, with its extensive collection of minerals and mining equipment, and another building nearby that displays historic photographs, locally produced art, and doubles as a gift shop.

While children are likely to be bored with a long stay here, the admission is relatively inexpensive. If you're in the neighborhood and want to give your children a painless history lesson, it's worth a quick stop.

● Maggie's

In the Colorado Grande Casino, 300 Bennett Avenue. (719) 689-3517. Daily, 7 A.M. to 1:30 A.M. **All ages.**

Amid the ringing of the slot machines and the push of the crowd in the casinos, Maggie's sits like a prim and proper lady, waiting to serve those eager to escape the madness. This is a restaurant decked out in Victorian finery, with elegant tablecloths, floral curtains, chandeliers—and none of the fanfare that usually goes along with such amenities. Dress is casual and prices are reasonable, with breakfasts from $2 to $6, lunches (including burgers and fries) around $4, and dinners from $5 to $13. The restaurant offers large portions, enough to split between two younger kids. And for those who don't want their children soaking up a hefty dose of gambling fever, it's one of the few eateries you can get to without first walking through a casino. (The restaurant entrance is on 3rd Street.)

● Mollie Kathleen Gold Mine

One and a half miles north of Cripple Creek on Highway 67. (719) 689-2466. Approximately May to October: daily, 9 A.M. to 5 P.M. Adults, $8; ages 3 to 11, $4; ages 2 and under, free. **Ages 6 and up.**

Opened in 1892, the "Mollie" offered up gold until 1961, when mining stopped due to soaring costs. Fortunately, tourists now keep the mine open, flocking to the 35-to-40-minute tours all summer long. Few will leave disappointed; the Mollie Kathleen features a well-run tour that offers a real feel for what it was like to work all day underground. Within minutes of the start of this visit, you'll understand just how difficult a miner's life must have been. "Make sure everybody keeps their fingers in," says the guide, after stuffing his charges into two tiny elevators, "or else they'll be gone." The elevators then plunge a thousand feet down a tight shaft, which is mostly pitch black—and may be frightening for some children. Visitors may feel water dripping on their heads on this ride (luckily, everyone is given a rain slicker to wear, just for this reason), and claustrophobics will understandably want to stay home.

Once in the mine, patrons wend their way along underground, past ore carts and shafts where miners took on the difficult task of digging upward in search of gold. For a good look at the miner's lot in life, guides will also show you the "lunch room," consisting of three benches and a bare light bulb hanging above.

Tour leaders are often experienced miners and ours moved through the mine swiftly while offering clear, engaging information. If children aren't interested in the guide's talk, they will find plenty to look at, nonetheless, during this underground mini-adventure.

It is advisable to wear closed-toed shoes, as the ground can be wet with puddles. In the summer, visitors may face a wait, as tour groups are limited to the number of people who can fit in the elevator. Groups leave approximately every 20 to 25 minutes. There are rest rooms and a gift shop on-site.

DELTA

● Fort Uncompahgre Living History Museum ◆

West end of Gunnison River Drive, just west of Highway 50. (970) 874-8349. Tuesday to Saturday: Fort opens first Tuesday in March and closes mid-December. Second week in December: evening open house with fort lit up with candlelight (call for information). Hours: 10 A.M. to 5 P.M.; last tour at 4 P.M. Adults, $3.50; ages 6 to 12 and seniors ages 65 and up, $2.50; ages 5 and under, free. **Ages 4 and up.**

Fort Uncompahgre was established as a fur trading post around 1826. This is a small gem of a fort, with guides in period dress to show you around. The fort operates as authentically as possible, and the guides are wonderful at making history come alive. Best of all, they talk right to the kids, telling them stories about what happened when pioneers had a bad tooth or how an 11-year-old might have been traded for a blanket.

To add to the fun, the guides demonstrate barrel-making, fire their guns at a card on a stump (both missed), and toss a tomahawk at a target. After they show you how to toss the tomahawk, each member of the group, no matter how young or old, is allowed to come forward and try their luck at throwing it. For the kids, that activity alone will make the fort worth the price of admission.

Delta is about 20 miles from Montrose; if you're in that area, it's worth the drive. Note also that the fort is closed on certain days of the week, even in summer, so plan accordingly.

● Grand Mesa Scenic and Historic Byway

On Highway 65, approximately 30 miles east of Grand Junction on Interstate 70 at exit 49. Open year-round. **All ages.**

For sheer variety of scenery, this national scenic byway is an interesting drive, offering everything from desert-like canyons to orchards and alpine meadows, all dotted with more than 300 stream-fed lakes. Watching over this expanse—a 55-mile traverse—is the stout Grand Mesa, the world's largest flat-top mountain. Of course, none of this will necessarily impress the kids. To hold their interest, look into the many recreational opportunities this area offers, including cross-country skiing, downhill skiing at the Powderhorn Resort (see entry in skiing chapter), snowmobiling, fishing, horseback riding, mountain biking, camping, boating, and more.

DURANGO

● Animas Museum

31st Street and West 2nd Avenue. (970) 259-2402. May to October: Monday to Saturday, 10 A.M. to 6 P.M. Ages 12 to adults, $1.75; ages 11 and under, free. **Ages 6 and up.**

Housed in what used to be the Animas City School, this museum offers two floors of exhibits, including a re-created turn-of-the-century schoolroom. Children can sit behind the desks and look at old primers, or trot upstairs to explore a room with Indian artifacts, including baskets and pottery, or another room featuring old clothes, saddles, dolls, and toys. The museum also plans to open a furnished 1870s, hand-hewn log cabin on the grounds outside the main building.

While most of the displays here are of the behind-the-glass variety and, therefore, less engaging for children, it's worth a quick stop at this museum for a glimpse of local history. Plan to spend about 30 minutes.

● Bar D Chuckwagon Suppers

8080 County Road 250 (nine miles north of Durango). (970) 247-5753. Memorial Day weekend to Labor Day: daily, gates open at 5:30 P.M.; dinner at 7:30 P.M. Adults, $14; ages 3 to 8, $7; ages 3 and under, free. Reservations required. **Ages 3 and up.**

The sign at the entrance says "That-A-Way," the parking lot attendants wear 10-gallon hats, the shops sell coonskin caps, toy pistols, and holsters. This is an evening to revel in the myth of the Old West, where dinner is served on tin plates and the harmony of a cowboy tune wafts through the glorious night air. The Bar D is a small acreage surrounded by red, rocky cliffs. You are invited to enter the premises as much as two hours before dinner to stroll through the various gift shops, ride the miniature train ($1 extra), and listen to guitar-picking wranglers. When it's time for dinner, you'll take your spot at long, communal picnic tables and stand in a fast-moving line where your plate will be filled with the usual chuckwagon fare, including barbecue beef, biscuits, baked potato, and baked beans. Afterward, wranglers play Western tunes—some fun and feisty, others as mellow as the night. The show also includes some silliness to keep the kids engaged, such as the man dressed as a woman, whose anatomy consists of a few well-placed balloons, or the backward fairy tale of "Rendicella." (The shows are different on odd and even dates.)

While the Bar D serves a slew of people, the setting under the stars feels intimate, the entertainment is first-rate, and the food is excellent for a mass-produced affair. If you have young children, the Bar D provides help getting their dinner and drink to the table. In bad weather, a tarp covers the seating area.

The evening lasts until 9:30 P.M., which may be late for some children. But it's worth pushing the edge of the bedtime envelope for this evening, which is sure to leave you nostalgic for the time when a campfire and a few good tales were more than enough to pass the time.

(Bring sweaters. It's also a good idea to wear long pants to avoid mosquito bites.)

● Diamond Circle Melodrama

699 Main Avenue in the Strater Hotel. (970) 247-3400. First weekend in June to September: Monday to Saturday, 8 P.M. All seats, $14. Reservations recommended. **Ages 4 and up.**

Go ahead: boo the actors. It's not rude, it's just part of the fun at this much-loved melodrama that has been celebrating villains and their heroine love interests for more than 30 years. Founded in 1962, the Diamond Circle is obviously doing something right, and this is an evening your children will remember—from the introductory sing-along, featuring a piano player and tunes as divergent as "La Cucharacha" and "Grand Old Flag," to the hour-long melodrama, to the vaudeville-style variety show that wraps up the evening.

The show takes place in the historic Strater Hotel in a Victorian-style theater, complete with red velvet curtains and brass chandeliers. Families are seated at small tables, where members can order popcorn and drinks before the show gets underway. Although the sing-along is a bit drawn-out, children will perk up when the melodrama, with its flashy costumes and deliciously overwrought dialogue, hits the stage. And the vaudeville, with short skits and song and dance numbers, offers plenty of wholesome laughs.

This is a long evening, winding up at around 11 P.M. But the children we saw leaving the theater were excited and happy—not a tired eye in the crowd. Is this a not-to-be-missed event, as most travel information will tell you? Not really. But you will receive a full night of feisty entertainment, well worth the cost.

(One tip for parents of chldren who might have trouble sitting for such a long time: order seats in the side boxes. This will leave a small amount of room for your child to walk around, without disturbing other patrons.)

● Durango & Silverton Narrow Gauge Railroad

479 Main Avenue. (970) 247-2733. Train originates in Durango, stops in Silverton and returns; one-way trips available. Mid-June to end of October, daily. Departure times mid-June to mid-September: 7:30, 8:30, 9:15, and 10:10 A.M. Hours vary rest of year, call for times. Bus rides available to Silverton or from Silverton to Durango. Adults: $49.10; ages 5 to 11, $24.65; ages 4 and under, free. Concessions, rest rooms on board. Advance reservations (four to six weeks) advised. Winter holiday train (special five-hour, 26-mile run to Cascade Canyon): late November through late April (no train on December 24 or 25). Adults, $41.55; ages 5 to 11, $20.80; ages 5 and under, free. **Ages 7 and up.**

This venerable train has been chugging along pretty much since the tracks were first laid in 1881 and is a major attraction in the Durango area. You'll see dramatic scenery, including spectacular rivers and canyons, as the train makes its way to the quaint town of Silverton. And you'll experience the rare opportunity of an old-fashioned train ride. Keep in mind, however, that the train ride is an all-day affair: three hours to Silverton, a two-hour layover, and three hours back. This can be extremely long for young children. We advise taking the bus one way, which cuts one leg of the trip in half. When you take the train, you must choose open-air or closed car. With Colorado's variable weather, the closed car is generally the safer option, particularly with kids, who are likely to balk at the idea of sitting in the cold for hours should the weather turn ugly. Seats are reserved so you can't change or move from seat to seat. Pack the kids as you would for a car trip—with cards or little games to play when or if the novelty of a scenic train ride wears off.

● Durango & Silverton Narrow Gauge Railroad Yard Tour

479 Main Avenue. (970) 247-2733 or (888) 872-4607. May to October: daily, 10:15 A.M. and 2 P.M. Adults, $5; ages 5 to 11, $2.50; ages 5 and under, free. **Ages 3 and up.**

If you're visiting Durango, home of the ever-popular Durango & Silverton Narrow Gauge Railroad, you'll eventually wind up at the train station, if only to take a peek at the attraction and see what all the fuss is about. Once here, there's a good chance you'll be tempted to take the yard tour, which offers a behind-the-scenes look at the station. This is the only tour, reads the station's brochure, that offers "this degree of authenticity."

Perhaps. But authenticity isn't necessarily a compliment, as only the most die-hard of train fans will enjoy seeing scrap metal and tools used to repair trains and other day-to-day minutiae of operating this line. The tour is filled with mostly mundane sights. There is, however, one redeeming feature: the stop at the roundhouse, where children are let loose to roam inside a locomotive and caboose. Children love climbing aboard and, in the process, getting as grimy as a real engineer. We spent a good deal of time here, waiting for the children to tire of running in and out of the trains.

As we were leaving, our 3-year-old train fanatic—covered head to toe in soot—said, "Mom, that was fun!" Our 6-year-old rolled her eyes. "That was boring," she said. That about sums it up. If you or your children are train lovers, the tour will be worth your time. If not, the 45-minute to 1-hour talk will feel like centuries.

If you go, dress your children in old clothes. You will definitely be coming away with a souvenir you hadn't planned on: plenty of soot and grime.

● Durango Fish Hatchery, Visitor Center & Wildlife Museum

151 East 16th Street (north of the Animas River, just off Main Street at 16th). (970) 247-4755. Hatchery open year-round, daily, 8 A.M. to 4 P.M. Visitor Center and Wildlife Museum open May 1 to October: Monday to Friday, 10 A.M. to 5 P.M. Free. **Ages 2 and up.**

Children who love watching fish swim about will feel like they've hit the jackpot here, where long ponds hold hundreds of trout of varying colors and sizes. Visitors are free to stroll around the premises as well as feed the fish (a quarter buys a handful of food from a dispensing machine). An adjacent self-guided nature walk offers information about animals at various seasons of the year. And be sure to stop at the visitor center, which offers an interesting six-minute video on the workings of the hatchery. The center also houses taxidermy displays of animal and bird life.

● Durango Pro Rodeo ◆

LaPlata County Fairgrounds, 25th Street and Main Avenue. (970) 247-1666. First week in June to Labor Day: Tuesday and Wednesday, 7:30 P.M. Adults, $12; ages 12 and under, $5. **Ages 3 and up.**

There's nothing better for city slickers than a healthy dose of country entertainment. And it doesn't get any better than this: an evening of bull-ridin', steer-wrestlin', barrel-racin' fun. This is a small-town rodeo, where you can hear the pounding of the hooves in the dirt and the crunch of cowboys thrown to the ground by their snorting beasts. You'll take your place on the bleachers overlooking the arena, salute the flag, and watch as a host of premier cowboys and cowgirls—from little buckaroos to the big guys and gals—compete for Pro Rodeo Cowboy Association points. Rodeo clowns provide comic relief. And nearby concessions offer snack fare, such as burgers and nachos. Barbecue dinners are also available beginning at 6 P.M. Our 6-year-old ranks this as her second-most-favorite attraction statewide—so saddle up the family wagon and git on down, little doggies!

● Honeyville

33633 Highway 550. (970) 247-1474. Memorial Day to Labor Day: daily, 8 A.M. to 6 P.M. Labor Day to Memorial Day: Monday to Saturday, 9 A.M. to 5 P.M. **All ages.**

This gift shop north of Durango is filled with everything honey—from honey jars to honey recipe books to honey barbecue sauce, all for sale. The main attraction for children, however, is the glass-encased honeycomb filled with bees in the middle of the store. Where is the queen bee? With a clue printed on the glass enclosure, children will enjoy searching for the female insect. Make a quick, 10- to 15-minute stop if you're passing by and you'll never have to explain what you mean when you say "busy as a bee."

● Mesa Verde National Park ◆

Located 36 miles west of Durango and 10 miles east of Cortez on Highway 160. (970) 529-4461, (970) 529-4465, or (970) 529-4475. Park open daily, year-round. See below for hours of many attractions. Admission, $10 per vehicle; $3 per person entering via other means. **Ages 5 and up.**

There are few things more awe-inspiring than the dramatic cliffs of Mesa Verde, where the Anasazi Indians lived 700 years ago. The Indians built their homes and communities into the recesses of the impossibly steep canyon walls; today, visitors can see what remains of their villages. Driving through this park—consisting of 80 square miles—one can't help but marvel at the beauty of the surroundings in contrast to the ruggedness of the life these Indian ancestors must have lived. And one can't avoid pondering the mysteries of their existence: why did they choose to live here? How did they manage day-to-day life? And why did they disappear without a trace? These are just a few of the questions you'll no doubt ask your tour guides as you explore the many archeological sites that Mesa Verde offers.

There is much to do here, from strolling leisurely through a well-appointed museum to tackling 10-foot ladders as you climb up to the ruins of a spectacular Indian village. You can walk through major cliff dwellings as well as mesa-top villages, catch glimpses of wildlife, including deer and eagles, and view unforgettable canyons and plateaus. When planning your vacation, we suggest setting aside at least one full day for Mesa Verde, which is approximately 40 minutes from Durango (once you reach the park entrance, plan on another 30 minutes to drive up the winding road to the visitor center). You might also consider staying overnight in the park, which offers campgrounds and motel-style accommodations at the Far View Lodge, open mid-May to mid-October, (970) 529-4421 or (970) 533-7731 (during off-season).

In any case, get an early start: the park recently instituted a ticket system for Cliff Palace, Balcony House, and Long House (summer months only), three of the most interesting ruins, and the $1.50 tickets are available on a first-come, first-served basis. (Note that visitors can only obtain a ticket for Cliff Palace or Balcony House in one day. Either tour may be combined with Long House, if desired.) During mid-summer peak season at the park, the tickets are often gone by noon.

Here is a more detailed run-down of the park's various offerings. The information below is based on summer access. The majority of attractions, with the notable exceptions of the museum and Spruce Tree House, are closed to the public during the winter months. Call ahead for winter hours.

Far View Visitor Center (open daily, 8 A.M. to 5 P.M., 970-529-4543). Start your tour here, where you can obtain tickets for the Cliff Palace, Balcony House and Long House tours, as well as gather brochures and maps that will help guide you through the park. The center also offers exhibits of Native American arts and crafts and is 15 miles from the park entrance.

Archeological Museum (open daily, 8 A.M. to 6:30 P.M.). While children aren't always happy to be dragged through museums, this one is definitely worth a stop to help them visualize the ruins as they were years ago. You'll see many well-done dioramas of Indian life as well as pottery and other artifacts. The museum is just outside of the Spruce Tree Terrace, where you might want to stop for lunch or a snack. It is also situated at the head of the trail to Spruce Tree House. Combine all three for a nice morning or afternoon.

Spruce Tree House (open daily, 9 A.M. to 6:30 P.M.). Visitors can take a self-guided tour to this site, one of the easiest to access with young children. There are no ladders or steps. In addition, the path to the ruins, about half a mile round-trip, is paved, offering the only site accessible with strollers.

Cliff Palace (open daily, 9 A.M. to 5 P.M.). On the left fork of Ruins Road Drive, north of the museum, Cliff Palace is the largest ruin in the park, featuring 217 rooms and 23 kivas, and offers a first-rate look at Anasazi life in all its intricacies. Reach it via a 15-minute hike, about a quarter-mile round-trip. Although visitors must climb four, 10-foot ladders on this tour, we suggest Cliff Palace over Balcony House for parents traveling with young children, as Balcony House is more strenuous and difficult to manage. Remember that this is a guided tour only and requires tickets from the Far View Visitor Center. The tour is one hour and leaves from the Cliff Palace Overlook every half hour.

Balcony House (open daily, 9 A.M. to 5 P.M.). Also on the left fork of Ruins Road Drive, Balcony House is truly an adventure, in which visitors climb a 32-foot ladder to enter the ruin site and crawl through a 12-foot tunnel to exit. While Balcony House is fairly small, featuring 35 to 40 rooms, the view is spectacular, and the exertion required to reach the ruin leaves an unforgettable impression of what life must have been like for its inhabitants.

As stated above, young children may find this tour scary, although park spokesman Art Hutchinson notes that he has seen 3-year-olds tackle the climbs with zest. In addition, he adds that parents with children in Snuglis or backpacks also seem to manage the tour without a problem. (Hutchinson warns, however, that those with children in backpacks will have to take the backpacks off at the end of the tour and push them through the tunnel; for that reason, front carriers are preferred.) Children who aren't in front carriers or backpacks must be able to climb the ladder unassisted by parents.

Ruins Road Drive (open daily, 8 A.M. to sunset). At an intersection a quarter mile north of the museum, you'll find two, six-mile loops (one loop leads to Cliff Palace and Balcony House) that will take you past 10 mesa-top excavations and overlooks cliff dwellings in the canyon below.

Long House (open daily, 10 A.M. to 5 P.M.). The second-largest cliff dwelling in Mesa Verde, Long House offers guided tours only, which begin with a minitrain ride to the trailhead. The tour takes about one hour; walking distance is a half mile, round-trip.

Badger House and Step House (both open daily, 10 A.M. to 5 P.M.). Badger House features a three-quarter-mile trail that leads to four mesa-top ruins. Step House is a half-mile walk, round trip. Both are self-guided tours.

Other tips. The park offers food at the Spruce Tree Terrace (8 A.M. to 4:30 P.M.) as well as the Far View Terrace (7 A.M. to 9:30 P.M.) and at a concession outlet at the Wetherill Mesa area (box lunches, snacks, and cold drinks, 9 A.M. to 3:30 P.M.). Plan your trip so that you are fairly near to one of these spots at lunchtime. In addition, note that there are no rest room facilities at the archaeological sites. Be sure to stop at the concessions before any major venture to the ruins, so your children can use the bathroom.

If you have only one day in the park, we recommend visiting either the Cliff Palace or Balcony House, the museum, and Spruce Tree House for a relatively relaxed visit. Try to fit in at least one guided tour, as guides will offer invaluable information to make the Anasazi era come alive for you and your children.

Hutchinson notes that a visit to two sites per day is about as much as most children seem to enjoy without getting bored. Kindergartners through eighth graders, he adds, are at an optimal age to soak in the lessons of Mesa Verde and seem to enjoy their visits here the most.

However you choose to structure your trip here, be assured that this is a visit your family won't soon forget. Mesa Verde is worth planning a trip around, and combined with many of the Durango-area attractions, it makes for a wonderful vacation. The park ranks as one of our favorite attractions statewide, a not-to-be-missed journey through time.

● **Purgatory at Durango**
Twenty-five miles north of Durango on Highway 550. (970) 247-9000. Mid-June to Labor Day: daily, generally 9:30 A.M. to 5 P.M. Alpine slide: single ride, $8 with discounts for multiple rides; ages 5 and under, free. Scenic chairlift rides: single ride, all ages, free. Mountain bicycle lift: single ride, bike and passenger, $5 all ages; all-day pass, $12. Miniature golf: $3 per person.

(Fees for golf good for all day.) Bike rental, horseback and pony rides, and carriage rides also available. Inquire at the Activities Desk. **Ages 2 and up.**

Like many other ski areas trying to keep business going in the off-season, Purgatory offers a host of summertime activities on its slopes. You can take the chairlift to the top of the alpine slide and head down on sleds—always a hit with kids. (Toddlers can sit in a parent's lap.) You can rent bikes, load them onto the chairlift, and take advantage of the many bike trails that lead to the bottom of the mountain. And if more passive entertainment is the order of the day, you can also simply enjoy the scenery by taking the chairlift to the top of the mountain and back down.

Miniature golf is available, and toddlers can enjoy the small playground next to the chairlift. In conjunction with nearby Buck's Livery, the ski resort also offers horseback riding (including sunset dinner rides) and carriage rides.

Whatever your choice, Purgatory offers a beautiful setting, well worth the visit. Restaurants on the premises offer a variety of lunch and snack options. It's best to come early, as afternoon thundershowers can shut down the alpine slide and put a considerable damper on any other outdoor activities.

● Trimble Hot Springs

6475 County Road 203 (six miles north of Durango). (970) 247-0111. Daily: summer, 8 A.M. to 11 P.M.; winter, 9 A.M. to 10 P.M. Adults, $7; ages 12 and under, $5; under age 2, free. **All ages.**

After you've spent time running around town, frantically trying to see all the sights, you owe yourself a stop here, where relaxation is just a dip in the mineral pool away. Trimble Hot Springs features an Olympic-size outdoor pool with water that is maintained at 85 degrees. Winter or summer, children will enjoy playing in this warm pool, which is about four-to-five-feet deep throughout. There is no shallow end. For those who like to heat things up further, a smaller pool divided into two parts offers water at 102 or 108 degrees; a ledge around the perimeter is convenient for toddlers to stand on, yet still be immersed in the water.

Trimble offers a variety of snack food, including ice cream and candy. In the summer, burgers and yuppie treats, such as a chicken sandwich with mesquite sauce, are also available. The facilities offer changing rooms with lockers, showers, and bathroom stalls. A grassy area adjacent to the pool is perfect for setting up a lounge chair and soaking up some rays.

FLORISSANT

● Florissant Fossil Beds National Monument

Highway 24 West from Colorado Springs to Florissant, turn south at the town center toward Cripple Creek on Teller Country Road No. 1. The visitor center is 2½ miles. (719) 748-3253. Daily: summer, 8 A.M. to 7 P.M.; winter, 8 A.M. to 4:30 P.M. Adults, $2; ages 16 and under, free; family, $4. **Ages 5 and up.**

Despite the name, the only animal and insect fossils at this national monument are behind glass in the visitor center. Nevertheless, your kids will enjoy "A Walk Through Time," a half-mile trail in this 6,000-acre park that passes some pretty impressive giant petrified tree stumps. You can buy (50 cents) or borrow a brochure for the walk, which is coordinated with the sights along the trail. You might also want to walk the one-mile Petrified Forest Loop, which leads to Big Stump, the remains of a giant sequoia. In the summer, you can join one of the guided interpretative tours or wildflower walks. Also in the summer, stop at the 1878 Hornbek Homestead at the north end of the park, where the original cabin still stands.

Florissant is about 35 miles from Colorado Springs. To avoid over-taxing the kids, you might stop here on your way to Cripple Creek or plan a day trip here from Denver; sightseeing in Colorado Springs and heading here would make a really long day. If you're traveling Teller Road No. 1 early in the morning or at sunset, you'll find copious herds of elk along the highway.

FORT GARLAND

● Fort Garland

Off Highway 159, three blocks south of Highway 160, 25 miles east of Alamosa. (719) 379-3512. April to October: daily, 9 A.M. to 5 P.M. November to April: Thursday to Monday, 8 A.M. to 4 P.M. Adults, $2.50; ages 6 to 16, $1.50; under age 6, free; seniors ages 65 and up, $2. Self-guided tours. **Ages 6 and up.**

A natural stopping point on your way to the southernmost parts of Colorado, Fort Garland is worth a quick stop. The fort was established in 1858 to protect settlers in the San Luis Valley; its true claim to fame is that Kit Carson served as the post's commandant from 1866 to 1867.

The adobe buildings were restored in 1945 and are furnished with period and authentic pieces, such as Kit Carson's guns and cane-sword. Mannequins in period costume depict scenes from Carson's life at the fort.

Although much of the collection is for viewing only, kids can imagine great battles from inside a large furnished tent from the Civil War era.

GUNNISON

● **Gunnison Pioneer Museum**

East Highway 50 (last building on the east side of town; across from McDonald's). (970) 641-4530. Memorial Day to mid-September: Monday to Saturday, guided tours, 9 A.M. to 5 P.M. (last tour, 4 P.M.). Tours take about an hour and a half. Adults $4; ages 6 to 12, $1; under age 6, free.
Ages 6 and up.

The Gunnison Pioneer Museum is a collection of vintage buildings from Gunnison, gathered together in one spot and filled with period pieces from the area. You'll find Gunnison's first post office, a rural schoolhouse, dairy barn, railroad depot, and narrow gauge train.

To be sure, the Gunnison Pioneer Museum has the usual array of historical clothing, a collection of ranchers' hats, toys, dolls, blacksmith tools, and wagons, but each of the buildings has something just a little different to recommend it. This was the first time, for instance, that we city folks had climbed into the hayloft of a barn (now filled with equipment).

Our guide, whose family donated many of the treasures here, handed out the kind of information that makes a tour more fun—showing the kids a dog-and-horse-hair coat, pointing out the face of an Indian outlined on the hill. Our oldest child was fascinated by the large, airy, one-room schoolhouse with its old-fashioned cloakroom, different from others we've seen just by its sheer size and architectural design. Although much of the museum's collection is no-touch, our oldest was allowed to thumb through old report cards and spent a lot of time examining the school records of students long ago. We also liked the collection of old-fashioned steamer trunks and paraphernalia in the depot.

As the grand finale, kids are allowed to scramble around inside a caboose. Even if they've been on a train before, they'll get a kick out of climbing into the upper berths.

● **Monarch Aerial Tram**

At the top of Monarch Pass, on Highway 50 between Gunnison and Poncha Springs. (719) 539-4789. Memorial Day to Labor Day: daily, 7:30 A.M. to 6:30 P.M. (depending on weather). May and September: daily: 8 A.M. to 6 P.M. (depending on weather). Adults, $6; ages 2 to 12, $3, under age 2, free; seniors ages 55 and up, $5. **Ages 3 and up.**

Whew, looking for a stopping point on the way up or down Monarch Pass? This aerial tram is a nice place to stop and smell the flowers, so to speak. The four-person, enclosed gondola will take you to the top of the Continental Divide. The ride up is gradual and steady and takes about 15 minutes.

Once at the top, you'll find beautiful vistas, a little snow, and some of the vegetation that can survive at 12,000 feet. Because it can be cold and windy at the summit, the tram house keeps jackets on hand for sight-seers to borrow, a nice touch for those not expecting the extremes in temperature from bottom to top. At the base, you'll also find a gift shop with a wildlife display and a sandwich shop to pause at for refreshments.

MONTE VISTA

● Monte Vista Best Western Movie Manor
Highway 160, three miles outside of Monte Vista. (719) 852-5921. Drive-in movies shown April to mid-October (included in room rate). **All ages.**

Open the curtains of your motel room at dusk and it's show time. The drive-in movie next door can be seen and heard through the in-room speakers in almost every room of this motel.

All of the movies selected for viewing are family-oriented; however, if you don't want to watch, you can simply close your curtains and turn off the speakers. Call ahead for reservations and movies—this is a popular place.

MONTROSE

● Black Canyon of the Gunnison ◆
Fifteen miles east of Montrose via Highway 50 and State Highway 347. (970) 249-1915, ext. 18. Open year-round. Visitor center: Memorial Day to Labor Day, daily, 8 A.M. to 6 P.M.; hours vary in spring and fall and winter, usually within the range of 9 A.M. to 4 P.M. $7 per vehicle. **Ages 6 and up.**

Black Canyon of the Gunnison is nothing short of magnificent, with its dramatic cliffs and swirling rivers far below. Although the canyon is 53 miles long, only 12 miles of the gorge lie within the monument. The canyon is commonly referred to in terms of the North Rim and the South Rim. The North Rim (reached by a graveled, country road from Crawford, Colorado) is steep and should not be attempted by anyone who isn't used to mountain driving. The North Rim is closed by snow throughout the winter. The South Rim is an easy drive, at least partially accessible even in winter, with a visitor center and concession stand. The North and South Rim roads are not connected.

About six miles after entering the Black Canyon on the South Rim side, you'll come to your first overlook at Tomichi Point, just before the visitor center. Even kids who aren't generally bowled over by scenery will be wowed by the impressive view. Park the car and walk the short path that leads to the edge of the canyon for your first real look at its splendid beauty. Continue on to the visitor center down the road where you can pick up a map showing short hiking trails. The visitor center also has a few hands-on exhibits, such as a coyote skin and antlers to touch and feel.

Only experienced hikers are able to walk down into the canyon, but there are numerous short hikes to the many overlooks on the South Rim. Try the Cedar Point Nature Trail for an easy hike with kids for a spectacular pay-off. The trail has interpretative signs describing the brush and plants, and the view looks out over the painted walls of the canyon, a natural phenomena that makes the canyon look as if an artist has taken a brush to it.

You can easily spend a couple of hours here without tiring of the beauty of nature.

● **Curecanti National Recreation Area** ◆
U.S. Highway 50 between Montrose and Gunnison. Elk Creek Visitor Center: 15 miles west of Gunnison on U.S. 50. (970) 641-2337. Visitor center hours: Memorial Day to Labor Day, daily, 8 A.M. to 6 P.M. Rest of year: 8 A.M. to 4:30 P.M. (Winter hours are intermittent; call first.) **Ages 2 and up.**

The Curecanti National Recreation Area encompasses about 53 miles of the 70 miles between Montrose and Gunnison and neighbors on Black Canyon of the Gunnison (see entry). The area includes three man-made lakes: Blue Mesa, 20 miles long; Morrow Point Lake, 11 miles long; and Crystal Lake, 6 miles long. Both Morrow Point and Crystal lakes are also within the Black Canyon. All three lakes are prime fishing and boating spots. Some activities that don't require any special equipment:

Cimarron Visitor Center and Railroad Exhibits. Twenty miles east of Montrose, just off U.S. 50. (970) 249-4074. Visitor center: Memorial Day to Labor Day, daily, 9 A.M. to 4 P.M.. Closed rest of the year. Railroad exhibits open all the time.

These exhibits celebrate the heyday of Cimarron, a ranching and farming community, in the days when the railroad stopped here from 1882 to 1949. The visitor center has boxcars, a railroad stockyard, and a caboose on display. You can also drive a short distance nearby to see locomotive 278, a narrow-gauge locomotive sitting atop a railroad trestle over a stream. Here, a friendly ranger will give a short, interpretative talk (ask if they're not too busy) and kids can walk around inside the boxcar. Cimarron has rest rooms and picnic tables and is worth a quick stop.

Elk Creek Marina and Lake Fork Marina. Lake Fork, (970) 641-3048, is 25 miles west of Gunnison; Elk Creek, (970) 641-0707, is 16 miles west of Gunnison. Follow the signs on U.S. 50. Both marinas service Blue Mesa Lake. Rent a pontoon, a flat boat that drives as easily as a car, for a family outing on the lake ($25 to $27 an hour, plus fuel; rates subject to change). At Elk Creek Marina, you'll also find Pappy's restaurant, a nice place to eat with the kids and one of the few restaurants in the area.

Fish feeding at Elk Creek Visitor Center. Join the ranger every day between Memorial Day and Labor Day to feed the trout in the small holding pond in front of the visitor center. The 15-minute program includes a chat on the natural history of the area and each child gets a handful of fish food. Worth a stop if you're in the vicinity.

Boat ride on Morrow Point Lake. This narrated ride on a 42-foot open air pontoon takes you through the canyon on an hour and a half round trip. The ranger will talk about the natural and cultural history and the geology of the area and the canyon features. The boat leaves the dock at 10 A.M., 12:30, and possibly 2:30 P.M. (depending on interest). Note, however, that access to the boat requires climbing down 232 steps and hiking an additional three-quarters of a mile on level ground, although most people—and children—can handle it with ease. Reservations are required, although you often can catch a ride without advance notice. (970) 641-0402. Adults, $8.50; ages 13 to 17, $8; ages 12 and under, $5; seniors ages 62 and up, $7.50.

Guided walks, and afternoon and evening programs for families. Inquire at the Elk Creek Visitor Center.

Junior Ranger program. Kids ages 5 to 12 can earn a certificate and a badge in one day by completing a book of activities. The activities include answering questions on the fish feeding session and interviewing a ranger.

● Montrose County Historical Museum

Corner of Main Street and Rio Grande Avenue. (970) 249-2085. May to October: Monday to Saturday, 9 A.M. to 5 P.M. Adults, $2.50; ages 5 to 12, 50 cents; ages 5 and under, free; seniors ages 55 and up, $2. **Ages 6 and up.**

The Montrose County Historical Museum houses a collection of artifacts of early pioneer life. The museum is chock-a-block with farming equipment, household objects, clothing, medical items, and musical instruments in every corner. Outside you'll also find a homesteader's cabin, furnished with original pieces from the family who owned it.

As historical museums go, this is a child-friendly place without big "do not touch" signs everywhere. You can let your guard down. Many of the exhibits are behind glass, but others are out in the open. The kids can try "curling" the hair of a wig with an old-fashioned hair-wave machine and pump the pedals on a nonworking organ. The Children's Corner, although roped off, has a nice collection of dolls and toys, including the hundred-year-old hobby horse (a burro actually) that belonged to a former governor as a child.

● Ute Indian Museum

17253 Chipeta Drive. (970) 249-3098. Open year-round. (Days and hours are variable with the season.) Adults, $2.50; ages 6 to 16, $1.50; under age 5, free; seniors ages 65 and up, $2. **Ages 6 and up.**

This museum commemorates the life of Ouray, the famous Ute Indian Chief, and his wife, Chipeta. The museum houses the Colorado Historical Society's most complete Ute Indian collection with beaded clothing, feather bonnets, dioramas, and lots of photographs. The museum has a changing exhibit that often features hands-on displays. Chipeta is buried in a well-marked tomb on the grounds.

MOUNT PRINCETON

● Mount Princeton Hot Springs Resort

15870 County Road 162. (719) 395-2447. Pool hours: Sunday to Thursday, 9 A.M. to 9 P.M.; Friday and Saturday, 9 A.M. to 11 P.M. Adults, $6; ages 12 and under and seniors ages 62 and up, $3. Pool use is free to those staying at the hotel. Suit rental, $1; towel rental, $15. Rooms start at $65 in winter, $77 in summer based on two adults; surcharge added for children. **All ages.**

People claim these outdoor hot springs have cured everything from headaches to chronic arthritis. We can't attest to that, but we can vouch for the beautiful scenery, the hospitality of the staff, and the relaxation-inducing powers of the mineral water in the three hot springs pools here. After a few hours in these pools, your children will be so mellow they'll practically melt into their pillows come nighttime!

Mount Princeton Hot Springs Resort is about a 2½-hour drive from Denver, a few miles past the small town of Buena Vista. Don't let the word "resort" throw you: this is a funky, earthy place with no pretensions. You'll see locals soaking up the steam along with travelers. The small complex of buildings features a main lodge and restaurant. Down a small hill, you'll find a locker room, where your famiy can grab towels and stash street clothes, and two man-made pools that hold the springwater pumped in from below nearby Chalk Creek. On cold days, you can enter and exit directly from the locker room area. The more adventuresome can also walk down a rocky path to the river, where rings of large boulders contain small pools of hot water at river's edge. (This area is closed during months of high snowmelt run-off, generally May to July.) In the summer, a third pool with a waterslide is also open in a separate part of the facility. (The waterslide is an extra fee: $5 for 10 turns or $8.50 for all day.)

Lodging here is your standard motel variety. The restaurant serves excellent food, if a bit pricey for family dining. But children are welcome, and those who prefer something less expensive can drive a short distance into town, where there are plenty of restaurants to choose from.

The main attraction, of course, is the water. Stop for a few hours and get back on the road, or stay until the stars come out. It's a fabulous way to say goodnight to a cool summer evening.

OURAY

● Bachelor-Syracuse Mine Tour

One mile north of Ouray on Highway 550, then 1 1/4 miles east on County Road 14. (Follow the signs; part of the road is gravel.) (970) 325-0220. End of May to mid-June and September 1 to mid-September: 10 A.M. to 4 P.M. (last tour). Mid-June to August: 9 A.M. to 5 P.M. (last tour). Tours every hour on the hour. Adults, $10.95; ages 3 to 11, $5.95; ages 3 and under, free. Panning for gold, $4.95; with tour, $4. **Ages 4 and up.**

The Bachelor-Syracuse Mine got its name from the three single men who founded it in 1884. Since then, 15 million ounces of silver, valued at $90 million, and 250,000 ounces of gold, valued at $8 million, have been extracted here. While no longer a working mine, the Bachelor-Syracuse still delivers—in authentic tours that give visitors a solid feel for what life is like working underground. Visitors to the mine are given yellow slickers and hard hats to wear and are loaded onto a train, where they straddle the seat the way one would ride a horse. This is a long ride, often in total darkness (those who have claustrophobia or children afraid of the dark, take note). It takes about 10 minutes to reach the spot where the tour begins.

Once you're half a mile into the mine, the train stops, passengers unload, and a guide offers information on the history of the mine, old and new mining techniques, safety precautions, and more. The talk can be technical, and young children aren't likely to understand much of it. But the tour is relatively short (one hour total), the trip in and out of the mine is similar to an amusement park ride, and simply being that far underground is an adventure in itself.

The temperature in the mine is 50 degrees year-round. Wear long pants and closed-toed shoes (there is running water on the mine floor). If it's breakfast or lunch time when you come, take advantage of the Outdoor Cafe located outside the mine entrance; the café offers hearty breakfasts and barbecue lunches in a picnic-style setting.

● **Box Canyon Falls**

The southwest corner of Ouray, off highway 550. (970) 325-4464. Mid-May to mid-October: daily, 8 A.M. to 8 P.M. Adults, $2; ages 5 to 12, $1; ages 4 and under, free; seniors ages 65 and over, $1.50. **Ages 3 and up.**

One of our friends, who'd never seen a waterfall up close before, remembers this is as a spectacular attraction. Indeed, even seasoned Colorado travelers will enjoy a stop at these powerful and scenic falls, which are enclosed by granite walls that have formed naturally through the years. To see the point at which they crash through their rock prison, follow the sign that says "Falls." This is an easy walk, although it's best to leave strollers behind as the path is fairly rocky. You will come to a swinging bridge that spans the canyon (fenced in to prevent anyone from falling), where you can watch the water careen downward. You can also head for a set of stairs that leads to a half-mile trail to the top of the canyon. If you're with children ages 4 and under, we suggest foregoing this very steep and rocky part of the trail, which will be difficult for most toddlers. Otherwise, you'll find a lovely view from this vantage point.

The attraction offers a small concession stand, where you can buy candy and other snacks. There are also rest rooms on the far side of the parking lot.

● **Ouray County Museum**

420 Sixth Avenue. (970) 325-4576. May 1 to October 15: Monday to Saturday, 10 A.M. to 4 P.M.; Sunday, 1 to 4 P.M. October 15 to April 30: Friday to Monday, 1 to 4 P.M. Adults, $3; ages 6 to 12, $1; ages 5 and under, free. **Ages 6 and up.**

Housed on three floors (including a basement) of this large 1887 building, which was originally a hospital, this museum does the small town of Ouray proud, with attractive displays categorized by room. Of particular interest on the main floor is the elaborate Victorian dollhouse in the entryway; the Mineral Room, with large crystals, quartz, and even gold, and the Ouray Room, set up as a Victorian parlor.

Upstairs, children can peer into 10 re-creations of various rooms from the turn of the century, including a child's room, a dental office, a law office, and a general store. And kids will especially enjoy the basement exhibits, which include an old jail cell, complete with mannequin prisoner asleep on the cot, a re-created (and fairly realistic) mine, and a room where rocks glow under ultraviolet light.

The museum has several miniature models throughout and a sparse cabin outside that visitors can walk through. It is well worth a stop, even if you've seen other museums of this nature. Plan to spend 45 minutes to an hour.

● Ouray Hot Springs Pool and Park ◆

North end of Ouray on Main Street. (970) 325-4638. Summer: daily, 10 A.M. to 10 P.M. Winter: Monday to Friday, noon to 9 P.M.; Saturday and Sunday, 10 A.M. to 9 P.M. (closed one day a week, generally Tuesday). Adults ages 18 to 54, $6; ages 7 to 17 and seniors ages 55 and up, $4; ages 3 to 6, $3; under age 3, free. Season passes available. **All ages.**

In the fourteenth century, Ute Indians enjoyed the natural hot water springs of Ouray, believing in the healing qualities of the water. In the late 1800s, the settlers who came here followed suit. Now it's our turn. And who can resist? This giant pool, built in 1925 with water piped in from several local natural springs, offers a respite like none other—with a terrific view to boot. Set at the base of a huge rock mountain, the 250-by-150-foot oval structure offers seven sections of varying temperatures. The hottest ranges from 102 to 106 degrees; the coolest, from 78 to 85 degrees. There are areas set aside for lap swimmers, those with floats, divers, or patrons who just want to quietly soak.

Winter or summer, the pool is a popular spot, with plenty of amenities to make a stay comfortable. Visitors can rent floats, volleyballs, rafts, and other water "toys" on an hourly or all-day basis. There is a shop that sells swimsuits; an enclosed room with vending machines; and changing rooms that include showers, hair dryers, playpens, changing tables, and lockers. Swimming suits and towels can be rented ($2 for towels; $2 for suits). Both pool and locker rooms are handicap accessible.

The pool offers only one major drawback: during the summer months, when the attraction is crowded, it can be rather difficult to keep up with your children—a must, since one of the pool rules requires that children under age 7 have an adult within reach at all times, regardless of swimming ability (although lifeguards are on duty at all times). It's best to come at times that are likely to be less crowded, such as early morning.

Plan to spend at least an hour—and probably more. If you need to leave, you can get your hand stamped and return later the same day.

If you come around mealtime, consider bringing a picnic lunch or dinner to enjoy in the park adjacent to the pool. The park offers a decent playground and an old caboose that children can walk through at limited times throughout the summer.

PAGOSA SPRINGS

● Rocky Mountain Wildlife Park and Art Gallery

Five miles south of Pagosa Springs on Highway 84. (970) 264-4515. Spring, summer, fall: daily, 9 A.M. to 6 P.M. Winter (after the first snow): open only at feeding time, Monday, Tuesday, Thursday, and Saturday around 2 P.M. Adults, $5; ages 4 to 12, $3; under age 3, free. **All ages.**

This is as close to a zoo as you'll find in this part of the state, and with 23 animals, it certainly can't compete with a metropolitan zoo experience. But it also offers something city zoos do not: fabulous scenery where animals live in their natural setting. Spread out over 15 acres, the animals here are indigenous to the area and include deer, black bears, wolves, and mountain lions. Because their enclosures are large, with room to roam, they can be somewhat hard to spot. In addition, the admission fee is a bit pricey for what you will see. But the park is a pleasant diversion and especially nice if you have been traveling and need an outdoor respite. Plan to spend about 30 to 45 minutes.

● Spa Motel

317 Hot Springs Boulevard. (970) 264-5910. Year-round: daily, 10 A.M. to 9 P.M. (Closed every other Monday for cleaning.) Adults, $5; ages 13 to 18, $3.50; ages 12 and under, $2.50; ages 4 and under, free. **All ages.**

Pagosa Springs offers something of a mystery: the town promotional materials promise one of the largest hot springs in the country, but where can you go to soak in them? The answer to that question isn't as evident as you'd expect. After a small investigation, we turned up two low-key spots—a spa beside the Spring Inn (see entry) and here, at a swimming pool outside the Spa Motel.

While the Spa Motel offers indoor hot baths for adults, children are only allowed in the 25-yard-by-40-foot outdoor pool. Here, the water temperature is kept at a nice 88 degrees, fine for summer or winter swimming. Children will enjoy this spot, which gives them plenty of room to jump and splash. Floating devices are allowed; you'll find a changing room with showers and baskets to stash your clothes. In addition, a life-guard is on duty in the summer (but not during winter months).

If you're choosing between here and the Spring Inn, just across the street, gauge your mood. The Spa Motel offers a more active experience, while the Spring Inn is a more quiet, sedate environment.

● Spring Inn

160 Hot Springs Boulevard. (800) 225-0934. Year-round, daily, 24 hours. Adults and children, $6.50; ages 6 and under, free. Rooms begin at $64 in winter and $80 in summer. **All ages.**

One of two spots where patrons can soak in the hot springs of Pagosa (see Spa Motel entry), the Spring Inn offers, in addition to lodging, three hot tubs and 11 natural-looking pools, all of varying temperatures, from warm to toe-curdling hot. While the spa looks rather modest from the parking lot, once inside, you'll find an impressively designed layout with pools built into different levels to simulate water in a natural setting. Children will delight in testing the various pools and choosing their favorite. They will also love walking across a bridge that dips a few inches into the water and leads to more mineral-water pools. The spa offers changing rooms, lockers, and a bathroom.

One caveat, however: the pools here are rather confining and the atmosphere is sedate; if your children are more inclined to splash about, you might prefer the hot springs swimming pool at the Spa Motel, just across the street.

In any case, this is a lovely spot to soak for an hour or two, offering a particularly beautiful setting at dusk.

● Treasure Falls

Fourteen miles north of Pagosa Springs on Highway 160. Watch for signs. **Ages 3 and up.**

Just north of Pagosa Springs, off of Wolf Creek Pass, you'll see these dramatic falls cascading downward. The longest waterfall in the San Juan Forest, Treasure Falls is a pretty sight, even when viewed from the highway. But that hardly compares to experiencing the falls close-up. We highly recommend parking your car and taking the easy, quarter-mile hike to the spot where the falls pool midway in their drop. You can watch from a small bridge, where you'll feel the refreshing mist from the spray. Or dip your toes in the cool pool. Hike a short way farther, closer to the top, and you'll feel like you're practically standing underneath the powerful falls.

Our 3-year-old managed this hike with no problem. Wear tennis shoes, and bring water if you have a container with you. The round-trip hike takes less than an hour and makes for a wonderful respite if you're traveling by car.

SALIDA

⬤ Mount Shavano Fish Hatchery & Rearing Unit

7724 County Road 154 (half mile northwest of Salida). (719) 539-6877. Daily, 8 A.M. to 4 P.M. Free. **Ages 2 and up.**

With 4 million fish eggs hatched a year, this is one of the largest trout units in the state. The trout are raised to around 10 inches and used to stock Colorado lakes and streams.

Visitors are allowed to walk outside among the beds of fish, concrete ponds holding mostly trout of varying sizes. In June, July, and August, tour guides are available to conduct you around; otherwise you're free to walk around on your own.

Although automatic feeders keep the fish happy, visitors are allowed to buy large pellets of fish food dispensed from a quarter machine. Our kids, of course, thought this was terrific. When they tossed in the food, the fish swarmed for the pellets causing no end of excitement. The kids also liked choosing their favorites from among the various sizes and species. Bring a number of quarters (not dimes and nickels); otherwise you'll have to track down someone with change.

⬤ Salida Hot Springs

410 West Rainbow Boulevard. (719) 539-6738. Memorial Day to Labor Day: daily, 1 to 9 P.M. Winter: Tuesday to Thursday, 4 to 9 P.M.; Friday to Sunday, 1 to 9 P.M. Adults, $5; ages 6 to 17 and seniors ages 60 and up, $3; ages 5 and under, $2. Suit rental, $1; towel rental, $1. Adult-only swim, Tuesday to Thursday, winter only, 5:30 to 6:30 P.M. Concession stand on site. **All ages.**

There's nothing as soothing as hot springs after a day of sightseeing. The Salida Hot Springs, an indoor facility, has a wading pool for the little ones and a four-foot-deep pool for others where the temperature hovers between 96 and 100 degrees. The latter leads into a slightly cooler (92 to 96 degree) pool that is 10 feet at its deepest end.

Although the temperatures sound hot, they're really just right for a relaxing dip. The wading pool is directly in eyeshot and just a few feet from the bigger pool, which makes it easy to keep an eye on more than one child. There are lifeguards on duty. After a couple hours soaking in the hot springs, we all went back to the hotel and slept like babies.

SILVERTON

● Old Hundred Gold Mine Tour

Five miles east of Silverton. Go east on Highway 110 to Howardsville, turn right on County Road 4, then left at the fork in the road. (Signs point the way; three miles of the road are gravel.) (800) 872-3009. End of May to mid-October: daily. Tours depart every hour beginning at 10 A.M. Last tour leaves at 5 P.M. (4 P.M. during spring and fall). Adults, $11.95; ages 5 to 12, $9.95; ages 5 and under 5, free; seniors ages 60 and over, $10.95. $1 discount for AAA members. **Ages 4 and up.**

The Old Hundred Gold Mine is about 10 minutes outside of Silverton, but once you don a yellow slicker and hard hat and take a minitrain into the mine, you'll feel as if you're in another land altogether. The Old Hundred tour takes you a third of a mile into the historic gold mine, where bare light bulbs brighten what would otherwise be a pitch-black tunnel. A guide leads you through an underground maze, explaining mining techniques through the years. You'll see how miners used to drill holes in rock with a "widowmaker" (so-named because miners who used the instrument didn't live long), learn how they lit dynamite fuses, and come to appreciate modern salaries (miners brought home 40 cents a week in the early days, according to our guide). This tour lasts about an hour. Although the minitrain that takes you in and out of the mine goes through very dark spots in the tunnel, young children on our tour didn't appear frightened. They did get a bit restless, however, with the guide's talk, which was often technical. But simply seeing the underground mine will be an education for all ages. As our 6-year-old said emphatically as we left the tour: "Mom, I do not want to be a miner when I grow up!"

This is very similar to the Bachelor-Syracuse Mine Tour in Ouray. If you're traveling this part of the state, choose the one most convenient. As with all mines, wear long pants and closed-toed shoes. The temperature in the mine is about 49 degrees year-round, and the path through it is often spotted with water puddles.

● San Juan Historical Society Pioneer Museum

On upper Green Street, next to the county courthouse. (970) 387-5838. Daily, Memorial Day weekend to mid-September, 9 A.M. to 5 P.M.; mid-September to mid-October, 10 A.M. to 3 P.M. Adults, $2.50; ages 12 and under, free. **Ages 4 and up.**

This museum is housed in a building that was formerly the county jail. And while it features many of the same pioneer artifacts you'll find in museums throughout the state, it also offers something different: a floor where children can see the original jail cells, complete with ball and chain. Children enjoy looking through the steel bars, and can walk into the cells to see the view from inside, test the weight of the ball and chain, and feel the roughness of the canvas cots.

The museum contains three floors of exhibits (including the basement), which display everything from old pharmacy bottles to a telephone switchboard and snowshoes. Plan to spend about 30 minutes.

TELLURIDE

● Telluride Gondola

If embarking in the town of Telluride, go to Station Telluride Gondola Terminal at Lift 8, beside The River Trail. If embarking at Mountain Village, go to Station Mountain Village Gondola Terminal in the core of Mountain Village at the base of the ski hill beside Lift 3 and Lift 4. (970) 728-6900. June to October: daily, 7 A.M. to 11 P.M. Free. **Ages 3 and up.**

The Telluride Gondola links the town of Telluride to the Telluride ski area and the nearby town of Mountain Village. There are four possible stops: Station Telluride (8,750 feet), Station St. Sophia (10,540 feet), Station Mountain Village (9,600 feet), and Station Village Parking (9,500 feet). The ride is free, and each car can accommodate up to eight adults.

While some might board the gondola simply for the thrill of the ride and the sweeping scenery, the gondola also offers a lift to some terrific mountain hikes. For plentiful hiking choices, get off at Station St. Sophia. Just beyond the station, you'll find trails that offer long hikes for those so inclined, or small walks that can act as test-hikes for the young ones. This is also a good place for a picnic. Keep in mind that while the gondola operates until 11 P.M., access to the St. Sophia Station closes at 8:30 P.M. Also, the gondola shuts down during lightning storms.

When you've finished exploring the natural world, you might consider once again boarding the gondola and riding to Station Mountain Village, where you'll find a host of shops and restaurants.

For those who prefer a guided hike, or information on other outdoor possibilities in Telluride, such as rafting, fishing, and biking, staffers at the Telluride Sports Adventure Desk can offer complete information on what's available. Call (800) 828-7547 or (970) 728-4477.

TEXAS CREEK

● El Carma Rock Shop

24359 Highway 50. (719) 275-6129. Memorial Day to Labor Day: daily, 8 A.M. to 6 P.M. After Labor Day: hours vary, generally Friday to Sunday, 9 A.M. to 5 P.M. (The owners live next door. If no one's at the store, knock on the door of their house and they'll be happy to open for you.) **Ages 3 and up.**

El Carma Rock Shop rises like an oasis in the long canyon stretch of highway between Salida and Canon City. Attracted by the piles and piles of pink, green, and varied colored rocks, we pulled off the highway—and were rewarded. The shop has piles of rose quartz, shiny mica, and other stones, and the kids had a field day selecting their favorites (priced from about 50 cents a pound on up).

Inside the shop are all sorts of stone treasures, including key chains, necklaces, and everyone's favorite—"gold" nuggets. But the best buy was the grab bags. Priced at $1.98, the bags were packed with real kid-pleasing finds—Indian arrowheads, small rock animal figures, pieces of quartz. The kids happily traded for the rest of the ride. They were so excited about the Rock Shop that they begged us to stop again on our way back, and we were happy to oblige.

Northeast

IF YOU'VE TRAVELED in the western part of the state, the eastern side may seem like an entirely different country. Here, rugged, mountain terrain is replaced with flat, open plains; densely vegetated areas are replaced with wheat and corn fields. Aside from the college town of Fort Collins and a few small cities to the south, you may go for miles and miles without finding much in the way of activity. Even so, a drive through this part of the state will offer your children a view of small-town farm life and the calm of open space.

If you're heading due north of Denver, plan a stop in Fort Collins, which offers many wonderful child-friendly attractions, most at parent-friendly prices, if not free. Greeley boasts a popular re-creation of pioneer life at Centennial Village. And farther to the east, artist Brad Rhea's sculpted trees provide a fun minitour for travel-weary kids.

FORT COLLINS

● Anheuser-Busch

2351 Busch Drive, just past Fort Collins off Interstate 25 North (exit 271). (970) 490-4691. May to October: daily, 9:30 A.M. to 5 P.M. November to April: Wednesday to Sunday, 9 A.M. to 4 P.M. Closed Thanksgiving, Christmas, and Easter. Free. **Ages 10 and up.**

The Clydesdale horses are as much a drawing card as the beer at this pristine facility, one of several Anheuser-Busch brewing and packaging plants in the country.

The tour, about 90 minutes from start to finish, takes you through the brewing and bottling process; kids will be more interested in the grand finale—the show barn where the Clydesdales are housed. Although they only have a few horses in the stalls, the animals are large and impressive by anybody's standards.

After the tour, complimentary beer and soft drinks are served in the visitor's center. In nice weather, you can enjoy the beer garden, which looks out over the picture-postcard grounds.

● Avery House

328 West Mountain Avenue. (970) 221-0533. Sunday and Wednesday, 1 to 3 P.M. Free. **Ages 6 and up.**

Situated in the middle of town, this charming 1879 home of Fort Collins surveyor Franklin Avery and his family is a fine example of every-day life in an era when women waited for the ice man to replenish their refrigerators and men had "collar boxes" on their nightstands to hold their stiff, white, detachable collars. Tour guides here are eager to intrigue children, and they tailor their lively talks to the age of the group. Our guide took our children straight to the kitchen, where she showed them an old-fashioned popcorn popper, mousetrap, and toaster, explained how bath water was warmed in the coal stove, and showed them how a rug beater was used. Upstairs, she pointed out a dish women used to collect stray hairs, a chamber pot, and more. Our tour lasted 20 minutes, but tours can also be much longer, depending on the interest of the group.

● City Park

1500 Mulberry Street. (970) 221-6640 or (970) 221-6660 (to reserve sheltered picnic areas for special events). Daily, 6 A.M. to 11 P.M. Swimming pool open to public early June through late August, Sunday to Friday, 12:30 to 5:30 P.M.; Saturday, 10:30 A.M. to 5:30 P.M. Adults ages 18 to 59, $2.50; seniors ages 60 to 84, $2; ages 2 to 17, $1.75; under age 2 and seniors ages 85 and up, free. Paddleboat rental, $4 for half an hour (boats hold 4 people). Train runs daily in summer, 10 A.M. to 6 P.M.; $1 per person. Batting cages open May 17 to August 31, Monday to Friday, 5 to 9 P.M.; Saturday, 8 A.M. to 5 P.M. and Sunday, noon to 9 P.M. Junior golf course (nine holes), hours vary, $10 weekdays, $11 from noon Friday through Sunday. (Call 970-221-6650 at least one day in advance to reserve a tee time.) **All ages.**

At the center of the city, stretching for 85 softly sculpted acres, City Park offers a no-miss diversion, with something bound to appeal to everyone in your family. Consider the list of amenities: ball fields, tennis courts, soccer fields, fitness course, swimming pool, golf course, play-grounds, paddleboats . . . suffice it to say that if you can't find something to do here, you aren't looking very hard.

In the summer, children descend on the outdoor swimming pool, located at the northwest end of the lake, which features a baby pool and a separate pool with a graduated floor and a lap and diving area. The pool offers a water slide and concessions stand for popcorn, candy, and other snacks. Also in this area, paddleboats are available for rental. They seat four people comfortably.

Young children will enjoy the miniature train near the playground area in the northwest corner of the park, although the ride is fairly short for the $1 fee. The park also offers plenty of picnic tables in this vicinity, and the playgrounds are large, one for toddlers, another for older children.

Young golfers will enjoy the junior course, a nine-hole golf course located at 411 South Bryan Avenue.

● Discovery Center Science Museum

Formerly known as Barton School, 703 East Prospect Road. (970) 493-2182. Tuesday to Saturday, 10 A.M. to 5 P.M.; Sunday, noon to 5 P.M. Adults and ages 4 and up, $3; ages 3 and under, free; $30 annual membership available. **Ages 3 and up.**

The name may say "Science Museum," but this is no stuffy, behind-the-glass-display-case place. This is the closest thing Fort Collins has to a children's museum, a hands-on learning experience where kids can lift a 125-pound rock with the help of leverage, send a teddy bear strapped in a tiny car careening toward a crash (to study motion), take pictures of their own shadows on a wall, read a dinosaur story on a computer, and much more.

Situated in a former elementary school, the museum is divided into seven exhibit rooms devoted to the following topics: energy & motion, biology, communications, light & optics, home science, electricity, and zoology. Each room offers a variety of challenges for children, from simple experiments, such as making their own fingerprints, to more complicated projects, such as designing strong bridges. In addition to the many small experiments children are invited to try, computers are situated throughout the museum offering a glimpse at undersea animals, dinosaurs, the moon, and other topics.

While some of the equipment here was in disrepair when we visited, there is plenty to keep kids active and intrigued. Plan to spend the better part of a morning or afternoon exploring science in this play-like atmosphere.

● Edora Pool Ice Center at Edora Park

1801 Riverside Street. (970) 221-6683 or (970) 221-6679 (recorded information). Open swim and skating hours change often; call recorded information line for current times. Each activity: adults, $2.50; ages 2 to 17,

$1.75; ages 2 and under, free. Skate rental, $1; towel rental, 25 cents.
All ages.

With its 65 acres, filled with 16 lighted horseshoe courts, a BMX course, six tennis courts, two lighted ball fields, two playgrounds, an 18-hole Frisbee golf course, and bike trails, Edora Park is a feather in the city's cap, to be sure. Add to the mix the Edora Pool Ice Center (EPIC), situated in the southeast corner of this expansive park, and you have a premier recreation spot in anyone's book.

The EPIC center features five crystal-clear swimming pools in one large room: a therapy pool (94 degrees), a large, two-foot-deep wading pool (87 degrees), a three-and-a-half-foot-deep pool with wheelchair access, a four-foot-deep lap pool with 10 lanes, and a six-foot-deep diving pool. Numerous learn-to-swim programs are offered here. The center also offers a standard-size ice rink, with open skating, drop-in hockey games, open ice dance practices, and more.

The programs for both the pool and ice rink are far too numerous to list here. It's best to pick up a seasonal catalog at the front desk. The facility also offers a moderately priced concessions stand that sells lunch food, such as pizza and hamburgers, as well as popcorn, pretzels, and other snacks. For those with babies, the locker rooms include diaper changing tables.

● The Farm at Lee Martinez Park ◆

600 North Sherwood Street. (970) 221-6665. Winter (November to April): Wednesday to Saturday, 10 A.M. to 4:30 P.M.; Sunday, noon to 4:30 P.M. Summer (June, July, and August): Tuesday to Saturday, 10 A.M. to 5:30 P.M.; Sunday, noon to 5:30 P.M. Transitional months (May, September, and October): Wednesday to Saturday, 10 A.M. to 5:30 P.M.; Sunday, noon to 5:30 P.M. Call first; hours subject to change. Free. **All ages.**

It's hard to say what makes ducks, goats, sheep, pigs, and cows such terrific entertainment for children. But hey, why analyze? Step into The Farm and you'll find a sweet, no-miss adventure for kids, who will love watching and feeding the farm animals that are enclosed in various pens throughout this family-friendly attraction.

The Farm is situated just west of Lee Martinez Park, on a site that once held a dairy. Purchased by the city of Fort Collins in 1973, it opened to the public in 1985. Visitors are invited to stroll the paved walkways, stopping to pet cows, horses, goats, and other animals who peek their heads through and over fences. You can also walk through a barn, where baby chicks are kept warm under special lights, climb the stairs to the top of an old silo, watch cows being milked at various times of the day, and more. Be sure to stop in at the Silo Store and purchase a scoop of food for a quarter; children delight in watching cows and sheep lap it from their hands. On Saturdays and Sundays, from mid-March to October, The Farm also offers pony rides for children up to age 12—$2 for a 20-minute go-round.

When your children tire of the animals—and you can bet you'll tire long before they will!—you can head over to the nearby playground in Lee Martinez Park, which offers extensive play equipment. The playground is within yards of a covered picnic area, basketball and tennis courts, and paved pathways for joggers, bicyclers, and roller skaters.

If you're visiting Fort Collins, or just find yourself with a free afternoon, The Farm is a lovely, relaxing diversion. Highly recommended.

● Fort Collins Municipal Railway

One and a half miles of track between City Park and downtown Fort Collins. (970) 224-5372. First weekend in May to last weekend in September: weekends and holidays, noon to 5 P.M. Adults, $1; ages 12 and under, 50 cents; seniors ages 60 and up, 75 cents. Runs approximately every half hour.
Ages 2 and up.

Step onto Car 21 and you'll be riding one of the few original, restored city streetcars in operation in the West. The trolley ride takes you down the tree-lined Mountain Avenue and back again for a short but sweet adventure. Catch the ride at City Park, near Roosevelt Avenue and Oak Street. The seats in the trolley feature moveable backs so that riders can face either direction. When the trolley reaches the end of the line and is ready to return to City Park, your kids will get a kick out of moving the seat backs and turning around in the seat, suddenly seeing what was behind them appear in front! The trolley doesn't run when it's raining, so be sure to choose a fair-weather day.

● Fort Collins Museum

200 Mathews Street. (970) 221-6738. Tuesday to Saturday, 10 A.M. to 5 P.M.; Sunday, noon to 5 P.M. Free. **Ages 6 and up.**

This museum emphasizes local history in tastefully arranged display cases. Children will see old musical instruments, such as accordians and zithers, sewing machines, beautiful hair combs, toys, kitchen appliances, doctors' tools, farm implements, and more. On the lower level, visitors can enter a courtyard containing three historic buildings representing different eras in Fort Collins's past, including a fur trapper's cabin, a one-room schoolhouse, and a building that served, at various times, as an officers' mess, the town's first school, and a home. Ask an attendant at the front desk upstairs for a key, which will allow you to go inside the sparsely furnished cabins. The museum grounds offer a nice spot for a picnic; there are tables outside, next to a small playground, great for letting children blow off steam after their quiet time in the museum. You could easily spend an hour exploring this site.

● Historic Old Town District

Downtown Fort Collins in the block bordered by Remington Street, North College Avenue, Mountain Avenue, and Linden and Walnut streets, and side streets. Store hours are generally Monday to Friday, 9:30 A.M. to 8 P.M.; Saturday, 9:30 A.M. to 6 P.M.; Sunday, noon to 5 P.M. **All ages.**

In the early 1980s, this old retail section of the city underwent complete renovation. Today, it provides a lovely shopping district with a historic feel, featuring art galleries, clothing shops, outdoor cafés, and more. This is a good place to stroll, browse, and people-watch. For a nice, leisurely diversion, head to the fountain in the middle of this block, where you and your children can take a breather. The mall is broad, with plenty of room for the children to run, jump, and do what kids do.

We also recommend stopping in the Children's Mercantile toy store, one block from the fountain area. Stuffed to the gills with modern playthings—including plenty of toys in the open for children to test—this is great entertainment for kids and their young-at-heart parents alike.

● Horsetooth Reservoir

South on Taft Hill Road to road 38E, go west, follow the signs to the reservoir (about 10 minutes outside of Fort Collins). (970) 679-4570. Open year-round. Quiet hours are enforced from 10 P.M. to 6 A.M. Entrance per vehicle or boat, $5. **All ages.**

In the foothills of Fort Collins, a short distance from town, Horsetooth Reservoir stretches across six and a half miles, providing great relief from summer's heat. Visitors can enjoy waterskiing, boating, scuba diving, swimming, fishing, and camping. Campsites are available on a first-come, first-served basis. Covered picnic areas with rest rooms, water fountains, and a plethora of tables are located at the south end of the lake. A swim beach is at South Bay, just north of park headquarters. And visitors can enjoy a sitdown lunch or dinner at Horsetooth Yacht Club restaurant near the beach.

For great hiking trails, continue past the reservoir on road 38E west for approximately three miles to Horsetooth Mountain Park. The area offers 25 miles of trails of varying difficulty. Pick up a trail map near the parking lot, then head out—keeping an eye open for the plentiful wildlife in the area, including deer, bluebirds, raccoons, porcupines, and—last but certainly not least—rattlesnakes.

● Lincoln Center

417 West Magnolia Street. (970) 221-6730 or (970) 493-2489, ext. 118 (recorded information). **Ages 5 and up.**

A multitude of art, theater, and music events take place in this beautiful building near downtown, and fortunately, children haven't been forgotten in all the excitement. The Lincoln Center SuperSeries features family entertainment January through May, with national touring productions providing a handful of musical and theatrical events. The series is $20 for four shows. If you don't want to buy the whole series, single tickets—when available—go on sale one month before each show. In addition, local children's entertainers are often booked here, with seats generally selling for around $4.75. In the summer—typically Wednesdays—late June to early August, don't miss the center's free concerts on the terrace. Bring a picnic lunch and enjoy the music.

● Swetsville Zoo

4801 East Harmony Road. (970) 484-9509. Daily, dawn to dusk. Free. Donations appreciated. **Ages 3 and up.**

Call this kitschy and corny (it is!), but children enjoy walking through this modest sculpture park, which features more than a hundred whimsical creatures made from car parts, farm machinery, and scrap metal. Visitors will see a two-headed dragon, a knight guarding a castle, grinning dinosaurs, a spider's web, and much more. If you aren't intrigued by this steel zoo of sorts, this is still a good place to stretch your legs and let the kids blow off some steam. For those so inclined, there are picnic tables and barbecue facilities available.

GREELEY

● Bittersweet Park

35th Avenue and 12th Street. (970) 350-9390. Daily, 5 A.M. to 11 P.M. **All ages.**

Aside from the usual park facilities, such as grills and picnic tables, Bittersweet Park has a lake in the middle that will have you trilling like a songbird. The area immediately around the lake is marshland, making it a natural sanctuary for ducks and their ducklings and all kinds of interesting birds. The ducks have grown so tame that they will actually waddle right up to your picnic table.

The park covers 60 acres. Your kids will be interested in the well-designed playgrounds and the 1.2-mile paved path, suitable for jogging, walking, and in-line skating. All in all, this is a pleasant break from sightseeing that won't take you very far out of your way.

● Centennial Village

1475 A Street. (970) 350-9220. Memorial Day to Labor Day: Tuesday to Saturday, 10 A.M. to 5 P.M. Mid-April to Memorial Day and Labor Day to mid-October: Tuesday to Saturday, 10 A.M. to 3 P.M. Adults, $3.50; ages 6 to 12, $2; ages 5 and under, free; seniors ages 60 and up, $3. Admission includes entry to the 1870 Meeker Home (see entry). **Ages 6 and up.**

Centennial Village is a collection of buildings representative of life in the West from the period of 1860 to 1949. You'll find numerous homes, a schoolhouse, a fire station, a tepee, a silo, a blacksmith shop, and even a trolley. All types of dwellings, from the elegant homes of the upper crust to the cramped shack of the homesteader, are grouped together in startling contrast. Don't miss the 1921 Wagon House, the first mobile home perhaps, which transported a family from Lamar, Nebraska, to Colorado traveling at the rate of 5 to 10 miles per day.

Centennial Village has full guided tours available and partial tours of the elaborate homes on the "square" several times a day (many of the more upscale homes are otherwise kept locked). We found it was easy to glide in and out of tours and explore the grounds as we wanted, an idea well-suited to those with children. You can easily spend 60 to 90 minutes here; couple this with a visit to Bittersweet Park (see entry) and on to the Meeker Home.

● 1870 Meeker Home

1324 9th Avenue. (970) 350-9220. Memorial Day to Labor Day: Tuesday to Saturday, 10 A.M. to 5 P.M. Mid-April to Memorial Day and Labor Day to mid-October: Tuesday to Saturday, 10 A.M. to 3 P.M. Meeker Home may be closed during the noon hour on any given day. Adults, $3.50; ages 6 to 12, $2; ages 5 and under, free; seniors ages 60 and up, $3. Admission includes entry to Centennial Village (see entry). **Ages 6 and up.**

Indian uprisings. Massacres. Kidnappings. Such was the fate of Nathan Meeker and his family. Meeker, who started the Greeley Tribune, built this middle-class home in 1870 and lived here for eight years before he was sent to "civilize" the Indians and was killed in an uprising. His family was captured in the attack and rescued some time later. Much of the furnishings are original; the rest are period pieces.

The guided tour lasts no more than 30 minutes and takes you through the parlor, dining room, kitchen, and upstairs to the small bedrooms. Of special interest to kids: a 10-foot-tall diamond-dust mirror, and a 3-D, old-fashioned Viewmaster that kids are allowed to handle. Older kids will be fascinated by the story; younger kids will find enough to look at to hold their attention during the tour. Coupled with Centennial Village, the Meeker House gives a complete picture of how the various classes of people lived during this time period. We suggest viewing Centennial Village, breaking for lunch at Bittersweet Park (see entries), and finishing the tour with the Meeker Home.

LONGMONT

● Longmont Museum

375 Kimbark Street. (303) 651-8374. Monday to Friday, 9 A.M. to 5 P.M.; Saturday, 10 A.M. to 4 P.M. Free, donations requested. **Ages 3 and up.**

Children are invited to grind corn with a rock, "ride" a saw horse outfitted with a real Western saddle, and try on old pioneer clothes and more in this small, well-organized museum. Peek into a re-created general store and one-room schoolhouse; stroll through a stagecoach stop. The museum focuses mostly on the Old West, but also showcases early gas station memorabilia, quilts, and more in changing exhibits. While most displays are of the behind-glass variety, there are many hands-on features throughout.

And if your children grow restless, head to the KidSpace in the back of the museum. This colorful room, devoted to children's museum-type activities, will engage them with its arts-and-crafts project table, a puppet theater stocked with a variety of puppets, a science table with science-related experiments, a reading corner, and more.

LOVELAND

● The Loveland Museum and Gallery

Fifth Street and Lincoln Avenue. (970) 962-2410. Tuesday, Wednesday, and Friday, 10 A.M. to 5 P.M.; Thursday, 10 A.M. to 9 P.M.; Saturday, 10 A.M. to 4 P.M.; Sunday, noon to 4 P.M. Free. **Ages 6 and up.**

Recently expanded, this museum clearly shows the community's loving care: this is a well-done look at the history of the Old West and Loveland's history in particular. Visitors will see, for example, exhibits on the GW Sugar Factory, an important impetus to Loveland's past economy.

An art gallery on the first floor often offers "please touch" exhibits featuring local and national artists.

The biggest draw for children here will be the many re-created rooms that offer a peek into the past. A stroll down one hallway offers a look into a typical turn-of-the-century home: entryway, parlor, kitchen, bedroom, and child's room. Visitors can also walk into a general store, the lobby of an old hotel, and more. Upstairs, the musem offers an exhibit of valentines, old and new, a testament to Loveland's continuing role as the Valentine's Day capital of the world. (Romancers from near and far send valentines from this city for its elaborate Valentine's Day postmarks.)

● North Lake Park

Entrance one-half block south of 29th Street, off North Taft Avenue. (970) 962-2727. Daily, 6 A.M. to 10:30 P.M. Train runs June, July, and August: Tuesday, Thursday to Sunday, noon to 8 P.M.; Wednesday, 2 to 8 P.M. All rides, 50 cents. Swim beach: daily in summer, 10 A.M. to 4 P.M. **All ages.**

There's plenty of activity at this park, one of Loveland's most popular. North Lake offers two ball fields, 12 tennis courts, three athletic fields, and horseshoe, basketball, and raquetball courts. Visitors are invited to fish from the edge of the calm lake at its center or feed the ducks and geese who will happily gather for the occasion. In the summer, the park's swim beach, on the north side of the lake, is a major draw. Open Memorial Day to Labor Day, the swim beach is supervised by lifeguards and offers snack food at a concessions stand. There is no charge for beach use.

Children will also enjoy the two playgrounds, just left of the entrance. One is designed for toddlers, the other for older children. And you won't keep the young ones off the miniature train nearby, dubbed the Buckhorn Northern Railway; the train runs past a railroad crossing and a miniature water tank for a touch of pint-size authenticity.

The park is also home to the Lone Tree School, a one-room schoolhouse built in 1883 and operated by the Loveland Museum and Gallery. The school, however, is generally open only for special educational excursions.

STERLING

● Living Trees of Sterling

Throughout the city. Obtain brochure with map at Welcome Center, (970) 522-7649, junction of Interstate 76 and U.S. Highway 6. **Ages 2 and up.**

A herd of giraffes, their necks stretching up to the sky, a clown balancing blocks, a golfer, a Minuteman. These are 4 of the 20 images sculpted from dead trees by Sterling artist Brad Rhea. In most cases, the sculptures have been left standing where the trees once grew. Rhea's unorthodox technique can be seen all around Sterling; all but three are in outdoor locations. Children especially enjoy the giraffes, which seem to grow out of Columbine Park like, well, like a majestic grouping of trees. Pick up a brochure, which includes a map and addresses of each sculpture, at the Welcome Center. The tour covers approximately five miles and is a great way to see the city if you're in the area and have time to stop.

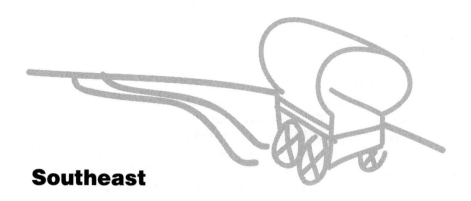

Southeast

THE SOUTHEAST REGION OF COLORADO is a diverse area that
borders Kansas to the east and New Mexico to the south. It's an area
steeped in pioneer history, and you'll easily imagine covered wagons
making the trek across the endless plains from Kansas, happy for the
respite offered by Bent's Fort in La Junta. Many of the towns—Pueblo,
Trinidad—sprang up to meet the needs of the travelers and later became
important to the mining industry.

Wherever you travel in this part of the state, you'll find a colorful
look at Colorado history. And just for fun, don't forget to stop for a ride
on the Kit Carson County Carousel in Burlington or take a whirl on the
Ferris wheel at the Colorado State Fair in Pueblo.

BURLINGTON

● Kit Carson County Carousel
*Kit Carson County Fairgrounds (Interstate 70, exit 437, turn left onto
Highway 385, turn right onto Webster, left onto 15th Street, cross the
railroad tracks to fairgrounds). (800) 288-1334. Memorial Day to Labor
Day, 1 to 8 P.M. All ages: 25 cents.* **Ages 2 to 10.**

This National Historic Landmark was hand-carved in 1905 and has
been fully restored with 46 wooden animals, including a giraffe, horses,
and zebras. The carousel animals turn to the tunes of a Wurlitzer Monster
Military Band Organ.

During the summer on Saturday and Sunday, 1 to 5 P.M. (boards 20
minutes before the hour), you can take a free horse-drawn wagon to and
from Old Town (see entry) to ride this splendid piece of yesteryear.

● Old Town

Interstate 70, exits 437 and 438, 13 miles from the Colorado/Kansas border. (800) 288-1334. Winter: Monday to Saturday, 9 A.M. to 6 P.M.; Sunday, noon to 6 P.M. Summer: Memorial Day to Labor Day: daily, 8:30 A.M. to 7 P.M. Self-guided tours only. Admission: Adults, $6; ages 12 to 18, $4; ages 3 to 11, $2; ages 3 and under, free; seniors ages 60 and up, $5. **All ages.**

Just shy of the Kansas border, you'll find Old Town, a collection of 20 historic buildings from Burlington and the environs, furnished in the period. The buildings include an old-fashioned drug store with a working 1940s Rockola and real soda fountain (open for malts, sodas, and sundaes, summers only, 11 A.M. to 6 P.M.), a white, steepled church where kids can pull the rope and ring the bell, a jailhouse with the original cells, and a dollhouse with hundreds of dolls. The town also has an Emporium, which specializes in hand-crafted collectibles and gifts, many by area craftspeople.

During the summer, Old Town has daily can-can shows every hour from 10:30 A.M. to 5:30 P.M. and Western gunfight shows on the weekends, 1:30 and 3:30 P.M. You can also take a horse-drawn wagon ride on the weekends (12:40 to 4:40 P.M., from Old Town to Kit Carson County Carousel, see entry).

Old Town is 165 miles from Denver through sparsely populated pasture and farmland. It's a must-stop if you're travelling to or from Kansas. You can easily spend a couple hours here.

LA JUNTA

● Bent's Old Fort National Historic Site ◆

Eight miles east of La Junta and 15 miles west of Las Animas on Colorado 194. (719) 384-2596. Daily, year-round. Labor Day to Memorial Day: 9 A.M. to 4 P.M. Memorial Day to Labor Day: 8 A.M. to 5:30 P.M. Guided tours on the hour in the summer, 9 A.M. to 5 P.M. Self-guided tours in winter. Admission: June 1 to August 31, $2 per person; children ages 16 and under, free. Rest of year, $2 per person, ages 5 and under are free. **Ages 6 and up.**

Oh, the thrill of the weary pioneer at seeing Bent's Fort rising majestically from the plains. One of the most important trading centers of the 1830s, Bent's Fort was meeting ground and stopping point for trader and traveler alike.

This fort is an amazing reconstruction of the actual Bent's Fort as it would have appeared in 1845. The real Bent's Fort, completed in 1833, was allegedly destroyed by William Bent in 1849, although no one really knows for sure why or how. Historians speculate that trading had subsided and he feared a cholera epidemic that was sweeping nearby Indian tribes.

There are numerous nooks and crannies to explore among the towers, trading rooms, and living quarters—our children were thrilled to happen upon a live chicken roosting in a window well. In the summer, the fort offers demonstrations, including cooking and blacksmithing. But in any season, this is one of the best historical sites for a true taste of trails West, although it's somewhat off the beaten track—the fort is nearly a four-hour drive from Denver and a 90-minute drive from the Pueblo area.

● Koshare Indian Museum

115 West 18th Street. (719) 384-4411. Daily, 10 A.M. to 5 P.M. Adults, $2; ages 17 and under and seniors ages 55 and up, $1. **Ages 6 and up.**

If you're in the area, stop at this museum for a quick look at a fine collection of Indian and Western art. Children will find the layout of the museum of interest, particularly its round ceremonial room.

The Koshare Museum is a Boy Scout–sponsored project; the Koshare Indian dancers, whose performances are a highly anticipated event, are Boy Scouts upholding a tradition begun in 1933. Performances are held in the evenings in summer and during Christmas week. Call for times and dates.

PUEBLO

● Children's Museum at the Sangre de Cristo Arts Center

Interstate 25 to exit 98B at 1st Street and follow the signs. (719) 543-0130. Monday to Saturday, 11 A.M. to 5 P.M. Adults, $1; ages 12 and under, 50 cents. **Ages 2 to 10.**

More of a children's center than a full-blown children's museum, this small but attractive facility is part of the Sangre de Cristo Arts Center. The major attractions are Stuffee, a seven-foot soft sculpture with zip out parts to teach kids about nutrition, digestion, and circulation; RT-2000, a walking, talking robot; Creation Station, where kids can make masks, collages, and pottery; and Soundsation, a light, sound, and movement exhibit.

Because this is a small place, it may be crowded and noisy on any given day. The kids, of course, will love it; when you've had enough, head for the more sedate El Pueblo Museum nearby (see entry).

Construction has recently begun on the Buell Children's Museum, a separate facility on the property. It's expected to be completed over the next two years.

● El Pueblo Museum

324 West 1st Street. (719) 583-0453. Daily: Monday to Saturday, 10 A.M. to 4:30 P.M.; Sunday, noon to 3 P.M. Adults, $2.50; ages 6 to 16 and seniors ages 65 and up, $2; under age 6, free. **Ages 6 and up.**

Our kids immediately found the exhibits that were hands-on and bypassed the rest at this museum that has Indian, Western, and Pueblo artifacts. The museum has two saddles to "ride" and a full-size tepee, complete with animal hides on the floor.

With a little wheedling from adults to come and look, however, they did find some of the other exhibits of interest after all—the Old Monarch, a cross-section of a 388-year-old tree where 14 men were hanged, and the clothes of an 1890 boy and girl.

This museum, up the street from the Sangre de Cristo Arts Center (see Children's Museum entry), is worth a stop if you're in the area, particularly if your kids haven't been to an Indian and Old West museum.

● The Greenway and Nature Center

Interstate 25 south to the Highway 50 exit, west to Pueblo Boulevard, turn left onto Pueblo Boulevard, continue to West 11th Street, turn right. Stay on Nature Center Road, past the Raptor Center (see entry). (719) 549-2414. Grounds open daily, dawn to dusk. Café on premises, open year-round, except Mondays. **All ages.**

Stop by the Raptor Center (see entry), which is actually part of the Greenway and Nature Center complex, and then drive here for a little change of pace. The younger kids can play on the playground; the older kids can stroll the walkway along the Arkansas River.

You can also rent a bike at the center and ride along the 36 miles of trails. The visitor center, which is being renovated, is open Tuesday to Saturday, 9 A.M. to 5 P.M.; Sunday, 10 A.M. to 5 P.M. and will have some interactive displays on local natural history.

● Lake Pueblo State Park

640 Pueblo Reservoir Road. (719) 561-9320. Rock Canyon Swim Beach: (719) 564-0065. North Marina: (719) 547-3880 and South Marina: (719) 564-1043. Park open daily, 24 hours a day. Visitor center: 8 A.M. to 4:30 P.M. From November to January, hours vary; generally closed on *weekends (call first). Rock Canyon Swim Beach: Memorial Day to Labor Day, 11 A.M. to 7 P.M. South Marina: April 1 to end of October, Monday to Thursday and Sunday, 8 A.M. to 6 P.M.; Friday and Saturday, 8 A.M. to 8 P.M. Admission: park, $4 per car; Rock Canyon Swim Beach, 50 cents per person. Water slide, $8 for all day.* **All ages.**

Lake Pueblo State Park covers 17,000 acres, 4,600 of which are lake surface. The visitor center has some interesting exhibits, including a huge aquarium and a live tarantula. Once you enter the park, you'll find several playgrounds and numerous picnic tables. In the northwest corner of the park, there's a model airplane field where you can watch—or bring a plane and join—the model airplane enthusiasts as they fly their remote-control planes.

There are two marinas. At the south marina, you can rent a pontoon, a boat that holds six to eight people and is easy to handle even for first-time boaters. However, the boats are first-come, first-served, and you'd be wise to call ahead and reserve one if you want to go boating. Rental is $60 for two hours. At the north marina, you can rent small fishing boats, $15 to $20 an hour.

The kids, of course, will want to head right for Rock Canyon Swim Beach, especially when they hear that it has a water slide, a sandy beach, bumper boats, and paddleboats. The water slide, reached via the beach, is a separate admission. There are no towel or suit rentals at the beach; there are picnic tables.

● Pueblo Zoological Gardens

Pueblo and Goodnight boulevards, in Pueblo City Park. (719) 561-8686. Memorial Day to Labor Day, 10 A.M. to 5 P.M.; rest of year, 9 A.M. to 4 P.M. Admission: Adults, $3; ages 3 to 12, $1; ages 13 to 18, $2, ages 3 and under, free. **All ages.**

This is a small, charming, very personal zoo featuring ranch animals and the usual run of zebras, llamas, and a lion or two. The zoo has 310 animals (about 110 species) on its 30 acres.

We particularly liked the "animal" house, home to lemurs, meerkats, and the fennec fox, and the ecocenter with its rainforest and indoor penguin exhibit. The penguin exhibit is constructed so that visitors can sit and watch the penguins as they dive and swim underwater.

The zoo also has a "touch and feel" discovery room. Our kids thoroughly enjoyed looking through microscopes and comparing their height to that of a cut-out kangaroo and gorilla. You can easily spend a couple hours at this enjoyable place.

● The Raptor Center

Interstate 25 south to the Highway 50 exit, west to Pueblo Boulevard, turn left onto Pueblo Boulevard, continue to West 11th Street, turn right. When you get to Nature Center Road, stay on the hard surface road and continue less than a mile to the Raptor Center barn. (719) 549-2327. Tuesday to Sunday, hours vary seasonally, generally 11 A.M. to 4 P.M. during the school year and 10 A.M. to 5 P.M. the rest of the year. (Call ahead for hours.) Donations.
Ages 3 and up.

With all our visits to parks and zoos, we had never seen a bald eagle this close before. The Raptor Center is a private, nonprofit organization that houses and rehabilitates injured birds of prey. The public can visit any birds (owls, falcons, and eagles) that are on hand, some of which have lived here for years. In early fall and late spring, the center has release days for the birds that have been rehabilitated, and you can come and watch the birds set free. Or if you adopt, that is, sponsor, a bird from the center, you are given the privilege of releasing it.

The naturalists who work here are gentle with kids. Every Sunday at 2 P.M., they showcase one of the birds in an educational program. After your visit here, continue down the road to the Greenway and Nature Center (see entry).

● Rosemount Victorian House Museum

419 West 14th Street. (719) 545-5290. Guided tours: June to August, Tuesday to Saturday, 10 A.M. to 3:30 P.M.; Sunday, 2 to 3:30 P.M.; September to May, Tuesday to Saturday, 1 to 3:30 P.M.; Sunday, 2 to 3:30 P.M. Closed January. Admission: adults, $5; ages 13 to 18, $3; ages 6 to 12, $2; ages 6 and under, free; seniors ages 60 and up, $4. **Ages 10 and up.**

This magnificent 37-room mansion is almost one of a kind because it contains nearly all the original furniture, wallpaper, and furnishings from 1893. Among the architectural gems of the house: a 9-by-13-foot stained-glass window at the landing of the dramatic staircase and fabulous wood-work throughout.

Be aware, however, that the tour is very structured and lasts every bit of an hour. Younger kids will be restless after a short time; older kids will find parts of the tour of interest here and there. The beauty of the home is certainly impressive by anyone's standards.

The third floor does house a small area that kids will enjoy, filled with artifacts—and even an Egyptian mummy. However, despite the obvious adult pleasure in viewing this Victorian masterpiece, if you're short on time or traveling with really young ones, you'll probably want to find another day to see it.

RYE

● Bishop Castle

Twenty-four miles northwest of Colorado City on State Highway 165, follow the signs. Open every day. Free. **Ages 6 and up.**

A truly amazing sight, Bishop Castle, modeled after a medieval castle, rises three stories high with a dragon's head leering from the top. The one-man project of owner Jim Bishop is being completed a little at a time; visitors can view the work in progress.

Note that the castle is located along a winding, 24-mile stretch off the highway flanked by the San Isabel National Forest. Although we were excited to spot deer and even a bobcat along the road, the trip to and from the castle took much longer than we had expected or anticipated—the castle is set back among the trees. In the winter, the short path from our parking spot was snowy and icy; the castle was deserted. Nevertheless, we found it worth the trip and were undeniably impressed by the scope of one man's dream. In the summer, you'll find lots of hustle and bustle at the castle as Bishop works to make his dream reality.

TRINIDAD

● Baca House and Bloom Mansion

300 East Main Street (across from the post office). (719) 846-7217. May 1 to September 30: daily, 10 A.M. to 4 P.M. Guided tour, both houses: adults, $5; ages 6 to 16, $2.50; under age 6, free; seniors ages 65 and up, $4.50. **Ages 6 and up.**

The Baca House was built by merchant John S. Hough in 1869 and bought by the prosperous Felipe Baca in 1870. The two-story adobe home is furnished with colorful Spanish textiles, religious objects, and ornately carved and upholstered furniture. The simplicity of the home stands in sharp contrast to the Bloom Mansion down the street, built in 1882 by Frank G. Bloom, one of the town's first bankers. The Bloom Mansion has the fussiness and intricate detail of a Victorian home.

Each home features around a 20- to 25-minute tour by guides, who will point out items of interest to the kids. Included in the admission price is the Santa Fe Trail Museum behind the Baca House, currently undergoing renovation to make it more hands-on.

Trinidad is 3½ to 4 hours from Denver, and a good stopping place if you're on your way to New Mexico.

Special Annual Events

BELOW, WE OFFER a partial list of festivals and special events throughout the state, alphabetized by town, compiled with the help of the
Colorado Tourism Board's Colorado Official State Vacation Guide. If
you're planning a trip, we recommend phoning the chamber of commerce
in the area where you'll be traveling for more detailed information.

JANUARY

Ullrfest, Breckenridge: Week-long celebration in honor of Ull, Norse
God of Snow. Includes parade, fireworks, torchlight display. (970)
453-6018.

Colorado Indian Market and Western Art Roundup, Denver: More
than 90 Native American tribes participate in this fair, which includes
crafts, music, and dance. (303) 534-8500.

National Western Stock Show and Rodeo, Denver: The largest annual
event in Denver, featuring rodeo performances, livestock auctions, and
children's pavilion with petting arena. Kicks off with a parade through
downtown Denver and runs for 10 days. (303) 534-8500.

Snowdown in Durango and at Purgatory, Durango: Five days of offbeat
activities, including chili cook-off, light parade, and waiter/waitress
obstacle races. (800) 525-8855.

Annual Norwest Bank Cowboy Downhill, Steamboat Springs: Ski
rodeo featuring more than 90 rodeo cowboys who compete in a slalom
course and wacky events, such as lassoing a resort employee. (800) 922-
2722.

FEBRUARY

KBCO Downhill Derby, Arapahoe Basin: Contestants race down the ski slopes in just about any vehicle made of cardboard. (800) 354-4386.
Denver Auto Show, Denver: Car buffs can view a host of automobiles, from classics to modern masterpieces at the Colorado Convention Center. (303) 534-8500.
Ice Fishing Contest, Walden: The nine largest fish win prize money in this contest on four lakes. (970) 723-4600.

MARCH

St. Patrick's Day Parade, Denver: The second largest St. Patrick's Day Parade in the nation. (303) 534-8500.
Denver March Pow Wow, Denver: Native American dancers, drummers, musicians, and artists perform at the Denver Coliseum. (303) 534-8500.
Monte Vista Crane Festival, Monte Vista: Bus tours, wildlife art exhibits, and more welcome the whooping and sandhill cranes back to the valley. (719) 852-2731.

APRIL

Aurora Arbor Day Festival, Aurora: One-kilometer family fun run and other races, as well as environmentally oriented activities. (303) 755-5000.
Taste of Breckenridge, Breckenridge: Breckenridge's best restaurants offer food tastings. (970) 453-6018.
Earthfest, Denver: Booths, entertainment, and workshops for kids in Larimer Square in downtown Denver. (303) 534-8500.
Red Rocks' Easter Sunrise Service, Morrison: Nondenominational service at the beautiful Red Rocks Amphitheatre at sunrise. (303) 697-8749.
Spring Splash, Winter Park: Winter Park Ski Resort closes the season with costumed racers negotiating an obstacle course that ends at an icy pond. (303) 422-0666.

MAY

Bolder Boulder, Boulder: Cheering crowds welcome world-class runners and more than 23,000 others along the 10K course through town. (800) 444-0447 or (303) 442-2911.

Kinetic Conveyance Sculpture Race, Boulder: Zany human-powered vehicles race across land and water at the Boulder Reservoir. (800) 444-0447 or (303) 442-2911.

Annual Music and Blossom Festival and Royal Gorge Rodeo, Canon City: Carnival, parades, and cowboy competitions. (719) 275-2331.

Territory Days, Colorado Springs: Games, contests, and a staged gunfight in the Historic District of Old Colorado City. (719) 635-7506.

Taste of Creede, Creede: Art demonstrations, bluegrass and classical music, and samples from local restaurants. (800) 327-2102.

Cinco de Mayo, Denver: Ethnic food and entertainment in several locations in honor of Denver's Hispanic heritage. (303) 534-8500.

Duck Race, Estes Park: Three thousand rubber ducks race down Fall River for charity. Includes entertainment and family activities. (800) 443-7837.

JUNE

Aspen Music Festival, Aspen: See entry under Aspen, Southwest.

Colorado Springs Spring Spree, Colorado Springs: Downtown closes to traffic for two days for this sidewalk festival. The highlight is a bed race down Pikes Peak Avenue. (719) 635-7506.

Crawford Pioneer Days, Crawford: Greased-pig catching contest, fast-draw shoot-out, entertainment, and arts and crafts. (970) 921-4725.

Capitol Hill People's Fair, Denver: Crafts, food booths, entertainment, and children's activities highlight this major gathering in Civic Center Park. (303) 534-8500.

Cherry Blossom Festival, Sakura Square, Denver: Dance, music, art, and food celebrating the Japanese culture. (303) 534-8500.

Juneteenth, Denver: A celebration of the end of slavery in Texas, with food and entertainment in Five Points. (303) 534-8500.

Estes Park Wool Market, Estes Park: Lamb cook-off, educational exhibits, and sales of llama, sheep, and angora rabbits at the Estes Park Fairgrounds. (800) 443-7837.

Glenwood Springs Strawberry Days, Glenwood Springs: Week-long event, featuring carnival, arts and crafts, and strawberries and ice cream after a parade. (970) 945-6589.

Greeley Independence Stampede, Greeley: Beginning in mid-June and culminating July 4 with fireworks. Features barbeques, parades, rodeo, concerts, and more. (970) 352-3566.

Renaissance Festival, Larkspur: The sixteenth century comes alive in this re-created village, where troubadors, jesters, and others entertain

244 FUN PLACES TO GO WITH CHILDREN IN COLORADO

visitors during weekends throughout the summer. (303) 534-8500.

Telluride Bluegrass Festival, Telluride: Four days of bluegrass and country music in an outdoor setting. (970) 728-3041.

Santa Fe Trail Festival, Trinidad: Arts and crafts, quilt show, music, and food. Held along the Santa Fe Trail in historic downtown Trinidad. (719) 846-9285.

JULY

Brush Rodeo, Brush: Fireworks, a parade, livestock, and the world's largest amateur rodeo. (970) 842-2666.

Carbondale Mountain Fair, Carbondale: Children's games, music, food, and more than 140 professional artists and craftspeople displaying their wares. (970) 963-1890.

Aerial Weekend, Crested Butte: Hot-air balloons, hang gliding, and a host of activities geared to children. (800) 545-4505.

Cherry Creek Arts Festival, Denver: Artists of local and national repute exhibit their wares in a festival setting that includes food, demonstrations, and a tent for children to create their own artworks. (303) 534-8500.

Denver Black Arts Festival, Denver: A celebration of African-American culture through art, dance, and food. (303) 534-8500.

Dinosaur Days, Grand Junction: A dinosaur parade, paleontology digs for the public, and band concerts during a four-day celebration. (970) 242-3214.

Lighted Boat Parade, Grand Lake: Boat owners decorate their crafts with lights for this evening event, followed by fireworks. (970) 627-3402.

Gold Rush Days, Idaho Springs: Events to celebrate Colorado's mining history, including panning for gold, mucking and drilling contests, horseshoe competitions, games, food, and a parade. (303) 567-4382.

Steamboat's Rainbow Weekend, Steamboat Springs: Hot-air balloon festival, with colorful aircraft from across the country, music, and a rodeo. (800) 922-2722.

AUGUST

Bill Pickett Invitational Rodeo, Denver: A rodeo to honor the memory of "the father of bulldogging," Bill Pickett, and other African-American cowboys. (303) 534-8500.

Evergreen Mountain Rendezvous, Evergreen: Mountain men demonstrate skills from days gone by. (303) 674-3412.

Palisade Peach Festival, Grand Junction: A tribute to one of Colorado's best-known crops. (970) 242-3214.

Daven Haven Downs Turtle Race, Grand Lake: Turtles race for charity. A turtle parade is held the night before the big event. (970) 627-3402.

Annual Boom Days Celebration, Leadville: Street fair, competitions, and the International Pack Burro Race. (719) 486-3900.

Colorado State Fair, Pueblo: Amusement park rides, livestock exhibits, petting arena, children's activities, and concerts during a 17-day period. (800) 233-3446.

Arkansas Valley Fair, Rocky Ford: The oldest continuous fair, with Watermelon Day, Fiesta Day, and more. (719) 254-7483.

SEPTEMBER

Broomfield Days, Broomfield: Arts and crafts, food, parade, and pancake breakfast. (303) 466-1775.

Colorado Springs Hot-Air Balloon Classic, Colorado Springs: One of the 10 largest hot-air balloon festivals in the country, a three-day event. (719) 635-7506.

Festival of Mountain and Plain . . . A Taste of Colorado, Denver: Large array of area restaurants offer their wares in booths along Civic Center Park. Includes entertainment and crafts. (303) 534-8500.

Larimer Square Oktoberfest, Denver: Munich's famous festival, celebrated with dancing and other entertainment. (303) 534-8500.

Native American Lifeways Festival, Montrose: Two days of Native American exhibits, dance, arts, and food. (800) 873-0244.

Telluride Hang Gliding Festival, Telluride: Pilots from around the world participate in the sport's longest-running and largest event in the U.S. Climaxed by the world hang gliding championships in Town Park. (970) 728-3041.

Vailfest, Vail: Children's activities, food, and entertainment. (970) 476-1000.

OCTOBER

Oktoberfest, Brush: Polka dance, antique auto show, and family activities. (970) 842-2666.

Apple Fest, Cedaredge: The Apple Olympics highlight this celebration of the apple harvest, which includes square dancing, arts and crafts, and food. (970) 856-6961.

Colorado Performing Arts Festival, Denver: Theatrical performances and free continuous entertainment at the Denver Center for the Perform-ing Arts Complex and other downtown locales. Special children's activi-ties. (303) 534-8500.

Western Arts, Film, and Cowboy Poetry Gathering, Durango: Authentic cowboys share their poetry, demonstrations, art, and film. (800) 525-8855.

NOVEMBER

Chocolate Festival, Creede: Sample a variety of chocolate in local shops and restaurants. (800) 327-2102.

Christmas Lighting Display, Denver: A dazzling display of holiday color at the Denver City and County Building through Christmas. (303) 534-8500.

Catch the Glow, Estes Park: Light displays, clowns, carolers, and nighttime parade, day after Thanksgiving. (800) 443-7837.

Georgetown Christmas Tree Lighting, Georgetown: Annual ritual signals the beginning of the holiday season in Georgetown. Held the Saturday after Thanksgiving. (303) 569-2888.

DECEMBER

Christmas Walk, Denver: Carolers, roasting chestnuts, and Father Christmas in Larimer Square every weekend from Thanksgiving to Christmas. (303) 534-8500.

Parade of Lights, Denver: Marching bands, floats, holiday-costumed marchers through the streets of downtown. Two nights of parades; one parade in the day. (303) 534-8500.

Georgetown Christmas Market, Georgetown: European-style celebra-tion featuring food, arts and crafts, madrigal singers, wagon rides, and more. (303) 569-2888.

Parade of Lights, Pueblo: Downtown parade with thousands of tiny lights. (800) 233-3446.

Yule Log Celebration, Silverton: Children search for the yule log, followed by refreshments and songs around a fire. (800) 752-4494.

Index

Index by Age Group

Alphabetical Index